Air Chief Marshals of India

AIR CHIEF MARSHALS OF INDIA

Capt (Retd.) Prem Singh

PRASHANT PUBLISHING HOUSE
DELHI-110094

Published by :
Prashant Publishing House
C-34, 28 Foota Road, Gali No.-3,
West Karawal Nagar, Delhi-110094
Phone : 011-22963970, Mob. : 9810396373

Air Chief Marshals of India

First Published 2012

ISBN 978-93-80565-31-6

PRINTED IN INDIA
Published by Mr. R.K. Jha M/s Prashant Publishing House and Published at **Dynamic Printers, Delhi**

Preface

For decades the IAF had largely been tethered to one non-western source. Much of the inventory acquired through this route has now been overtaken by obsolescence. As a result, in recent years, there has been an alarming erosion in combat power and other capabilities. Even after prolonged and reportedly vigorous effort, the indigenous Research & Development Organisations and the Aerospace Industry have not been able to provide a respectable degree of self reliance to the IAF.

The near total dependence on foreign sources for cutting edge technology and frontline equipment is potentially perhaps the most debilitating factor that often threatens to seriously undermine the capability of the IAF. Despite the limitations, the IAF has managed to attain and project an image of a potent force capable to preserving the sovereignty of the Indian skies and in more recent times, to project power albeit limited in quantum and reach. And even in the future there appears to be no option but to procure advanced technology and hardware from abroad. There is however an attempt to indigenize products through co-development, co-production and the difficult, but innovative, concept of "Offsets". Though not the best, this route is the most expedient under the circumstances to accord military hardware a semblance of Indian character.

Armed Forces offer excellent career opportunities to the adventurous young candidates. Its a career that offers immense facilities, a privileged lifestyle and of course, honour in serving the country. The major activity of the air force is that of flying combat air crafts and helicopters. Other activities include technical work such as aeronautical engineering, electronics, and computer engineering, as well as administrative, financial and planning duties.

—*Editor*

Contents

1

Indian Air Chief Marshals

INDIAN AIR FORCE

The first Indian Air Force officer to hold the rank of air chief marshal was Arjan Singh who was promoted in the second half of the 1960s while he served as Chief of Air Staff. Since that time all Indian air chiefs have held the rank. From the 1960s to 2010, 17 Indian chiefs of the air staff have held the rank.

MOHAN SWAROOP CHATURVEDI

The Early Years

M S Chaturvedi was commissioned in the Indian Air Force as a Pilot Officer on 20th July 1940. He was one of the first batch of recruits taken directly as 'Observers' into the IAF, in light of his flying experiences as well as academic qualifications. He began his training at the No. 20 Squadron RAF at Lower Topa, Muree Hills and Risalpur in the Northwest Frontier Province. He was assigned to the General Duties Observer Branch as an Observer (as Navigators were then known). At that time they flew open cockpit aircraft like the Westland Wapiti and the Hawker Harts.

The Navigator had four roles in such aircraft-navigator, air gunner, bomb aimer and wireless operator. The complexity of the role was compounded by the fact that the Navigator was not harnessed to the aircraft but was attached to it by a chain and had to cling tightly to the gun ring during manoeuvres. After his training, Plt Offr M.S. Chaturvedi was inducted into the Coast Defence Flight at Bombay (initially called the Indian Air Force Volunteer Reserve). He flew Wapitis and Dragon Rapides. Their main assignment was to exercise vigilance over the coast and escort convoys into and out of the ports. Patrols in the Dragon Rapide offered more than the fair share of excitement to the aircrew. About one of the missions, he wrote:

"Being a twin engined aircraft, the safety margin of the Dragon Rapide was far greater than that of the Wapitis and Audaxes. However, instances of engine falures were not uncommon. I had a horrifying experience when, once flying with Minoo Engineer on a patrol mission, the oil pressure of one of the engines started dropping rapidly. The engine had to be trimmed and the bombs jettisoned in the sea. We started back-trekking and just made the Juhu airport when the second engine also stopped. The landing was made by Minoo Engineer with both engines dead! It was a touch and go affair and both of us were very badly shaken".

The World War had come to India's Eastern border by 1942 with the Japanese having conquered most of Burma. This led to the formation of new squadrons in the IAF. Chaturvedi joined the newly formed IAF Squadron No. 7 and was trained in the OTU at Peshawar on the Vultee Vengence Dive Bomber aircraft. The Squadron was a mobile squadron, with its own equipment and personnel, to keep it independent of the ground stations. After Peshawar, training was completed in Phaphamau (near Allahabad) to Bairagarh (near Bhopal). Then the Squadron moved to Cambelpore in the NWFP for operations.

He served on the Burma front in 1942-3. He was providing reconnaissance and close air support to the ground troops. Despite difficult operational circumstances due to the monsoon, with slush filled roads and airfields, cloud covered targets and enemy attacks, the Squadron flew almost 100% serviceability doing the maximum possible sorties per aircraft per day. Besides providing invaluable reconnaissance photos of Japanese positions, he took part in bombing enemy dumps, troop concentrations and supply lines. After the Burma Campaign, M S Chaturvedi was posted in different capacities in Dehradun, Bangalore and Madras. In July 1946 with post War demobilization at its height, he was inducted into the Staff

College at Quetta (Baluchistan). His excellent performance led to his joining the Air Headquarters as Squadron Leader Plans II in October of the same year.

He was personally hand-picked by Gp Capt Aspy Engineer for a trip to the UK to study the RAF Record Office in London and Ruislip. This was done so that Chaturvedi can take over the RIAF Record Office on his returning, Chaturvedi returned as Wing Commander to take over as Officer in-charge of Record Office in Red Hills, Madras in 1947. Just after independence, he moved to IAF Records Office in New Delhi.

The Strategist with Foresight

MS Chaturvedi's contribution to the country until now had been in various capacities, but what was to follow would propel him to the highest echelons of the Indian Air Force. In 1949 he was appointed Director of Policy and Plans with the rank of Group Captain. This marks the beginning of his role as the strategist, which lasted through till the end of his career. It was under his leadership that a strong foundation for the modern IAF was conceived and created from scratch, an achievement that merits him a place among the greatest leaders of the Indian Air Force.

At the time Gp Capt Chaturvedi took charge of the post of Director of Policy and Plans, the IAF was in a state of confusion and change. The withdrawal of the British officers and equipment, followed by reduction of squadrons due to the formation of Pakistan and finally the Kashmir conflict had taken their toll on the IAF and planning processes were practically non-existent. Gp Capt Chaturvedi began formulating the strategy of developing an Air Force capable of both offensive and defensive roles to succeed against external aggression. This force also needed the transport & support capabilities and well-trained, well-equipped manpower. Chaturvedi developed detailed plans to create a balanced Air Force of twenty squadrons (from the six and a half in use then) that would meet the needs of the Air Force for the next several years. This plan was submitted to the Government after approval from the Chief of Air Staff. The government decided due to budgetary constraints to immediately upgrade to a ten squadron Air Force and to build the training and infrastructure for a twenty-squadron force.

The first task in the implementation of the policy was to expand the IAF's training facilities for all branches including Flying, Ground Operations, Technical Training and Armaments. Chaturvedi was involved in planning and setting up a number of these facilities from scratch, even before any ground infrastructure was in place. Initially British instructors were used to tide over the shortage of trained people and gradually replaced by Indian instructors as they became ready to take their place. By about 1951 most of the training infrastructure of the IAF was in place, which would stand it in good stead over the next several decades.

Chaturvedi felt that while normal training of the pilots in squadrons was going on well, the pilots were not getting the proper exposure to live armament firing. He was instrumental in identifying Jamnagar as the location to set up the Armament Training Wing. He personally visited the place for a recce on 28 Sep 50, with a view to set up the ATW. Jamnagar at that time was only a small runway and a civil airport. But Chaturvedi recognised its potential and the possibilities and immediately recommended the place to be developed as the ATW. Soon afterwards, Operations Directorate started the Training Wing which operating under tents at Jamnagar, till the time the construction works were completed.

During 1951 MS Chaturvedi was also a part of the North and North Eastern Border Committee, setup by the Prime Minister Pandit Jawaharlal Nehru to study the effects of the occupation of Tibet by China and to recommend steps to counter any possible threats. This Committee also included high-ranking representatives from the Army, the Ministry of External Affairs and the Defence Ministry. He was also on a two person Committee with the Deputy Chief of Army Staff to evaluate the situation in Nepal. Both these Committees submitted comprehensive recommendations that unfortunately got lost in a bureaucratic maze, which if put into practice may have reduced the problems India faced in the Chinese conflict of 1962.

By the end of 1952 the government had accepted the IAF's proposal to increase to a 15 squadron force. This shifted

Chaturvedi's focus as the Director of Policy and Plans towards procurement of the right aircraft. Until now, the IAF had used British aircraft like the Hurricanes, Spitfires and Tempests all of World War II vintage. For the new fighter aircraft the choice was between the British Meteor and the French Ouragon. Gp Capt Chaturvedi recommended the French Ouragon to reduce the risk to the IAF of having a single supplier (Britain) for all its purchases. Chaturvedi had already felt the risks during the heightened tensions of 1951 with Pakistan, when it was realised that enough spares for the Vampire were not stocked with the IAF, even though it was the frontline fighter.

The Chief of Air Staff (Air Marshal Gibbs) was not in favour of the Ouragon, but nevertheless he acted fairly and asked the Prime Minister to decide on this matter. The Prime Minister after due consideration decided that the Ouragon should be procured from France. Similarly, for purchasing of transport aircraft Chaturvedi chose the American C-119 with Wright cyclone engines. This policy of diversification of procurement from different countries has been used by the Air Force ever since.

The Multi Faceted Leader

After formalizing the policies of the IAF, M S Chaturvedi moved rapidly through a number of leadership roles. In each of these roles his contribution was always as a visionary. In this phase his roles were varied, holding almost all the top positions in Airstaff, Personnel and Maintenance. In 1954, still in the rank of Group Captain, Chaturvedi took charge as Station Commander, Air Force Station, Tambaram (near Madras), the largest Air Force Station at the time.

After serving there for about a year, he returned to Delhi as Station Commander, Air Force Station, Delhi. Many of the Air Force facilities in Delhi that are currently in use owe their existence to Chaturvedi's sting as the Station Commander. In addition to the current Air Force Station he also set up two Air Force Schools-the Air Force Bal Bharti School and the Air Force Central School. Over the next few years Chaturvedi rapidly progressed through the posts of Director of Reserves and Director of Personnel Services.

The Technical and Equipment services of the IAF had lagged behind the rapid development of the technology and introduction of sophisticated equipment that were being introduced into the Air Force. In 1957 he chaired a Committee consisting of the senior-most officers of these branches to reorganize these services and enhance coordination at all levels. The recommendations included setting up of Air Stores Parks near each operational area to reduce the size and response time of the supply lines. The Technical and Equipment services were kept at the same reporting level and were divided by the types of aircraft. To increase cooperation the respective officers at all levels from Air Headquarters downwards were asked to sort any problems by discussing it directly with their counterparts.

In 1958 M S Chaturvedi was promoted to Air Commodore and appointed Air Officer in Charge Maintenance. This gave him the chance to implement the recommendations of the Committee and revitalize the Technical and Equipment services. This task was complicated by the fact that the IAF was servicing more than twenty different aircraft at the time, many of which were obsolete and spares for them had to be procured by cannibalization of other aircraft or local manufacturing. Air Commodore Chaturvedi also put in place the right systems over the next few years to increase the effectiveness of the maintenance services and strengthen them to withstand the pressures of war. These measures ensured the success of the IAF when tested by the war against Pakistan in 1965.

Not soon afterwards, Chaturvedi become Air Vice Marshal at the young age of 48, in 1963 and took charge as Air Officer in charge Administration. After the 1962 war against China the IAF felt the need to develop a strong defense on India's eastern border. During his tenure he set up a number of Air Wings and Stations in North Bengal and Assam. Many of these bases were nothing but World War II airstrips and the entire infrastructure for these bases was developed during his tenure.

Air Vice Marshal Chaturvedi was among the key contributors during the war against Pakistan in 1965 and his work in augmenting the IAF's personnel, aircraft and serviceability gave the IAF a decisive edge leading to air superiority being established very quickly. With the upgradation of the ranks of the IAF in 1966, he became an Air Marshal in 1966. At that point he was deputed to serve the nation in a different capacity as the Managing Director of Air India. Air India was among the top international airlines at that time, with JRD Tata as its Chairman. During Air Marshal Chaturvedi's seven years at the helm, Air India's revenue and profitability grew rapidly and it became one of the first non-US airlines to acquire the Boeing 747 aircraft. During this period he also served as President of the Aeronautical Society of India, using his vast experience in military as well as civilian aviation to promote the growth of aviators and aerospace technologists in India.

Retirement

After his retirement in 1973, Air Marshal Chaturvedi used his knowledge and understanding of the IAF to write a book entitled "History of the Indian Air Force". This book is considered a must read for anyone who wants a deeper understanding of the evolution of the IAF into the great fighting forces of the world. Much emphasis was given to the evolution of electronics and the description of training units in the book, which is not available anywhere else. Air Marshal M.S. Chaturvedi was a great aviator, a farsighted thinker and a capable leader. Many of his policies have withstood the test of time and the framework that he created for the IAF still exists, despite the unimaginable changes that have taken place in technology. This is his legacy to the nation that will endure for a very long time to come.

ASPY ENGINEER

Air Marshal Aspy Merwan Engineer DFC (15 December 1912 – 1 May 2002) was an officer in the Indian Air Force who rose through the ranks to become Chief of the Air Staff and later served as India's ambassador to Iran.

ARJAN SINGH

Marshal of the Indian Air Force Arjan Singh, DFC (15 April 1919-) is the only officer of the Indian Air Force to be promoted to five star rank, equal to a Field Marshal, to which he was promoted in 2002. He was born in the Punjab Lyalpur, British

India, into a Aulakh family. With the death of Field Marshal Sam Manekshaw in June 2008, he is presently the only living Indian military officer with a five-star rank.

Education and training

Singh was educated at Montgomery India (now in Pakistan). He entered the RAF College Cranwell in 1938 and was commissioned as a Pilot Officer in December 1939. He led No. 1 Squadron, Indian Air Force into command during the Arakan Campaign in 1944. He was awarded the Distinguished Flying Cross (DFC) in 1944, and commanded the Indian Air Force Exhibition Flight in 1945. Almost faced a court martial, when he tried to raise the morale of an air force pilot, by conducting a low level air pass over a house in Kerala. Though he apologised for his mistake, but he insisted that such tricks are needed for every cadet to be a fighter pilot.

Career and commands held

He was Chief of the Air Staff (CAS), from 1 August 1964 to 15 July 1969, and was awarded the Padma Vibhushan in 1965. He was Lt. Governor of Delhi from Dec 1989-Dec 1990 and was made Marshal of the Air Force in January, 2002.

Career Highlights

- 1938 — Commissioned in Royal Air Force as a Pilot Officer
- 1940-Flying Officer
- 1942-Flight Lieutenant
- 1944-Squadron Leader
- 1945 — Awarded Distinguished Flying Cross
- 1947 — Wing Commander, Royal Indian Air Force, Air Force Station, Ambala
- 1948 — Group Captain, Director, Training, Air Headquarters
- 1950 — Air Commodore, Indian Air Force AOC, Operational Command
- 1959 — Air Vice Marshal
- 1961 — Air Officer in Charge, Administration, Air HQ

- 1963 — Deputy Chief of Air Staff and subsequently Vice Chief of Air Staff
- 1964 — Chief of Air Staff (Air Marshal)
- 1965 — Chief of Air Staff rank upgraded to that of an Air Chief Marshal
- 1965 — Awarded Padma Vibhushan
- 1966 — Chairman of the Chief of Staff Committee
- 1969 — Retired from Indian Air Force
- 1971 — Ambassador to Switzerland and the Holy See
- 1974 — High Commissioner to Kenya
- 1980 — Member of the Minorities Commission
- 1989 — Lt. Governor, Delhi
- 2002-Marshal of the Air Force

Marshal of the Air Force Arjan Singh, DFC, was one pilot who grew up in the annals of the air force as the first chief for leading the force into war. He was Chief of Air Staff when the IAF saw action in its first combat of the modern age in 1965. He was hardly 44 years of age when entrusted with the responsibility of leading the Indian Air Force, a responsibility he carried with considerable flamboyance and élan.

Arjan Singh was born on 15 April 1919, in Lyalpur, completing his education at Montgomery. He was still in college in 1938, 19 years of age when he was selected for the Empire Pilot training course at RAF Cranwell. His first posting on being commissioned was flying Westland Wapiti biplanes in the North Western Frontier Province as a member of the No.1 IAF Squadron. Arjan Singh, flew against the tribal forces, before he was transferred for a brief stint with the newly formed No.2 IAF Squadron. Later he moved back to No.1 as a Flying Officer, when the Squadron re-equipped with the Hawker Hurricane.

Promoted to Squadron Leader in 1944, Arjan Singh led the squadron against the Japanese during the Arakan Campaign flying close support during the crucial Imphal Campaign and later assisting the advance of the allied forces to Rangoon, Burma. For his role in successfully leading the squadron in combat, Arjan Singh received the Distinguished Flying Cross

(DFC) in 1944. He was given command of the IAF Display flight flying Hawker Hurricanes after the war which toured India giving demonstrations. On 15 August 1947, he had the unique honour of leading the fly-past of over a hundred IAF aircraft over Delhi, over the red fort.

Promoted to Wing Commander, he attended Staff College at UK, and immediately after Indian independence became the AOC, Ambala in the rank of Group Captain. In 1949, promoted to Air Commodore, Arjan Singh took over the Air Officer Commanding of Operational Command, which later came to be known as Western Air Command. Arjan Singh had the distinction of having the longest tenure as the AOC of Operational Command, from 1949-1952 and again from 1957-1961. Promoted to Air Vice Marshal, he was the AOC-in-C of Operational Command. Towards the end of the 1962 war, he was appointed the DCAS and became the VCAS by 1963. He was the overall commander of the joint air training exercises "Shiksha" held between the IAF, RAF and RAAF.

On 01 August 1964, Arjan Singh took over as the Chief of Air Staff in the rank of Air Marshal, which became the pinnacle of this career. Arjan Singh was the first Air Chief who kept his flying category till his CAS rank. Having flown over 60 different types of aircraft from Pre-WW-2 era biplanes to the more contemporary, Gnats & Vampires, he also had flown in transports like the Super Constellation. Arjan Singh's, testing time came in September 1965, when the subcontinent was plunged into war. When Pakistan launched its Operation Grand Slam, in which an armoured thrust targeted the vital town of Akhnur, he was summoned into the Defence Minister's office with a request for air support.

With a characteristic non-chalance, he replied "...in an hour." And true enough, the air force struck the Pakistani offensive in an hour. He led the air Force through the war showing successful leadership and effort. Though at a certain level, mistakes were made and planning could have been better, in all fairness, it must be said that the credit for thwarting Ayub Khan's grandiose plans to capture Kashmir is shared by the Indian Army and the Indian Air Force, and Arjan Singh for leading the air force through the war.

Arjan Singh was awarded the Padma Vibhushan for his leadership of the air force, and subsequently in recognition of the air force's contribution in the war, the rank of the CAS was upgraded to that of Air Chief Marshal and Arjan Singh became the first Air Chief Marshal of the Indian Air Force. He retired in August 1969, thereupon accepting ambassador ship to Switzerland. He remained a flyer to the end of his tenure in the IAF, visiting forward squadrons & units and flying with them. Arjan Singh was a source of inspiration to a generation of Indians and Officers. In recognition of his services, the Government of India conferred the rank of the Marshal of the Air Force onto Arjan Singh in January 2002 making him the first and the only 'Five Star' rank officer with the Indian Air Force.

A delightful account of an ace pilot

In these depressing days of a scam a day, a biography of a living legend of our armed forces, the first Marshal of the Indian Air Force, Arjan Singh, brings some hope that all is not lost yet. This intrepid soldier stands out as an example of how one man with his dignified behaviour and soldierly élan, can truly be called a leader of men and of a mighty force that he has so energetically lead with distinction in war and in peace over the last many decades.

Roopinder Singh, now on the editorial staff of *The Tribune*, has put together a very readable account of an ace pilot who handled with distinction every assignment, be it in the Air Force, in the field of governance or in diplomacy. As Ambassador to Switzerland and the Vatican, and later as High Commissioner to Kenya, he rubbed shoulders with the high and mighty. Back home he served with the Minorities Commission of India and later on became the Lieutenant Governor of Delhi in the V. P. Singh government in 1989. While with the commission he said, "There were not too many problems of the Sikhs, since by nature they are problem-solvers themselves. In 1984 when the anti-Sikh riots took place, he narrates that he, along with Kuldip Nayar and Patwant Singh, went and met President Zail Singh and asked him to call out the Army without delay. Arjan Singh says, "He (Zail Singh) attempted to contact the Prime Minister and the Home Minister but without success.

Unfortunately, the deployment of the Army was delayed till the evening. As a result, many lives were lost. It was a politically inspired situation which went out of control by omission and commission and I do not blame any particular community for it". Polite yet firm, the Marshal has his own way of spelling out the truth. Ever a farmer at heart and a son of the soil, he, as the Lieutenant Governor of Delhi, ensured that the farmers whose lands were bought out by the builders and the Delhi Development Authority, were paid reasonable rates of compensation.

Born at Lyallpur, now in Pakistan, Singh was commissioned into the IAF in 1939, and shortly thereafter awarded the Distinguished Flying Cross in 1944 during World War II.

He commanded the IAF station at Ambala and was the Deputy and Vice Chief of Air Staff, before being selected to command the elite Air Force in the critical days of the Indo-Pak war of 1965, when he was awarded the Padma Vibhushan. He retired from the IAF in 1969, but continued to lead an active life. In 2002, at long last, one has to say, because this recognition should have by right come to him much earlier (Manekshaw who was the COAS in the 1971 war became the Field Marshal well before Singh), this soldier-cum-diplomat was appointed the Marshal of the Indian Air Force.

The NDA government did what the Congress governments should have done long ago. Roopinder Singh, in his taut and captivating account, written in simple yet effective prose, has brought centre stage a man who never asked for anything himself, not even the honorary Marshalship of a force that he had nurtured from its very inception in the early days in the NWFP, when the single-engined Wapiti aircraft that he so ably flew as a youngster, was the mainstay of the IAF.

Arjan Singh set exacting standards for his command, and sent home many who had not done well in the 1965 war. "You have to maintain discipline. If someone has done wrong, punish him, if he has done well, reward him", he states. How one wishes that some of our very senior armed forces commanders remember this piece of advice from a war veteran. There is no dearth of testimonials that Singh has earned from his superiors and peers. In 1965, Defence Minister Y. B. Chavan said while referring to him, "When he is asked to go on a new task, CAS walks as a dancing bird. A real fighting Sikh: and yet how soft and gentle". And then again Chavan said, "Air Marshal Arjan Singh is a jewel of a person; quietly efficient and firm, unexcitable but a very able leader".

Recently, George Fernandes said about him, "The significant changes that you brought about in the structuring and functioning of the Air Force took it towards becoming a strong professional force. Successive generations of officers and men in the Indian Air Force have looked up to you as a father figure".

Some of the photographs from the Marshal's personal collection that appear in the book are, indeed, priceless. From his earlier days at the RAF Flying College at Cranwell in UK, to the active flying days with the fearless Baba Mehar Singh and Pritpal Singh, to the pinning of the DFC by Admiral Lord Mountbatten at the Imphal airstrip in 1944, and then in an achkan and chooridar pyjama with bride Teji on their wedding day, all bring to mind an active and energetic personality, who lived life to the hilt. Now that a beginning has been made with this book, this writer hopes that Arjan Singh will find time to pen down his memoirs in his own words for posterity.

A delightful read of a man who towers above most of today's Generals, Admirals and Air Marshals. And also above the majority of our politicians, who somehow persist in calling themselves leaders.

A Many Splendoured Career

Air Chief Marshal Arjan Singh, who was Chief of Air Staff of the Indian Air Force from 1964 to 1969, is the epitome of a military leader and it is in the great fitness of things, and truly a grand morale booster to the officers and men of the Indian Air Force that he was honoured with the rank of Marshal of the Indian Air Force (equivalent to the Army's Field Marshal), on the Republic Day of 2002. This is appropriate and timely even as the world's fourth largest Air force prepares for a major upgradation of its capabilities in the new millennium.

Born on 15 April 1919 in Lyallpur and educated first in Montgomery (now Sahiwal in Pakistan) and then at the

Government College in Lahore, Arjan Singh joined the infant Indian Air Force in 1938. He was commissioned from the RAF College Cranwell on 23 December 1939, and as a Pilot Officer with 'A' Flight at Drigh Road, Karachi first saw operations on the North West Frontier Province (NWFP).

Arjan Singh's two operational tenures on the Burma Front during World War II—the first as a Pilot Officer with No.1 Squadron ("Tigers") and subsequently in 1944, as Commander of the same Squadron, are outstanding landmarks of his enviable flying career. In the first, he assiduously learnt the techniques of air warfare in the thick of battle, during ceaseless sorties that he flew day in and day out.

During the second, as a consummate Squadron Commander, he displayed masterly leadership to the maximum advantage of the IAF during the seige of Imphal. In recognition of his leadership and gallantry in the air, he was awarded the Distinguished Flying Cross (DFC) on the spot, the first Indian pilot to be so honoured by the Supreme Allied Commander, South East Asia. The citation read:

Squndron Leader Arja11 Singh is a fearless and exceptional Pilot, with a profound knowledge of his specialised branch of tactical reconnaissance and he has imbued those under him with the same spirit. The success of No. 1 Squadron Indian Air Force reflects the greatest credit on him.

When India became a Republic in 1950, Arjan Singh was commanding the Operational Group, then responsible for all air operations from Kashmir to Kanya Kumari. Arjan Singh held the Command of this Group, the only fighting arm of the IAF, till December 1952 and again from December 1955 to April 1959, initially in the rank of Air Commodore and then in the rank of Air Vice Marshal for over 6 years, longer than any other officer of the IAF.

After India became independent, Arjan Singh was detailed to undergo a number of prestigious courses in the United Kingdom:

- RAF Staff College, Brackwell
- Joint Services Staff College, UK
- Imperial Defence College, London.

His long tenure of the all-embracing Operational Group well groomed and equipped Arjan Singh for higher Command. In between, from December 1952 to December 1955 he was Air Officer-in-Charge Personnel Organisation and Air Officer-in-Charge Administration from May 1961 till December 1962, which provided him with necessary administrative experience so essential for an Air Chief in the making.

On 1 August 1964, Air Marshal Arjan Singh took over as the IAF's third Indian Chief of Air Staff. With the well-recognised qualities of leadership, experience and inborn confidence, Arjan Singh consummately directed the air campaign during the war of September 1965, but for the timely and effective action by the Indian Air Force in the Chhamb sector on 1st September, history could well have had been different. In the subsequent weeks, the IAF consolidated its air superiority by deep penetration attacks against enemy targets, including the farthest Pak airfields like Peshawar and Mauripur before the conflict came to an end.

Arjan Singh, who on 1 August 1964 had become Chief of Air Staff in the rank of Air Marshal at the young age of 45, was the first officer of the Indian Air Force to don the tapes of Air Chief Marshal, on January 15th 1966. By the time he was 50 he had completed his tenure and retired, after having held the exalted office of Chief of Air Staff for 5 1/2 years, the longest of any Chief of the three Services. The career graph of Arjan Singh is an inspiration, and he remains an icon for subsequent generations of the Indian Air Force.

Arjan Singh has flown no less than 65 different types of aircraft and continued his passion for flying till the last day of retirement. Arjan Singh's zest for flying percolated right down the line, which enthused the flyers for combat flying training and who then gave ample proof of their readiness in the 1965 war. Arjan Singh's leadership from the cockpit won him not only the confidence of the flyers, but earned him their complete reverence too. In 1967, Arjan Singh had the unique honour of being invited to take the salute at the passing out parade of the Royal Air Force Flying College, Cranwell, where he had first learnt flying 28 years earlier, and presented the 'Sword of Honour' to the best Cadet.

Arjan Singh is an amiable, softspoken man of few words, and by nature averse to confrontation. He does not believe in throwing his weight about, nor likes to tread on others. However, despite his discreetly maintained soft exterior, he is a man of firm action.

He did not hesitate in discarding three senior officers ("directed to resign"), on account of their inept performance during the 1965 War. During Arjan Singh's tenure as Chief of Air Staff, the IAF was equipped With new generation supersonic fighters, strategic reconnaissance aircraft, tactical transport aircraft and assault helicopters, still in service today. The long overdue establishment of the Air Force Academy at Hyderabad was started. Work on modern radar and communication network also commenced.

Measured by any standard, Arjan Singh has had some fine innings. Even after retirement he continued to serve the country. In 1971, he was accredited as India's Ambassador to Switzerland. From there, in 1974 he went to Kenya, as the Indian High Commissioner, and returned to India in 1976, after having had a Six year long ambassadorial stint, longer than any other officer from the Armed Forces. Some years on, he became the Lt. Governor to Delhi. For his meritorious services in the conduct of the 1965 Indo-Pak War, Arjan Singh was honoured with the Padma Vibhushan.

Arjan Singh Leads the Tigers

In May 1943, a detachment of the famous No. 1 Squadron (the Tlgers) went to Miranshah farr bombing trials and then moved to Kohat where command was assumed by Sqn. Ldr. Arjan Singh on 3 September 1943. During the next few months, No. 1 Squadron detachments carried out army co-operation exercises at Adampur, in the Punjab. In early December 1943, Field Marshal Sir Claude Auchinleck visited the RAF Station at Kohat and inspected No. I Squadron. Sqn. Ldr. Arjan Singh advocated the intense desire of his Squadron to go back into battle. This was supported by the RAF Station Commander. Within a week of this request, No. 1 Squadron (now with Hurricane IIBs) was ordered to move immediately to Imphal on the Manipur front where massive buildups were taking place on both sides of the Assam-Burma border. The next year was to be breathless with action and epoch marking in the already chequered history of the Tiger Squadron.

No. 1 Squadron reached Imphal (Main) on 3 February 1944 and were to remain in action thereafter for a record period of 14 months, taking vital part in the fateful seige of Imphal followed by the trans-Chindwin and transIrrawaddy offenses Once again, No. 1 Squadron IAF shared the base with their old colleagues-in-arms No. 28 Squadron RAF, both being Tactical Reconnaissance Units (Tac R), cooperating closely with the Army. The Tigers under Sqn. Ldr. Arjan Singh commenced operational flying immediately, with sector reconnaissances flown on 5 February, carrying out offensive, tactical and photographic reconnaissance to observe Japanese movements on the Chindwin, beyond Tiddim, and as far east as the Mytkyina-Mandalay railway, much valuable information being obtained by the Squadron.

The Japanese offensive against Imphal started on 8 March, attempting to cut off the 17th Indian Division as it retreated. No. 1 Squadron's task was to locate the position of the retreating troops day to day and to keep the tracks leading from the Tiddim road under observation for Japanese movements. Fighting in the thick jungle-hills was confused. On 29 March, during-late evening reconnaissance by Arjan Singh, Japanese troops were seen clambering down the hills. Landing back at Imphal Main to refuel, the entire Squadron was led back into the area by him before sunset and the Hurricanes hammered the enemy with machine guns and bombs, decimating the Japanese advance battalion, with 14 officers and 217 men killed and wounded.

During March, the Squadron had flown 366 sorties but April 1944 was to be a crucial month when the seige of Imphal tightened and the Japanese came so close that the Imphal airfields were within range of enemy artillery fire. Maximum air effort was put in by No. 1 Squadron, flying 412 sorties in April, tactical reconnaissance mostly over the Tiddim road, Palel-Tamu-Sittaung road, Imphal Kohima road and Ukhrul road. The Tigers strafed bashas, mechanical transport, gun positions and troops. In turn, Japanese Kawasaki Ki-48 and Mitsubishi Ki-21 bombers raided Imphal on 15 April, damaging two of No. 1 Squadron's Hurricanes. During May 1944, the weather deteriorated with early monsoon rains which curtailed flying yet No. 1 Squadron flew 372 sorties, including 32 by night, that month, which also had the loss of a long range reconnaissance Hurricane to prowling Japanese Nakajima Ki-43 (Oskar) fighters. No. 1 Squadron's aircraft ranged over almost the entire battlefield, carrying out continuous tactical reconnaissance as in the area north-east of Imphal the Japanese were being gradually pushed back.

June 1944 was an even more trying month, the runways waterlogged and rain storms which made flying hazardous. No. 28 Squadron RAF has been pulled out of Imphal, leaving No. 1 Squadron TAF solely responsible for tactical reconnaissance in the area, flying 327 sorties that month. The Tiger's Hurricane IIBs (with machine guns) were replaced by Hurricane IICs (with cannon) for greater effect in ground attack missions. The seige of Imphal was broken by the month-end and the Squadron was tasked to keep harrassing the retreating Japanese, mainly in the Ukhrul area and south of Imphal. Reconnaissance was carried out over the roads and tracks from Palel to Sittaung on the Chindwin, from Tamu to Kamjong, from Htinzin to Yazagyo, the Chindwin river and so on, a total of 307 sorties being flown in July.

During the ensuing battle for Central Burma, the British Indian forces mounted relentless pressure on the retreating Japanese beyond the Chindwin and No. 1 Squadron, as part of the 221 Group, operated from forward bases covering a front of some 200 miles to the limits of their endurance and range. In August, No. 1 Squadron flew 354 sorties, with targets of opportunity being attacked, but deteriorating weather in September reduced sorties, to 292, but these were longer in duration, the Hurricanes fitted with extra fuel tanks. On 17 September, the Tigers attacked bunkers on a hill feature in the Yazagvo area and Taukkyan airfield south-west of Kalemyo. And so into October, with the Squadron flying a record 439 operational missions totalling 780 hours, the Tigers operating to as far as the Mandalav Myitkyina railway. The value of No. 1 Squadron's tactical reconnaissance was gratefullv acknowledged by XXXIII Corps, the Squadron commended "for the skill and speed with which aerial photographs have been produced and dropped on forward troops".

The Japanese continued to fall back and in November, No. 1 Squadron were discovering their lines of retreat. With an average strength of 17 pilots, the Tigers flew 524 operational sorties, totaling just over 1000 flying hours, a most fantastic effort !

On the night of 3 November, Sqn.Ldr.Arjan Singh had carried out a vital low level tac-recce of the bridge at Hpaungzeik, enabling the allies to move across and No.1 Squadron received a notable appreciation of its efforts from GOC 20th Indian Division who presented them with a Japanese sword of honour captured in the battle of Imphal in recognition of "assistance readily and courageouslv given by its pilots and crews".

PRATAP CHANDRA LAL

Air Chief Marshal Pratap Chandra Lal (1916–1982) was the Chief of Air Staff, Indian Air Force during the Indo-Pakistan War of 1971. He served in the IAF from 1939 until his retirement in 1973. He served as CO of No. 7 Squadron, AOC-in-C of Western Air Command, VCAS and Managing Director of Hindustan Aeronautics Limited. He also served as Chairman, Air India after retirement. During his service, he received the Distinguished Flying Cross, the Padma Bhushan and finally the Padma Vibhushan. He embarked on writing his memoirs My Years with the IAF, but died before completing them. His wife Mrs. Ela Lal finished the book and published it in 1983.

Pratap Chandra Lal was born in December 1917. Though his ancestors were lawyers he had inclination in aviation from his childhood. At the age of 17 he got the Amateur Pilot's license as the youngest Indian pilot. Pratap Chandra Lal graduated in journalism from King's College, London in 1938. After that Pratap Chandra Lal took Empire Pilot training at Royal Air Force and was commissioned into the Indian Air Force in Karachi in 1940 as a navigator. Later Pratap Chandra Lal worked as a navigation instructor at Risalpur. In 1941 he was appointed to No.3 Coast Defense Fight, Calcutta. After two months he was appointed as a Navigation Instructor to No.1 Flying Training School at Ambala. After two years Pratap

Chandra Lal was posted flying and navigational instructor to the Operational Training Unit at Peshawar.

In 1943 he joined the No.7 Squadron as a combat pilot. During Burma campaign this squadron was involved in several major battles including Imphal, Kohima, Aryan and Rangoon. In 1945 Pratap Chandra Lal was made squadron leader for his exceptional performances. For his courageous leadership in the war against Japan he was awarded the Distinguished Flying Cross medal. In 1946 he was promoted to the rank of Wing Commander and posted to the Inter-Services Recruiting Office, Calcutta. After five months Pratap Chandra Lal moved to U.K to attend a senior commander's course. After returning back to India Air Chief Marshal Pratap Chandra Lal was appointed as Director of Planning & Training in the rank of Group Captain. He again moved to U.K to attend a course at Royal Air Force Staff College. After a year he came back to India and was promoted to the rank of Air Commodore. In 1951 Pratap Chandra Lal captained the Indian Air Force team, which supported the then Nepal King Tribhuvan to face palace coup. Air Chief Marshal Pratap Chandra Lal was also the military secretary to the cabinet for two years. In 1954 he was sent to Europe as a team leader for the assessment of the new aircraft for Indian Air Force. Pratap Chandra Lal was the first Indian to fly supersonic and the Gnat.

In 1957 he was appointed to the Ministry of Civil Aviation as General Manager of the Indian Airlines Corporation. It was during this time he resigned from his service. After few months his service was again reinstated. He was promoted to the rank of Air Vice Marshal and posted as Air Officer Maintenance. In 1963 Air Chief Marshal Pratap Chandra Lal was appointed as Air Officer Commanding-in-Chief Western Air Command. After a year he was posted to Air Headquarters as the Vice Chief of Air Staff. In 1965 Air Chief Marshal Pratap Chandra Lal was awarded Padma Bhushan for his exceptional performances in the war against china. For a short while he was posted in the Training Command. After that he was appointed as the managing director of the Hindustan Aeronautical Ltd. In 1969 he assumed the charge of the Chief of Air Staff. During the war against Pakistan in 1971 his performance was remarkable. It would not be an exaggeration to say that P.C. Lal was the main brain behind the Indian Air Force's most significant triumph. For exemplary leadership Air Chief Marshal Pratap Chandra Lal was awarded the Padma Vibhushan in 1972. He retired from the Indian Air Force, on 15th January 1973. He also held some crucial advisory posts after his retirement. Air Chief Marshal Pratap Chandra Lal died in 1984.

It was under the able leadership of Air Chief Marshal Pratap Chandra Lal, that the Indian Air Force won its most decisive victory in 1971. Paradoxically, unlike the earlier Chiefs, Lal was no fighter jock. He was an instructor and a manager, par excellence. His contribution to India's aviation industry via tenures with the Indian Airlines Corporation and Hindustan Aeronautics Ltd. bear testament to his professional abilities. He was just the sort of chap who could, and did, mould a large and rapidly expanding air force into an efficient fighting force. Pratap Chandra Lal was born in December 1917, into a family of Allahabad-based lawyers. He had an early interest in aviation, and became the youngest Indian to earn his Amateur Pilot's license at age 17, in January 1934. Having qualified for a diploma in journalism at King's College, London in 1938, Lal expected to return to full-time study of law at the Inns of Court in the fall of 1939.

However, the outbreak of war in Europe precluded his return to England. As part of Britain's efforts to strengthen India's defence in such perilous times, the government decided to expand the Indian Air Force (then one squadron of Wapitis). Consequently, everyone in India with a pilot's license was invited to join up. With little else to do in the fall of 1939, Lal decided to give the air force a try.

P.C. Lal arrived at the training establishment at RAF Station, Risalpur on 12 November 1939. An acute shortage of navigators in India (both RAF and IAF) led to Lal being recruited as a navigator, with the proviso that he would later be trained as a pilot. He was commissioned into the Indian Air Force in Karachi during May 1940. Three months later he was posted back to Risalpur as a navigation instructor. During his tenure there he instructed both RAF and IAF pilots (both of whom he considered rather weak in navigation). In January 1941 he was posted to No.3 Coast Defence Fight based at Calcutta. Two months later he was recalled as Navigation Instructor to No.1 Flying Training School at Ambala.

It was during his tenure at Ambala, that Lal earned his 'wings' flying Audaxes and Hawker Harts. Early in 1943 Lal was posted as flying and navigational instructor to the Operational Training Unit at Peshawar where he oversaw the conversion of two RAF Squadrons and the IAF's No.7 and No.8 Squadrons to Vultee Vengeance dive bombers. In October of 1943, after much persuasion, Lal was allowed to join Hem Chaudhuri's No.7 Squadron as a combat pilot. The squadron, however, didn't see action until February of 1944, by which time it had converted to Hawker Hurricanes. Between February 1944 and March 1945 No.7 Squadron (along with No.1 IAF) was very active on the Burma front and took part in every major battle: including, Imphal, Kohima, Akyab and Rangoon. In that one year Lal had managed to log 210 hours and ended the campaign as a Squadron Leader. In October 1945, P.C. Lal earned a Distinguished Flying Cross for undertaking hazardous recon flights deep into Japanese held territory.

In 1946, Sqn. Ldr. Lal applied for and received a permanent commission in the IAF. He was thereafter promoted to Wing Commander and sent to Calcutta to take charge of the Inter-Services Recruiting Office in August 1946. This stint lasted a mere five months, and in December that year left to attend a senior commander's course in the U.K. Upon his return in was promoted to Group Captain and appointed in 1947 to the post of Director of Planning & Training. In 1948 he relinquished training responsibilities to Group Captain (later Marshal of the Air Force) Arjan Singh. In May 1949, Lal was sent to attend courses at the RAF Staff College for nearly a year. He returned to India in June 1950 and was shortly promoted to Air Commodore.

In November 1951, P.C. Lal led the Indian Air Force team that helped bring King Tribhuvan of Nepal to safety in the face of abortive palace coup. Between 1953 and 1955 P.C. Lal worked as the Military Secretary to the Cabinet. In October 1954, P.C. Lal went to Europe at the head to a team to evaluate new aircraft for the IAF. He became the first Indian to fly supersonic (in a Mystere IVA) and to fly the Gnat. This team was also instrumental in ensuring that the IAF didn't end up buying the Supermarine Swift. In 1957, P.C. Lal was deputed to the Ministry of Civil Aviation as General Manager of the Indian Airlines Corporation (IAC). During his six years there he oversaw its successful evolution as a corporate entity. It was during this period that he fell out with then Defence Minister V.K. Krishna Menon over the purchase of replacements for the Airlines' aging Dakotas. Menon was convinced that IAC's requirements could be met with the Hs. 748s that the Air Force was acquiring. Lal thought otherwise. In the end Krishna Menon prevailed. And at the end of P.C. Lal's tenure as GM of IAC on 30 September 1962, Krishna Menon ensured that his services with the Indian Air Force were terminated.

By a quirk of fate Krishna Menon's inept handling of the China crisis in October 1962 forced his resignation before the year was out. In December 1962, P.C. Lal's services were reinstated by the Air Force as Air Officer Maintenance with the rank of Air Vice Marshal. On 24 November 1963, he was posted as Air Officer Commanding-in-Chief Western Air Command. And on 01 October 1964, he moved to Air Headquarters as the Vice Chief of Air Staff. He served in that capacity during the war in 1965. For his contributions during the war P.C. Lal was awarded the Padma Bhushan. At the end of the war he was appointed to head Training Command with the rank of Air Marshal. This was to be a short stint, and in late 1966, he was deputed to head Hindustan Aeronautical Ltd. as Managing Director. During his three years at HAL, P.C. Lal was instrumental in overseeing the establishment of the production lines for HAL's new MiG-21 and Gnat fighters, and the Hs.748 freighters (the very aircraft he had crossed swords with Krishna Menon over!). What was more ironic is that P.C. Lal, who had almost been thrown of the Air Force, was asked to take over as Chief of Staff effective, 16 July 1969.

Upon taking office, Lal was determined to ensure that the Indian Air Force contribute more decisively to the outcome of any future war. And to this end spent much time reorganizing training and logistics. Early on during his tenure, P.C. Lal made it a point to visit various army units in order to better understand their needs for air support. His efforts did not go un-rewarded. In the winter of 1971, P.C. Lal found himself leading the air force in a war against Pakistan. Indeed, who better to lead the IAF in these crucial years than a distinguished pilot, a skilled instructor and a manager par excellence. Improved tactics, training and careful planning all contributed the ascendancy of the IAF as one of Asia's most effective air arms.

The air force was involved at every stage of this intense conflict which led to the creation of an independent Bangladesh on 16 December 1971. For Lal, the war in 1971 marked the pinnacle of his career. It would not be an overstatement to say that P.C. Lal was the architect of the IAF's most decisive victory.

In 1972, P.C. Lal was awarded the Padma Vibhushan for his leadership of the air force. He retired from the IAF, on 15 January 1973 as the IAF's most successful chief and its most highly decorated officer. After his retirement from the Air Force P.C. Lal continued to serve in various advisory capacities to the Government of India. Air Chief Marshal Pratap Chandra Lal passed away in 1984 while he was still working on his memoirs and a history of the IAF. The book was eventually completed by his wife and provides an eminently readable history of the IAF's first 25 years.

OM PRAKASH MEHRA

Om Prakash Mehra was Chief of the Air Staff (India) from 1973 to 1976. He received Param Vishistht Sewa Medal in 1968. He was awarded Padma Vibhushan in 1977. He later became governor of Maharashtra from 1980 to 1982 and governor of Rajasthan from 1982 to 1985.

Air Chief Marshal OP Mehra was born on 19th January 1919 at Lahore. His basic education was at the Sacred Heart Convent. He finished school at the Central Model School in 1933 and joined Government College, Lahore, and completed a Masters Degree from the Punjab University in mid 1940. After a short spell of flying at the Northern India Flying Club, Lahore, he was selected for the Indian Air Force and joined the services as Pilot Officer on 30th November 1940.

On completion of his training, he was posted to No.1 Squadron in August 1941. In March 1946 Mehra was selected to serve as the Indian Air force representative at the Joint Chiefs of Staff in Australia-An organization set up to provide Administrative and Logistics support to the British Commonwealth Occupation Forces located in Japan. In view of Nationalization of the armed forces, he was recalled and posted in February 1947 as the Chief Ground Instructor at the No.1 Advance Flying School Ambala, to replace the RAF Officer who was returning home. In August 1947 he was promoted to the rank of Wing Commander and posted as Commandant of the Elementary Flying Training School at Jodhpur.

On promotion to the rank of Air Vice-Marshal in August 1963 he look over as AOC in Chief Maintenance Command, in which capacity he served during the 1965 War. In January 1968 he was awarded the PVSM and promoted Air Marshal in March 1968. Soon thereafter he was posted as Deputy Chief of Air Staff, Air Headquarters. Early 1971 he was deputed as Chairman Hindustan Aeronautics Ltd Bangalore. On 15th January 1973 he returned to Air Headquarters, designated as the new Chief of Air Staff, succeeding Air Chief Marshal PC Lal.

Air Chief Marshal Mehra relinquished the post to Air Chief Marshal Moolgavkar on 31st January 1976, on completion of his tenure. After his retirement, he represented India at a UNESCO meeting in Paris as Deputy Leader of India's Team. He was the recipient of Padma Vibhushan in January 1977. He went on to serve as the Governor of Maharashtra (1980) and later as Governor of Rajasthan (1982).

Air Chief Marshal Mehra was elected President of the Indian Olympic Association and was responsible for the hosting by India of the Asian Games in 1982. From 1978 to 1980 he was President of the Asian Games Federation, currently known as the Olympic Council of Asia and continues to be the Honorary Life President of the Olympic Council of Asia.

Academic Qualifications

- M.A. History from Panjab University in 1940
- Air Force Career Commisioned on 30th November, 1940

- Appointed Chief of Air Staff on 15th Jan.1973.

Constitutional Appointments

- Governor of Maharashtra (3rd November 1980 to 6th March,1982)
- Governor of Rajsthan (6th March 1982 to 4th Nov. 1985)

Other Important Professional Assignment

- IAF representative on Join Chiefs of Staff in Australia-1946 to 1947
- Dean, Institute of Armament Technology, Pune from 1960 to 1963
- Chairman, Hindustan Aeronautics Ltd. Bangalore from March 1971 to Oct. 1973.

Association With Professional Bodies

Follow of Aeronautical Society of India

- Aeronautical Society of India from 1947 to 1977 — President
- Center for Air Power Studies-Vice Chairmen
- Center for Strategic and International Studies-Member
- Management Committee for Shri Satya Sai International Canter and School for propagation of human values.-Member

Sports and allied Activities

- Olympic Council of Asia Hony life — President
- Indian Olympic Association from 1975 to 1980 — President
- Asian Games Federation since Re designated OCA 1978-1980 — President
- Delhi Gymkhana Club (2 years) — President
- Delhi Golf Club Ltd.(2 Years till Oct.1994) — President
- Delhi Race Club Ltd.(4 Years) — President
- Services Sports Control Board for 4 Years — Vice President
- Indian Hockey Federation (6 Years) — Vice President
- Delhi Lawn Tennis Association(2 Years) — President

- Durand Cup Football (1973 to 1975) — Member and later Chairman

Association with International, Organisations

- C.I. International Hotels Ltd. — Director
- Polyplex Corporation Ltd. — Director
- Mayar India Ltd. New Delhi — Director
- Adyar Gate Hotels Ltd. Chennai — Director
- Ansal Properties & Industrial Ltd. — Director
- ROPSSA Properties & Enterprises Pvt. Ltd. — Chairman

Honours & Awards

- Param Vishistht Sewa Medal — Jan. 1968
- Padam Vibhushan — Jan. 1977
- Srimoni Award — 1988
- Rajiv Ratna Award — 1991
- Help Age India Golden Award--1999
- Distinguished Leadership Award for Services to the Indian Air Force
- National Security Awarded by the American Biographical Institute.

Air Chief Marshal OP Mehra was born on 19th January 1919 at Lahore. His basic education was at the Sacred Heart Convent. He finished school at the Central Model School in 1933 and joined the Government College Lahore and completed a Masters Degree from the Punjab University in mid 1940. After a short spell of flying at the Northern India Flying Club Lahore, he was selected for the Indian Air Force and joined the services as Pilot Officer on 30th November 1940.

On completion of his training, he was posted to No.1 Squadron in August 1941. On the formation of No.3 Squadron, He was posted to the new Squadron. He had the distinction of serving only with No.3 Squadron throughout, till he commanded the Squadron in 1945. No.3 Squadron was initially equipped with Hawker Hart and Andax Aircraft and saw extensive service in the North West Frontier Province. With just over two years service in January 1943 he was selected to undergo a course at the Defence Service Staff College at

Quetta. He was the youngest and the junior most Officer on that Course. On successful completion of the course he was reposted to No.3 Squadron, which by then had been equipped with Hawker Hurricanes. Towards the end of 1944 after doing a course at SLAIS (Specialised Low Attack Instructors School)- the Squadron moved to the Arakan Coast.

Though he was the adjutant of the Squadron, his operational flying was as much if not more than the other Officers of his seniority. The Squadron operated for a few days from Coxs Bazar on the Arakan Coast and was then moved to Bawali Bazar and later to Akyab. The task of the Squadron was offensive operations against the Japanese army, which by then had started retreating.

Around mid March 1945 the Squadron was pulled out and deployed at St. Thomas Mount Airfield near Madras. After a short period the Squadron was repositioned at RAF Station Risalpur in the North West province to be re-equipped with spitfire Vs and VIIIs. At about this time he was promoted to the Rank of Squadron Leader and he assumed Command of the Squadron, which on completion of the re-equipment and armament training was shifted to Bangalore and within 3 days of its stay, the Squadron was re-deployed at Kolar, an air-field which had not been in use for years. The Squadron had a trying time at that base as it was called upon to manage every aspect of running a base with even the basics not in position.

In March 1946 Mehra was selected to serve as the Indian Air force representative at the Joint Chiefs of Staff in Australia- An organization set up to provide Administrative and Logistics support to the British Commonwealth Occupation Forces located in Japan. In view of Nationalization of the armed forces, he was recalled and posted in February 1947 as the Chief Ground Instructor at the No.1 Advance Flying School Ambala, to replace the RAF Officer who was returning home.

In August 1947 he was promoted to the rank of Wing Commander and posted as Commandant of the Elementary Flying Training School at Jodhpur, later on designated as No.2 Air Force Academy. In August 1950, he was promoted to the rank of Group Captain and he took over Command of No.2 Ground Training School at Tambaram Madras where he spent three years. He was, in September 1953 posted to Air Headquarters as Director of Training.

Having had a long spell heading Training Institutions, he was posted as Senior Air Staff Officer (SASO), Operational Command,(later designated as Western Air Command). After a span of nearly four years he was shifted to Jamnagar as Commanding Officer of Armament Training Wing effective April 1958. On promotion to the rank of Air Commodore in January 1960, he returned to Air Headquarters as Principal Staff Officer in charge of the Policy and Plan Division, which he held only for 10 months as his services were loaned to the Defence Research and Development Organisation as Dean of the Institution of Armament Technology.

On promotion to the rank of Air Vice-Marshal in August 1963 he look over as AOC in Chief Maintenance Command, in which capacity he served during the 1965 War. His next assignment was at Air Headquarters as Air Officer Maintenance (AOM). In January 1968 he was awarded the PVSM and promoted Air Marshal in March 1968. Soon thereafter he was posted as Deputy Chief of Air Staff, Air Headquarters. Early 1971 he was deputed as Chairman Hindustan Aeronautics Ltd Bangalore. On 15th January 1973 he returned to Air Headquarters, designated as the new Chief of Air Staff, suceeding Air Chief Marshal PC Lal.

Air Chief Marshal Mehra relinquished the post to Air Chief Marshal Moolgavkar on 31st January 1976, on completion of his tenure. During his over 35 years in the Air force he flew a very wide variety of aircraft-from the early days flying the Tiger Moth and finally the Jaguar (in UK) and the MiG-21. He also flew most of the Helicopters and Transport aircraft from time to time. In his flying career, He had amassed over 6000 flying hours.

Retirement did not mean an end to his eventful career. He represented India at a UNESCO meeting in Paris as Deputy Leader of India's Team. He was the recipient of Padma Vibhushan in January 1977-a recognition of his 35 years services covering a wide range of responsibilities within and outside the Air Force. He went on to serve as the Governor of Maharashtra (1980) and later on Rajasthan (1982). Air Chief Marshal Mehra was actively involved in the Olympic movement right from 1954. In 1975 he was elected as President of the Indian Olympic Association and was responsible for the hosting by India of the Asian Games in 1982. From 1978 to 1980 he was President of the Asian Games Federation, currently known as the Olympic Council of Asia and continues to be the Honorary Life President of the Olympic Council of Asia.

Since retirement and after completion of his constitutional assignments he is actively engaged in Community service projects. For such work he has received the Srimoni Award in 1988, the Rajiv Ratna Award in 1991 and the HELP-Age Indian Golden Award in 1999.

HRUSHIKESH MOOLGAVKAR

Air Chief Marshal Hrushikesh Moolgavkar, PVSM, MVC

Hrushikesh Moolgavkar was commissioned in the Royal Indian Air Force on 30 November 1940. He was posted to No.1 Squadron flying the Hawker Harts after commissioning and soon converted to Lysanders. In January, when No.1 Squadron moved to Toungoo airfield in Burma in operations against the Japanese, young Moolgavkar was one of the lucky few who was part of the squadron. In the short time No.1 was involved in ops, Moolgavkar emerged as one of the keen pilots who would hog the flying..

After returning from the Burma Ops, Moolgavkar served with No.4 Squadron as a Flying Officer, flying the Hurricane and Spitfire fighters. During operations on the Burma front, he did a total 280 hours of operational flying which included bombing, rocketing and gunnery. During the time he was promoted to Flt Lt and took over command of a Flight within the Squadron.

Providence saved young Moolgavkar early in January 1945. While operating from Hove, near Cox Bazar, Moolgavkar took off in a Spitfire. Just after takeoff the engine of the Spitfire cut out. While attempting to forceland the Spitfire on the sea beach, the aircraft nosed over and lay upside down in the shallow water, with Moolgavkar hanging upside down from his seat still in his straps. As the tide rose, Moolgavkar faced the prospect of drowning slowly as the water rose above his head level. A One in a million chance saw two British Commando Officers notice the wrecked Spitfire. They pulled out Moolgavkar from the aircraft, saving his life.

Moolgavkar suffered from several crushed vertebrae, and had to spend six months with his back in plaster. After returning from the Hospital, Moolgavkar commanded No.10 Squadron flying the Spitfire XIV from 09 May 1947 to 21 Feb 1948. He was posted to the DSSC to undertake a staff course.

Moolgavkar took over as the Commanding Officer of No.1 Operations Wing at Srinagar from Wg Cdr M M Engineer in late September 1948 when the Kashmir Operations were underway. Moolgavkar was responsible for planning and execution of close air support during the famous Zoji La battle. Sometimes Moolgavkar himself flew on these sorties. The venture exposed him to grave dangers. His determination, initiative and drive enabled the RIAF to render effective support to the Army. For his contribution in these operations, Moolgavkar received the Maha Vir Chakra for exceptional gallantry and leadership. His was one of the four MVC's awarded to the IAF for the Kashmir Operations.

In February 1949, an Aircraft Testing Unit was formed consisting of pilots of No.7 Squadron. The ATU received four Vampire F3 fighter bombers which were the first Jet fighters for an Asian air arm. Wg Cdr Moolgavkar was put in charge of the ATU on its tour of India. He was one of the first to convert to the Vampire at Poona and soon after took the aircraft to Bombay, and Madras on pubic displays around the country.

In 1951, Moolgavkar was Director of Operations in the rank of Group Captain. He was in France in 1953 for the evaluation of the Ouragan aircraft and He led the first flight of four Ouragan fighters flown to India all the way from France. It was during time that he flew a Mystere II fighter bomber and became the first Indian to fly faster than sound.

In 1954, he was part of the team under Air Cmde P C Lal along with Flt Lt Roshan Suri, which went to France and UK to test and procure a second generation Jet Fighter for the IAF. He test flew both the Mystere IVa and later the Supermarine Swift. The team came back after having decided on the procurement of the Mystere IVa. During the same trip, He was also one of the first to fly the Midge fighter, which later became the Folland Gnat.

1957 found him as the Station Commander for Palam, which then had Vampires of No.7 and No 10 Squadron under him. He was promoted Air Commodore in 1964 and posted to Maintenance Command HQ as the Senior Air Staff Officer, in which position he was serving during the 1965 War. He came back to Air HQ as a staff officer and later on, after promotion to Air Vice Marshal was appointed the AOC-in-C Central Command. It was during his tenure that the Sukhoi-7 BMK fighter bombers were inducted into his command. After the tenure at Central Command was over, Moolgavkar took over command of the National Defence College in Delhi at the special request of Air Chief Marshal PC Lal.

He took over as the AOC-in-C Western Air Command in 1973. and soon after in 1976, he was awarded the PVSM for distinguished service. Not soon after, on 1 Feb 1976, he took over as the Chief of Air Staff of the Indian Air Force. From then till the end of his tenure in Oct 78, when he handed over the baton to Air Chief Marshal Idris Latif, Moolgavkar took upon himself the task of bringing under control, the IAF's accident rate. He was always known as a stickler for flight safety, even from his Station Commander days. Now as the CAS, Moolgavkar implemented several reforms and rules that saw improvement of flight safety across the whole of the Indian Air Force. Moolgavkar always maintained his flying status. Even as the CAS, he would go on flights on IAF MiG-21s, which also included the first flight of the HAL built MiG-21M [C-1531].

IDRIS HASAN LATIF

Air Chief Marshal Idris Hasan Latif was Chief of Air Staff of the Indian Air Force from 1978 to 1981. He also served as the Governor of Maharashtra during 1981-85 and later as the Indian ambassador to France (till 1988). He was the first Indian Muslim to become the head of the Indian Air Force.

Latif was born in Hyderabad, Andra Pradesh into a Sulaimani Bohra family in 1923. He was educated at Nizam College, Hyderabad and was commissioned into the Royal Indian

Air Force in 1942. He took part in the Burma Campaign on the Arakan Front during World War II. Later he was a member of the Indian Advisory Group to Indonesia that helped the Indonesian Air Force induct jet fighters. Latif is a Graduate of the Defence Services Staff College and the National Defence College and served as Air Defence Commander and Senior Air Staff Officer in Eastern Air Command. During 1961-65 he was the Air Attaché at the Indian embassy in Washington D.C. During the 1971 Indo-Pakistani war, he was Assistant Chief of Air Staff (Plans). In 1971 he was awarded the Param Vishisht Seva Medal in 1971. He led Air Force Relief operations during the Patna floods in 1975. In 1985 IAF submitted the Air Staff Requirements (ASR) for LCA in October 1985.

He is married to Bilkees Latif, a social worker.

Air Chief Marshal Idris Hasan Latif, PVSM

Air Chief Marshal Idris Hasan Latif, was appointed Chief of the Air Staff with effect from September 1, 1978 and relinquished this appointment on his retirement from the Indian Air Force after nearly 40 years of distinguished service. As an officer in the flying branch of the Air Force, his operational experience covered a wide spectrum at various levels of responsibilities. He has flown several thousand hours on fighter, bomber and transport aircraft, ranging from the pre-Second World War Vintage bi-planes to the supersonic MiGs and India-made Maruts.

Born on June 9, 1923, he was commissioned into the Air Force in 1942. He was then 18 and studying at Nizam's College, Hyderabad. The Air Chief's father, Mr. Hasan Latif, was Chief Engineer of Hyderabad State and after his retirement he became Principal of Osmania Engineering College. On completion of his training at Ambala, he was posted to the Coastal flight at Karachi to carry out anti-submarine duties. He was among the first few pilots to be sent to England in 1943 for training on Hurricanes and Spitfire fighters which were soon to be inducted into the Indian Air Force.

Air Chief Marshal Latif had his first taste of war in the air when as a ground attack pilot in a Hurricane Squadron, he took part in the Burma Campaign on the Arakan Front in the

Second World War. Earlier in 1943-44, he flew with the Royal Air Force in the United Kingdom. Soon after the war, he was back in Burma with No. 9 Squadron. The same Squadron now flying the famous Sabre Killer Gnats is today proud of having him as its Commodore Commandant. He was only 26 years old and a Squadron Leader when, at the dawn of Independence, he commanded No. 4 Squadron equipped with Tempest fighters. This distinction was followed by another honour conferred upon him in recognition of his rich experience of operational flying. He was sent on a special mission to Indonesia as a member of our Advisory Group which helped the Indonesian Air Force induct jet fighters.

A Graduate of the Defence Services Staff College and the National Defence College, Air Chief Marshal Latif served as Air Defence Commander and Senior Air Staff Officer in Eastern Air Command. During 1 971 operations, he was Assistant Chief of Air Staff (Plans), and in that capacity he carried out the onerous task of making first-hand assessment of the problems and achievements of frontline squadrons and the modernisation plans of the Air Force. For nearly five years (1961-1965), he was our Air Attache in Washington and was concurrently accredited to Canada and it was during his tenure there that he flew the USAF, F-S fighter.

On his promotion to the rank of Air Marshal in January 1974, he was posted as Air Officer Incharge Administration at Air Headquarters. Later he took over as Air Officer Commanding-in-Chief, Central Air Command and subsequently Maintenance Command.

In May 1977 he was appointed Vice-Chief of the Air Staff which post he held until he assumed office as Chief of the Air Staff. In recognition of his distinguished service of the most exceptional order, Air Chief Marshal Latif was awarded the Param Vishisht Seva Medal in 1971.

Air Chief Marshal Latif combines in his dynamic personality an extraordinary measure of the operational with the humanitarian. One of the memorable landmarks in his career was the Air Force Relief operations under his stewardship during the Patna floods in 1975. Under his inspiring guidance and directions, the helicopter pilots flew as many as 20 sorties a day to carry out humanitarian tasks that called for great precision and accuracy and flying skill of a very high order. All available air and ground crews were inducted into the operation—an operation which earned them the gratitude of the people saved from the ravages of the floods.

Flying has always been the first passion of Air Chief Marshal Latif and in all his higher appointments in the Air Force, he always found time to carry out as much flying as his other onerous responsibilities would permit. His interest in flying continued till almost the very last day in office and during the course of the recent months he made it a special point to fly the latest aircraft inducted into the Air Force—Jaguar, MiG-23 and MiG-25. During his official visit to France in 1981, he also had an opportunity to fly the Mirage-2000. Within a few days of his retirement from the Air Force, the Government has also announced his appointment as a Member of the reconstituted Public Enterprises Selection Board.

Air Chief Marshal Latif has also a long and intimate association with Maharashtra and its people. His forefathers came and settled in Bombay and their old family house Latifia can be seen on Pandita Ramabai Road and their property in Bombay extended right upto Chowpatty. For him also for many years Maharashtra was an important field of his active service in the Indian Air Force. It was in this State at Poona in the late '40s that he first commanded an operational squadron. Two decades later he returned to take over command of the Air Force at Poona which by then had become one of the most important operational base of the Air Force. Thereafter from the early '70s, right till the end of his career, his links with the State remained unbroken and intimate as Air Officer Commanding-in-Chief, Central Air Command, later Air Officer Commanding-in-Chief, Maintenance Command and finally as Chief of the Air Staff.

Air Chief Marshal Latif is fond of riding, and has been a keen player of Cricket and Tennis. Ever since he was a boy, his greatest passion, besides flying in later years, has been photography. His love for Urdu poetry is shared by his wife Bilkees Latif. Though soft-spoken, Air Chief Marshal Latif is a strict disciplinarian and attaches great importance to punctuality as an attribute. He believes in the dignity of man—trusting human beings and reposing faith in their capabilities for achieving results. He encourages free debate to precede a decision but once it has been taken he expects complete compliance.

Air Marshal Idris Hassan Latif was born on 09 June 1923 at Hyderabad. His father, Mr. Hasan Latif was a Chief Engineer. After completing his formal education from Nizam's College, Hyderabad, he joined Royal Indian Air Force in 1941. He was commissioned in 1942 and was appointed to the No.2 Coastal Defense Flight in Karachi. During this time he flew vintage bi-plane aircrafts like the Wapiti, Addaxes and Harts. In 1943 Air Chief Marshal Idris Hassan move to United Kingdom and took training on Hurricane and Spitfire aircrafts.

During Burma campaign he flew Hawker Hurricane for No.3 and no.9 Squadron. At the time of partition in 1947 he remained in India. After the war against Pakistan Air Chief Marshal Idris Hassan was promoted to the rank of Squadron Leader and posted as the commanding officer of No.4 Oorials, flying the Hawker Tempest. He was sent to Indonesia to assist newly born Indonesian Air Force. After coming back to India joined Defence Services Staff College at Wellington. In 1961 Air Chief Marshal Idris Hassan went to USA as the Air Attaché. At that time he was also the Air Attaché to Canada.

In 1965 Air Chief Marshal Idris Hassan came back to India and was appointed to Eastern Air Command as the Air Defense Controller and subsequently became the Senior Air Staff Officer. Next year he was posted to Lohegaon Airbase at Pune as Station Commander. On promotion to the rank of Air Vice Marshal, he was appointed to the Air Head Quarters Assistant Chief of Air Staff.

At that time he was responsible for making plan for development of Air Force. In 1971 Air Chief Marshal Idris Hassan was awarded the Param Visist Seva Medal. In 1974 he was promoted as Air Marshal and became Air Officer In-Charge of Administration at Air HQ. Afterwards he was appointed as AOC-in-C at Central Air Command. In 1975 during the Patna floods he led the Air Force relief operations team. At that time Air Chief Marshal Idris Hassan did outstanding performance. Before being appointed as chief staff of Indian Air Force in 1978 he was the Vice Chief of Air Staff.

Air Chief Marshal Idris Hassan had very modern outlook and tried a lot for the modernization of Indian Air Force. He retired in 1938. After retirement Air Chief Marshal Idris Hassan Latif was sent to France as an Indian Ambassador.

DILBAGH SINGH

Air Chief Marshal Dilbagh Singh (March 10, 1926-Feb 9, 2001) was the head of the Indian Air Force from 1981 to 1984, as Chief of the Air Staff. He was the second Sikh to hold that position. Dilbagh Singh was commissioned as a pilot in 1944. His operational flying career spanned the Spitfire to introducing the MiG-21 into service in India. He had earlier made the first official "Supersonic Bang" over India in New Delhi when the Mystere IV-A was showcased in a public demonstration.

He served as India's Ambassador to Brazil from 1985 to 1987. Air Marshal Dilbagh Singh was born on 10th March 1926 in Punjab. From his childhood he was very interested in flying. He was commissioned in the Indian Air Force in 1944 and was appointed to the No.1 Squadron flying Hurricanes. Dilbagh Singh was the second Sikh Chief of Air Staff of the Indian Air Force after Air Marshal Arjun Singh. Dilbah Sing participated in the operation during the tribal invasion of Kashmir in 1947. He actively took part in the fly operations in a Spitfire from Srinagar and flew stories as part of No.10 Winged Daggers Squadron against Pakistan forces. For his exceptional courageousness in this operation he was Mentioned-in-Dispatches.

After that Air Marshal Dilbagh Singh was sent to Afghan Air Force cadets for Flying Instructors training programme. On promotion to Squadron Leader he was posted to the Ambala Air Base as Officer In Charge of Flying in 1954. In the next year he got his first command and was given the charge of No.2 Squadron flying Spitfire XVIIIs. In 1956 he moved to France for training on Mystere IV-A fighter. After completing training Air Marshal Dilbagh Singh came back to India and commanded the No.1 Squadron flying the Mystere IV-A at Kalaikunda. He assumed the first official 'Supersonic Bang in New Delhi. After few years Air Marshal Dilbagh Singh was appointed as the chief instructor of Armament Training Wing. He was the chief trainer of the first batch of seven 'chosen' pilots and 15 engineers at an airbase in Kazakhstan. In 1962 he was selected for the training on MiG-21F, which was bought from the USSR. After completing five months training Dilbagh Singh returned to India and created No.28 First Supersonics Squadron-the first supersonic squadron of India.

In 1965 Air Marshal Dilbagh Singh was appointed at the Air Headquarters as Deputy Director (Weapons). After the 1965 war he was promoted to the rank of Group Captain and served at Halwara AFB. During 1971 war against Pakistan Dilbagh Singh was the commanding officer of Lohegaon AFB, near Pune. He fought bravely in this war. Later he was appointed as Senior Air Staff Officer in the Western Air Command. In 1978 he rose to the rank of Air Officer Commanding in Chief (AOC-in-C) of Western Air Command. Air Chief Marshal Dilbagh Singh was awarded the Vayu Sena Medal and Param Vishist Seva Medal for dedicated service to the nation. 1981 he assumed the charge of Chief of Air Staff of Indian Air Force and served next three in this post. He had over 5000 hours flying experiences in 40 years of service. Dilbagh Singh was the second Sikh Chief of Air Staff, the Indian Air Force had after Marshal of the Air Force Arjan Singh. Born in Punjab on 10 March 1926, Dilbagh took an interest in flying at a very early age. He joined the IAF in 1944 at the height of World War 2. Heflew operational sorties with No.10 Squadron and later posted to the No.1 Squadron flying Hurricanes at Kohat in 1945.

When the tribal invasion of Kashmir came in October 1947, Dilbagh Singh was actively involved in the operations. He was one of the first to fly operations in a Spitfire from Srinagar. Later on he joined No.10 Winged Daggers Squadron and flew sorties against the raiders in the Hawker Tempest aircraft. For his role in the operations, Dilbagh Singh was Mentioned-in-Despatches. After the Kashmir Operations, he was deputed to attend Flying Instructors training after which Dilbagh Singh was involved in training Afghan Air Force cadets.

Promoted to Squadron Leader in 1954, he assumed the responsibilities of Officer In Charge of Flying at the Ambala

Air Base. Command of a Squadron came his way in August 1955, when he took over No.2 Squadron flying Spitfire XVIIIs. Dilbagh did not stay with No.2 Squadron for long, he handed over command in February 1956 and went to France to get trained on the Mystere IV-A fighter. After returning from France, Dilbagh took over as the CO of No.1 Squadron flying the Mystere IV-A at Kalaikunda.

After arriving in India, Dilbagh undertook the first official 'Supersonic Bang' over India in New Delhi when the Mystere IVa was showcased to the Nation. After four years of operational flying, Dilbagh Singh went to Jamnagar as the Chief Instructor at the Armament Training Wing.

Dilbagh shot into the limelight in late 1962, when he was selected to be trained on the MiG-21F which was being acquired by India from the USSR. He led the first batch of seven 'chosen' pilots and 15 engineers for training at Lugovya, an airbase in Kazakhstan in the erstwhile USSR for training on the MiG-21F fighter. After undergoing training for five months, the team came back to India to form the core of the first supersonic squadron, No.28 *First Supersonics* Squadron. Dilbagh Singh raised the unit in Chandigarh with an order of battle of six MiG-21s in early 1963.

In May 1965, Dilbagh handed over the command of No.28 Squadron to Wg. Cdr. M.S.D. Wollen (later Air Marshal) and joined Air Headquarters as Deputy Director (Weapons). He was holding the staff job till the end of the 1965 war with Pakistan, when he took over command of Halwara AFB in the rank of Group Captain. His services were recognised with the award of the Vayu Sena Medal in 1966. More staff appointments followed.

At the outbreak of the 1971 War, Dilbagh Singh was under Central Air Command, as Air Officer Commanding of Lohegaon AFB, near Pune. From his base, No.35 Squadron flying Canberras struck Karachi Oil Tanks and Harbour Installations. Dilbagh's responsibilities included providing facilities to aircraft of the maritime air operations. Dilbagh became the Senior Air Staff Officer in the Western Air Command in 1976 and finally became the Air Officer Commanding in Chief (AOC-in-C) of Western Air Command in 1978. In 1979, He received the Param

Vishist Seva Medal for distinguished service. In 1981, Dilbagh Singh became the Chief of Air Staff, in the rank of Air Chief Marshal. His tenure lasted three years till 1984, in which time the IAF saw the induction of the MiG-25, MiG-23 and the selection of the Mirage 2000. He was also the Commodore Commandant of No.28 Squadron. Dilbagh Singh laid down the office of CAS in 1984, by which time in a career spanning four decades, he had about 5000 hours of flying on different types of aircraft, was decorated by the government for distinguished service thrice.

DENIS ANTHONY LA FONTAINE

Air Chief Marshal D.A. La Fontaine, PVSM, AVSM, VM

Air Chief Marshal Denis Anthony La Fontaine became the Air Chief on the sudden demise of Air Chief Marshal L.M. Katre. La Fontaine was the Air Officer Commanding in Chief of the Western Air Command at that time. La Fontaine was born in Madras on 17 September 1929. He was the son of Major Je La Fontaine of the Indian Army Medical Corps. La Fontaine's family boasted a lineage of Army service. Both his Grandfathers served with the Indian Army as officers.

Educated at St. Anthony's High School at Lahore and at St. George's College at Musoorie, he enrolled into the Indian Air Force in October 1947. He did his training on the Tigermoth aircraft, moving on the Harvards, Spitfires and the Tempests aircraft. He was commissioned into the flying branch at Ambala in April 1950.

La Fontaine's first posting was to the No.7 Battle Axes Squadron flying the Tempests. When No.7 converted to the De Havilland Vampires in 1951, La Fontaine was one of the first pilots in the Indian Air Force to undergo training in flying the jets, which were the first jet fighters operated by any country in Asia.

Soon after, La Fontaine was selected to undergo the All Purpose Instructors Course. Over the next three years, he spent his career imparting Beginner, Intermediate and Operational Instructions in flying in a variety of aircraft including the Tigermoth, the Harvard, Spitfire and Vampires.

In 1956, he returned to operational flying, when he was posted to the No.2 Squadron flying the Toofanis. Then La Fontaine moved onto No.29 Scorpions as a Senior Flight Commander. Command of his own unit came in 1960, when he was promoted to Squadron Leader and was entrusted to raising a new squadron, No.47 Black Archers. This Squadron, flying the Toofani, became the first Fighter Combat Squadron to win the Mukherjee Trophy in its first year of raising. After the upgradation of ranks of the Squadron Commanders of Fighter Squadrons, to Wing Commander, La Fontaine took over command of No.14 *Fighting Bulls* Squadron at Kalaikunda.

Flying the Subsonic Hawker Hunter, he was involved in the Indo-Pak Ops of 1965. La Fontaine led a unfruitful fighter interception sweep over the East Pakistani city of Jessore and an abortive interception to Barrackpore. Aircraft from his unit did take on the Pakistani Sabres over Kalaikunda and No.14 Squadron was the only Hunter unit in 1965 that encountered the enemy Sabres and got the best of them and were still unscathed by the end of it. Told to lay off operations against targets within East Pakistan, La Fontaine and his team did not see much action later on.

After the operations, as a Group Captain, La Fontaine was the Chief Instructor with the Air Force Academy. He was responsible for developing a system of graded performance standards that improved the quality of flying training. At the outbreak of the 1971 War, he was deputed as a Senior Staff Officer to the Maritime Air Operations Cell in Bombay to help out civilian airline operations. Throughout the 1970s, he held a variety of staff appointments with Western Air Command. He was Ops 1, Air 1 and later Senior Air Staff Officer (SASO) of WAC. In between these staff appointments, he also held some operational appointments in the form of command of two fighter bases.

As Air Marshal, he first was Air Officer Commanding-in-Charge of Personnel in the Air Headquarters. The first AOC-in-C Command came with the Central Air Command. Later shifted to command the Western Air Command. On the untimely demise of the then CAS, Air Chief Marshal L.M. Katre, La Fontaine took over as the Chief of Air Staff. After becoming

CAS, he oversaw the IAF inducting state-of-the-art defence fighters like the Mirage 2000 and the MiG-29. Both were procured primarily to counter the Pakistani F-16 threat. The IAF was involved in operations for the first time since 1971, when it undertook supply and relief sorties over Sri Lanka. Later after the induction of the IPKF, the IAF was involved in supply and COIN operations. However La Fontaine could not oversee the complete operations of the IPKF. He retired in 1988, succeeded by Air Chief Marshal S.K. Mehra.

In the course of his career he was decorated thrice. He was a recipient of the PVSM, AVSM and VSM for distinguished service. La Fontaine now leads a retired life in a farmhouse at Brahmanapally Village in Medak District.

NIRMAL CHANDRA SURI

Born on 26 July 1933, Nirmal Chandra Suri went on to become the Chief of Air Staff of the Indian Air Force on 1 August, 1991. He is an alumnus of the famous Royal Indian Military College, Dehradun. He was a part of the First course of the Joint Services Wing, the present-day National Defence Academy, Pune. During the 1965 Indo-Pak war, Suri was selected to lead the detachment from No.20 Hawker Hunter Squadron and he flew several sorties during the war. In 1969, he was awarded the Vayu Sena Medal for his contributions and devotion to service.

During the 1971 War, Suri had to take over the Number 7 Hunter Squadron and he flew several sorties during this war as well. He was awarded the Ati Vishisht Seva Medal or AVSM in 1982. He became the Chief of Air Staff on 1 August 1991 and was instrumental in various initiatives – including the induction of women officers in the IAF first as ground duty officers and later as pilots. He has always been a passionate flyer and he is not known to have passed on any opportunity to fly. Air Chief Marshal N.C. Suri, PVSM, AVSM and VM, retired from service on the 31st of July 1993 and was succeeded by S. K. Kaul.

Nirmal Chandra Suri was born on 26th July 1933. He studied in St Xaviers School in Calcutta and then continued his schooling with the Royal Indian Military College at

Dehradun. He was a member of the First course of the Joint Services Wing (the precursor of today's National Defence Academy) and trained as part of the 57th Pilots Course at the No.2 Air Force Academy in Jodhpur.

He was commissioned as a fighter pilot on 15th March 1952 and joined No.4 Squadron, flying Vampire fighter bombers. He subsequently served with Nos 2 and 27 Squadrons. After a period of operational flying, he was selected for the QFI training. He was rated as an A1 Instructor, this enabled him to become a QFI at FIS itself. Subsequently, in 1960, he completed the Pilot Attack Instructors Course.

He returned to operational flying with No.20 Squadron soon after and converted to the Hawker Hunter. He was still with No.20 Squadron when war broke out in September 1965. No.20 Squadron was based at Hindon during the war and only sent half of its aircraft to the frontline on attachment with No.7 Squadron. Suri was selected to lead the detachment from No.20 Squadron. He flew several sorties during the war. At the end of the war he was mentioned in the dispatches for his contribution.

After the war, Suri took over command of No.20 Squadron. He was instrumental in converting the squadron to the newly inducted Type 56a, and also modifying them so that they could carry the inboard tanks on the outboard pylons. At the end of his tenure in 1969, Suri was awarded the Vayu Sena Medal (Devotion to Duty).

After a brief stint in Iraq on instructional duties Suri returned in 1971 to join the Aircrew Examination board as an examiner. Fate would decree that Suri would have to lead yet another Squadron. During the 1971 War, No.7 Squadron which was operating Hunters in the Western Sector lost their commanding officer when Wg Cdr BA Coelho had to eject in Pakistani territory. Suri was sent from AEB to Nal to take over the Squadron for the rest of the duration. He flew several sorties with No.7 Sqn during the war.

After the war, on promotion to the rank of Group Captain, Suri took over AFS Hindon in August 74. Subsequently, in January 1976, he was with the National Defence College for a course. In January 1979, Suri received his second command stint of an air force base, this time the much larger AFS Lohegaon at Pune, which was at that time inducting the newly acquired MiG-21 Bis fighter. AFS Lohegaon performed outstanding during this period,l winning all the trophys instituted by central air command during his tenure. At the end of the tenure, Suri was awarded the AVSM in 1982

A series of staff postings followed, SASO Central Air Command, coinciding with the induction of the Mirage 2000 and other equipment like the An-32 and Il-76. After promotion to Air Marshal, Suri held the appointments of AOC Personnel. In 1987, he was awarded the PVSM. He subsequently took over Central Air Command as the AOC-in-C. During this time CAC was active in the Sri Lankan Operations, lending its Mirage 2000s, Il-76s and An-32s in the build up to Op Pawan. Subsequently Suri moved to Air HQ as the VCAS.

Suri was appointed as the Chief of Air Staff on 1st August 1991 after 41 years in uniform. During his tenure as chief, He was instrumental in various initiatives – including the induction of women officers in the IAF first as ground duty officers and later as pilots. The entire process for the ground breaking decision was taken in a matter of months!

He also kicked off the golden jubilee celebrations of the IAF – during which time several initiatives were taken to preserve the historical aspects of the Air Force. The IAF's Golden Jubilee film "Salt of the Earth" was produced during this phase. Throughout his air force career, Suri was a passionate flyer, even after achieving Air Rank, he never passed on an opportunity to fly. He actually logged his 6000th flying hour at Gwalior during the Golden Jubilee celebrations of No.7 Squadron, flying in a Mirage 2000. By the time of his retirement he had over 6200 flying hours under his belt.

Air Chief Marshal Suri retired on 31 July 1993 and was succeeded by Swaroop Krishna Kaul. After retirement Air Chief Marshal Suri had another remarkable achievement when he was awarded the PhD a from the Intercultural University in Netherlands at the age of 63. He still continues his higher learning studies and is currently settled in NOIDA. General Nirmal Chander Vij was born January on 1943 in Jammu. He was the 21st Indian Chief of Army Staff Preceded by

Sundararajan Padmanabhan. He assumed the office of Indian Chief of Army Staff on 31 Dec 2002. His received his early education from SRML Higher Secondary School in Jammu and than joined the National Defence Academy at pune in 1959. He was commissioned into the Dogra Regiment on 11th December 1962.

After few weeks of his joining in the Indian Army, he saw Indo-China War in Walong sector in 1962. He served in the eastern region six times. It is a record in the Indian Army. He was the General Officer Commanding of the 4 Corps while he was serving last time in the eastern sector. IN 1971 Indo-Pak war, his troops was the first one to capture the 'Chicken Neck' and also occupied the 'Chhote Chak' post of Pakistan in Miran Sahib Sector. During his long tenure in the Indian Army, he served as the General Staff Officer of an Infantry Division, a Director in the Military Operations Directorate as a Colonel and Deputy Director General of Perspective Planning (Strategic Planning) as a Brigadier at Army HQ in New Delhi.

General Vij was the Major General at the Western Command at Chandimandir in Chandigarh. In 1999 during Kargil war against Pakistan, he served as the Director General Military Operations. He was decorated with Uttam Yudh Seva Medal for outstanding performances as DGMO in the Kargil war. General Nirmal Chander Vij got several professional acclaim for successfully carrying out the Operation Khukri He also accomplished a great job for the trapped Indian peacekeeping troops in Sierra Leoneafter successfully commanded a mountain brigade involved in active counter-insurgency operations in the north east, an elite RAPID (Reorganised Army Plains Infantry Division) unit, the 1 Strike Corps based at Bhopal, Madhya Pradesh and the IV Corps based at Tezpur, Assam. General Nirmal Chander Vij was conferred with Param Vishisht Seva Medal for his extraordinary performances as a army staff. General Vij served also as a commander in some major fronts including a Strike Corps and a Corps positioned in active counter-insurgency operations in the North East on 01 October 2000. After that he was posted to Southern Command as the GOC at pune. In 2001 at the time of Gujarat earthquake he was the leader of the Indian Army's rescue team. General Nirmal Chander Vij was selected for the post of Vice Chief of Army Staff (VCOAS) at New Delhi and in January 2002. He was appointed as the 10th Colonel of the Dogra Regiment and the Dogra Scouts in the same year. While he was the Chief of Army Staff, the Royal Bhutan Army and the Indian Army undertook a joint operation and force to leave the United liberation Front of Assam (ULFA) from their base camps in Bhutan in December 2003. In 2004 General Nirmal Chander Vij was nominated as the Chairman Chiefs of Staff Committee (COSC). After completing 42 years of distinguished military service he retired as the Indian Chief of Army Staff on 31 January 1962. He was succeeded by Joginder Jaswant Singh. He was the honorary Colonel of the Dogra Regiment & Dogra Scouts and also Deputy Chairman of National Disaster Management Authority, Govt of India. He was also closely associated with the Married Accommodation Project (MAP), establishment of Professional Colleges and Ex-Servicemen's Health Scheme (ECHS). General Nirmal Chander Vij is married to Mrs. Rita Vij and they have a son, Nalin, who is a software engineer in the United States.

S. K. KAUL

Air Chief Marshal (Retd.) Swaroop Krishna Kaul, born on the 20th of December, 1934 was the chief of the Indian Air Force between 1993 and 1995. Kaul was born in Kashmiri Mohalla, Lucknow and now lives in Gurgaon.

He was commissioned in the IAF on 17 July 1954 and retired in December 1995. During his service, he was awarded the Param Vishisht Seva Medal and the Maha Vir Chakra for a show of conspicuous gallantry during the 1971 war.

SATISH KUMAR SAREEN

Air Chief Marshal Satish Kumar Sareen, PVSM AVSM VM ADC

Satish Kumar Sareen's family originally hailed from Rawalpindi, in present-day Pakistan where he was born on 01 March 1939. His family moved to Delhi during Partition. Sareen joined the IAF in 1954, where he was part of the Joint Services Wing (JSW) in Dehradun. The JSW was a predecessor of today's

National Defence Academy. Sareen graduated from the first batch of the JSW and went onto the AFFC for flying training. He was commissioned on 29 May 1957. He stood first among the fighter stream pilots and was awarded the Himmatsinghji trophy.

He was posted to No.20 Squadron flying Vampire Fighters. He moved on to No.4 Squadron flying the Ouragans. It was with No.4 Squadron that he took part in the Goa Operations in 1961, when he flew several sorties against Portuguese targets. After the operations in Goa, Sareen took up his first non-operational appointment when he attended the Pilot Attack Instructor (PAI) course. He distinguished himself in the course and was retained as an instructor in the PAI Program, where he helped impart training to others following in the same stream.

When war broke out in 1965, Sareen was with No.29 Scorpios Squadron flying the Ouragans at Gauhati. He undertook some sorties against targets in East Pakistan, but the fighting was minimal in the Eastern Sector. After the war, Sareen moved to No.27 Flaming Arrows Squadron flying the Hawker Hunter. After a brief stint, he was part of a detachment of pilots earmarked for conversion to MiG-21s. He moved back to No.29 Squadron after it converted back to the MiG-21.

In January 1970, Sareen attended the Defence Services Staff College at Wellington. He passed out of DSSC in November 1970. Now a Squadron Leader, Sareen joined Eastern Air Command as the Chief Operations Officer with Agartala AFB in Tripura near the East Pakistan border.

Agartala was base to some Gnat fighters during the 1971 War. He was responsible for planning and launching extensive fighter, helicopter, transport operations including several successful strikes on the Chittagong City. For his role, Sareen received the Vayu Sena Medal.

After the war, Sareen took over as Ops 1 Officer with Eastern Air Command HQ. In 1973, he was posted to No.1 Squadron flying MiG-21s in Adampur as Senior Flight Commander. After more than two years with the Squadron, Sareen received an opportunity to be posted to the Iraqi Air Force as an instructor. This was part of a longstanding bilateral arrangements between the two air forces in the 1970s. Sareen took up the offer and was posted to Al-Kut military airbase in Iraq. During his tenure in Iraq till 1977, Sareen undertook more than a 1000 instructional sorties.

In 1977, Sareen was the Chief Operations Officer of No.15 Wing at Barielly. He got his first command soon after at the same airbase, No.24 Squadron flying the MiG-21bis. After promotion to Group Captain, in 1981, he took over an Air Defence Signals Unit in the Eastern Sector. Numerous Staff Appointments followed, he was Air Defence Commander, WAC and SWAC. Air Attaché to the High Commission of India, in the UK. In 1989, he returned to India and was commander of Srinagar Air Force Station in the Jammu & Kashmir Valley. He was awarded the AVSM for distinguished service in 1990. Soon afterwards he took over as ACAS (Ops) at Air HQ in the rank of Air Vice Marshal.

After a short stint as SASO Central Air Command, Sareen took over South Western Air Command as AOC-in-C. After about a year, he moved onto as the AOC-in-C Western Air Command-India's Premier Air Command. It was in this capacity he received the PVSM in 1995. Sareen was posted back to Air HQ as the Vice Chief of Air Staff responsible for all IAF defensive & offensive operations and intelligence activities.

Finally in December 1995, he was promoted to Air Chief Marshal to take over as the Chief of the Air Staff, Indian Air Force. His tenure saw the nuclear tests in Pokhran. Within the Air force, it saw wide ranging changes in the strategic, operational, training, maintenance and flight safety doctrines & performance of the IAF. Particular attention paid to the welfare of serving and retired Air Force personnel and their families. Air Chief Marshal Sareen retired on 31 December 1998, handing over the charge to Air Chief Marshal Anil Yashwant Tipnis.

Satish Kumar Sareen was born on 01 March 1939 in Rawalpindi (Now in Pakistan). At the time of partition his family shifted to Delhi. In 1954 he joined the Indian Air Force. Sareen did his graduation from Joint Services Wing in Dehradun (presently known as National Defence Academy) and also completed his flying training. Satish Kumar Sareen received the Himmatsinghji trophy for standing first among the fighter stream pilots. After that Satish Kumar Sareen was appointed to No.20 Squadron for flying Vampire Fighters. During Goa operation in 1961 he flew many sorties against Portuguese attack as part of No.4 Squadron. After that he attended the Pilot Attack Instructor (PAI) course and subsequently served as instructor of PAI Program. In 1965 war against Pakistan he flew several Ouragans at Gauhati as part of No.29 Scorpios Squadron. After the war he was appointed to the No.27 Flaming Arrows Squadron.

After completing the Defense Services Staff College course in 1970 Satish Kumar Sareen led the Eastern Air Command as the Chief Operations Officer at Tripura. During the 1971 War for his courageous leadership he was awarded the Vayu Sena Medal. After the war Satish Kumar Sareen was appointed as Ops 1 Officer at Eastern Air Command HQ. As Senior Flight Commander he flew MiG-21s in Adampur as part of No.1 Squadron. After that he was sent to Al-Kut military airbase in Iraq as an instructor of Iraqi Air Force. In 1977 he returned to India and joined No.15 Wing as a Chief Operation Officer. After that he commanded the No.24 Squadron flying the MiG-21bis. In 1981 Satish Kumar Sareen was promoted to the rank of Group Captain and led an Air Defense Signals Unit in the Eastern Sector.

After that Satish Kumar Sareen held many posts like-Air Defense Commander of WAC and SWAC, Air Attaché to UK. After returning back to India he commanded the Srinagar Air Force Station in the Jammu & Kashmir Valley. In 1990 he was awarded the Ati Visist Seva Medal in 1990 for his good performances and subsequently promoted to the rank of Air Vice Marshal. As AOC-in-C he served South Western Air Command and Western Air Command. In 1995 he was awarded the Param Visist Seva Medal. After that Satish Kumar Sareen served as Vice Chief of Air Staff responsible for all IAF defensive & offensive and intelligence activities at Air Head Quarter. In December 1995 he assumed the charge of Chief of the Air Staff as Air Chief Marshal.

Air Chief Marshal (Retd) Satish Kumar Sareen, PVSM, AVSM, VM, ADC was born on 1st March 1939 in Rawalpindi,

Pakistan. After Partition his family moved to Delhi. Sareen joined the IAF in 1954, where he was part of the Joint Services Wing (JSW) in Dehradun. He graduated from the first batch of the JSW and went onto the AFFC for flying training. Sareen was commissioned on 29 May 1957. He stood first among the fighter stream pilots and was awarded the Himmatsinghji trophy.

Flt Lt Sareen was posted to IAF 20 Squadron flying Vampire Fighters. He moved on to IAF 4 Squadron flying the Ouragans. It was with 4 Squadron that he took part in the Goa Operations in 1961, when he flew several sorties against Portuguese targets. After the operations in Goa, Sareen took up his first non-operational appointment when he attended the Pilot Attack Instructor (PAI) course. He distinguished himself in the course and was retained as an instructor in the PAI Program, where he helped impart training to others following in the same stream.

When war broke out in 1965, Flt Lt Sareen was with IAF 29 Squadron "Scorpios" flying the Ouragans based at Gauhati. He undertook some sorties against targets in East Pakistan, but the fighting was minimal in the Eastern Sector. After the war, Sareen moved to 27 Squadron "Flaming Arrows" flying the Hawker Hunter. After a brief stint, Sqn Ldr Sareen was part of a detachment of pilots earmarked for conversion to MiG-21s. He moved back to 29 Squadron after it converted back to the MiG-21.

In January 1970, Sqn Ldr Sareen attended the Defence Services Staff College (DSSC) at Wellington and passed out in November 1970. He then joined Eastern Air Command as the Chief Operations Officer with Agartala AFB in Tripura near the East Pakistan border. Agartala was base to some Gnat fighters during the 1971 War. He was responsible for planning and launching extensive fighter, helicopter, transport operations including several successful strikes on the Chittagong City. For his role, Sareen received the Vayu Sena Medal.

After the war, Sqn Ldr Sareen took over as Ops 1 Officer with Eastern Air Command HQ. In 1973, he was posted to IAF 1 Squadron flying MiG-21s in Adampur as Senior Flight Commander, in the rank of Wing Commander. After more than two years with the Squadron, Wg Cdr Sareen received an opportunity to be posted to the Iraqi Air Force as an instructor. This was part of a longstanding bilateral arrangements between the two air forces in the 1970s. Sareen took up the offer and was posted to Al-Kut military airbase in Iraq. During his tenure in Iraq till 1977, Wg Cdr Sareen undertook more than a 1000 instructional sorties. In 1977, Wg Cdr Sareen was the Chief Operations Officer of No.15 Wing at Bareilly. He got his first command soon after at the same airbase, IAF 24 Squadron flying the MiG-21bis. After promotion to Group Captain, in 1981, he took over an Air Defence Signals Unit in the Eastern Sector.

Numerous Staff Appointments followed, he was Air Defence Commander, WAC and SWAC. Air Commodore Sareen was then posted as Air Attaché to the High Commission of India in London, UK. In 1989, he returned to India and was commander of Srinagar Air Force Station in the Jammu & Kashmir Valley. He was awarded the AVSM for distinguished service in 1990. Soon afterwards he took over as ACAS (Ops) at Air HQ in the rank of Air Vice Marshal.

After a short stint as SASO Central Air Command, Air Marshal Sareen took over South Western Air Command as AOC-in-C. After about a year, he moved onto as the AOC-in-C Western Air Command-India's Premier Air Command. It was in this capacity he received the PVSM in 1995. Sareen was posted back to Air HQ as the Vice Chief of Air Staff responsible for all IAF defensive & offensive operations and intelligence activities.

Finally in December 1995, he was promoted to Air Chief Marshal to take over as the Chief of the Air Staff, Indian Air Force. His tenure saw the nuclear tests in Pokhran. Within the Air force, it saw wide ranging changes in the strategic, operational, training, maintenance and flight safety doctrines & performance of the IAF. Particular attention paid to the welfare of serving and retired Air Force personnel and their families.

In 1997, former Indian Prime Minister, I.K. Gujral commissioned the Su-30MKIs into the 24 Squadron of the IAF based at Lohegaon near Poona with great fanfare. On that occasion, Air Chief Marshal, S.K. Sareen praised the new multi-role fighter as an effective force multiplier, which would enable the IAF to quickly establish air superiority (against perceived foes, i.e. Pakistan China, Iran etc.). He stressed that the Su-30MKI is a weapons system of vast strategic dimensions, whereby the reach and lethality of the IAF would be extended many times. With the Prithvi SSM and the Su-30MKI combination, the lethal range of Indian air power has been extended from merely 150 kilometres (km) to 2500 km. The Su-30MKI will be able to hit selected targets anywhere in Pakistan and well beyond in Saudi Arabia, Iran, Syria, Jordan, Iraq, Oman, Qatar, UAE, Bahrain, Afghanistan, all Central Asian states, China, Bangladesh, Myanmar (Burma), Thailand, Malaysia, Indonesia, Cambodia, Brunei Dar-us-Salam and deep into the Indian Ocean. According to the former Chief of the Air Staff of the IAF, Air Chief Marshal P.C. Kaul, 40 of the Su-30MKI aircraft have the destructive airpower of 240 present-day fighter-bombers of the IAF.

India's aquisition of the Su-30MKI caused great apprehension in Pakistani defense circles. At the Farnborough Air Show in 1996, Pakistan's Air Chief Marshal Muhammad Abbas Khattak is reported to have told his Indian counterpart, Air Chief Marshal S. K. Sareen, "You don't buy the Su-30 and we will not purchase the Mirage 2000-5". India bought 40 Su-30MKIs two months later, little concerned that the deployment of the Prithvi SSM and the procurement of the Su-30MKI multi-role fighter-bombers would accentuate the fear of ulterior Indian motives in Pakistan. A missile and air power race had now begun. In an April 1997 press conference at Air Headquarters, PAF Base, Chaklala (Rawalpindi), Air Chief Marshal Muhammad Abbas Khattak had admitted that the qualitative edge that the PAF had over the IAF in 1992 was fast eroding."

Aerial bombing display by the Su-30's

In March 1998, the IAF demonstrated its superior fire power at the Vayu Shakti '98' exercices held at Pokhran. An array of Indian Air Force aircraft carried out displays. The centrepiece was the Su-30 with its high agility, its high scope for combat maneuvering & low-level aerobatics. As it fired eight bombs on a simulated runway with perfect marksmanship, its capability for accurate weapons delivery was also showcased. This spectacular display served as a riposte to doubters. Air Chief Marshal S.K. Sareen said, "This exercise should once and for all put at rest all controversies. The aircraft(Su-30) performed creditably in its bombing mission and showed its superlative agility in the mock dog fight. Its solo aerobatics display proved beyond doubt that it is the finest aircraft available today. Besides, over the next few years, the Su-30 would be further upgraded with latest avionics and electronic warfare equipment to improve its mission effectiveness". He said that another 12 Su-30 aircraft, which are expected by early next year, would be equipped with beyond-visual-range Precision Guided Missiles. The Su-30 contract was worth Rs 6,300 crore for 40 aircraft with complete infrastructure.

In April 1998, tens of thousands of people converged on downtown Bombay or crowded onto rooftops to view an airshow, the city's first since 1959. The air show commemorated 50 years of India's independence from British rule. The newly aquired Su-30 jets showed off their might for the first time to the Indian public. When a television reporter asked ACM Sareen what he felt, pointing to the roaring Sukhois flying overhead in tight formation, Sareen laughed and said: "Yeh dekh kar tumharey rongte khadey nahin hotey?

ANIL YASHWANT TIPNIS

Air Chief Marshal Anil Yashwant Tipnis, PVSM AVSM VM ADC

Anil Yashwant Tipnis was born on 15 September 1940, and did his education at Barnes High School, Deolali. His initiation into the services started with him joining the 15th Course of the National Defence Academy (NDA) in January 1956. After which he moved on, for flying training to the Air Force Flying College in January 1959. Anil Yashwant Tipnis was commissioned into the Indian Air Force (IAF) as a fighter pilot on 28 May 1960. He finished his training with flying colours, receiving the coveted Majumdar Trophy for his excellent performance. The initial years of Tipnis' service were spent as an operational pilot in several frontline fighter squadrons.

His first posting was to a Hunter Squadron. In 1963, when Wg. Cdr. Dilbagh Singh (later Air Chief Marshal and CAS of the IAF) raised the first MiG-21 Squadron, Tipnis was one of the few pilots to be sent to No.28 Squadron to fly the MiG-21s. He was still serving with the First Supersonics when war broke out in September 1965, and he served with the Squadron during its operations in the war.

In 1966 he graduated as a Pilot Attack Instructor (PAI) and won the Naronha Trophy for standing first. This was followed, in January 1970, by a deputation to Iraq as a PAI. On return he was posted as the Flight Commander of No.45 Sqn which then served as a MiG-21 Operational Conversion Unit. He qualified as a Fighter Combat Leader at the IAF's prestigious Tactics & Air Combat Development Establishment (TACDE) in 1973 winning the Sword of Honour; he continued on staff as a flight commander of the Combat Development & Training Flight.

In 1975 he underwent the Defence Services Staff Course at Wellington following which, in July 1977, he took over as the Commanding Officer of No.23 Sqn equipped with MiG-21bis aircraft. Tipnis was one of the four officers short listed for the Indo-Soviet Joint Space mission. He underwent all the training required for the mission in the course of the final selection. After a couple of staff appointments and a stint at the National Defence Academy as the Chief Instructor (Air) and Battalion Commander, he was posted to France in October 1983 as the Team Leader for the Mirage Project Team in the rank of Group Captain, where he was responsible for the negotiation and purchase of the Mirage 2000 aircraft into the IAF.

On returning back to India three years later, he was posted to the Mirage 2000 base of the IAF, as the Air Officer Commanding, Air Force Station Gwalior in the rank of Air Commodore. In 1989 he attended the Defence Studies Course at the National Defence College, New Delhi, and successfully completed it. Later on he was posted as Deputy Personnel Officer at Air HQ in New Delhi.

More important staff appointments at Air HQ and Command HQ followed. On promotion to the rank of Air Vice Marshal in

June 1992, he was appointed the Assistant Chief of the Air Staff (Inspection) at Air Headquarters. In June 1993 he took over as the Air Officer Commanding J&K area. On being promoted to the rank of Air Marshal in September 1994 he took over as the Senior Air Staff Officer (SASO) of Eastern Air Command and later, in February 1995, was posted as the SASO of Western Air Command, the largest operational command of the Indian Air Force. In August 1995 he assumed charge as AOC-in-C of Western Air Command. He was appointed as the Vice Chief of Air Staff (VCAS) in April 1997. On 31 December 1998, he was promoted as Air Chief Marshal and took over as the 18th Chief of Air Staff. Upon his retirement on 31 December 2001, he completed 41+ years in uniform.

His tenure saw the first deployment of Indian Air Force combat aircraft in action since the 1971 War. When the fighting at Kargil erupted, the IAF was deployed to attack intruders positions in the high altitude areas. Needless to say the IAF acquitted itself very well in these limited actions. Throughout the course of operations, the Air Chief Marshal was deeply involved in overseeing the conduct of operations. Along with the then-Army Chief, General V.P. Malik, he visited the frontline units and forward areas to get a feel of the progress of the operations.

In his career in the Air Force, Air Chief Marshal Tipnis received the Param Vishisht Seva Medal, Ati Vishisht Seva Medal and Vayu Sena Medal for distinguished service.

He is keen on outdoor activity and plays golf and tennis regularly. His other outdoor activities include gliding and sailing. His passion for flying continues till today, and he loves being in the cockpit, be it that of a glider, helicopter, transport aircraft and particularly of a fighter. He continued to maintain his currency on fixed wing (fighters and transport aircraft) as well as rotary wing aircraft during his service as Air Chief.

SRINIVASAPURAM KRISHNASWAMY

Air Chief Marshal Srinivasapuram Krishnaswamy, PVSM AVSM VM and Bar

Air Chief Marshal Srinivasapuram Krishnaswamy became the 19th Chief of Air Staff on 31 December 2001. Air Chief

Marshal S. Krishnaswamy was commissioned in the Indian Air Force in 1961. He is operational on a number of combat aircraft including the Mirage 2000.

He flew the Gnat fighter aircraft during the 1965 Indo-Pak War and was awarded Mention in Despatches for his contribution. Subsequently, he was sent to UK to undergo Test Pilots Course. On his return, he joined the Air Force Flight Test Centre – Aircraft and System Training Establishment (ASTE).

Air Chief Marshal Krishnaswamy, as a test pilot, was involved in flight testing and evaluation of Military as well as civil aircraft and weapon systems. For his outstanding contribution in indigenous development programme he received the 'Agni Award for Self Reliance' in August 1999. He has more than 4000 hours of flying experience and has captained over 30 varieties of aircraft and helicopters. He was also trained as a Fighter Combat Leader (FCL) and served as Senior Instructional Staff at the Tactics & Air Combat Development Establishment (TACDE).

Air Chief Marshal Krishnaswamy specialised in Electronic Warfare (EW) and had the unique distinction of having raised and commanded the first EW Squadron of the Indian Air Force, comprising a mix of MiG-21 and Canberra aircraft. He has held a variety of operational and staff appointments during his career. Besides the command of a Squadron, he did a tenure as Chief Operations Officer of a Mirage-2000 base and commanded Air Force Station, Pune. In senior appointments, he has served as Assistant Chief of Air Staff (Plans), Deputy Chief of the Air Staff and Air Officer Commanding-in-Chief of three Operational Commands viz., Central, South Western and Western Air Command. He took over as the Vice Chief of the Air Staff in August 2001.

A graduate of Defence Services Staff College, he is an alumnus of the National Defence College. Air Chief Marshal Krishnaswamy is a recipient of Param Vishist Seva Medal, Ati Vishist Seva Medal and a bar to Vayu Sena Medal. He was born in Chennai in January 1943 where he went through his schooling and college education. He is married to Mrs. Harveen Krishnaswamy, has two daughters and two grand sons.

SHASHINDRA PAL TYAGI

Air Chief Marshal Shashindra Pal Tyagi, more commonly known as S P Tyagi (born 14 March 1945) is the former Chief of the Air Staff of the Indian Air Force. Prior to becoming chief of Indian Air Force, he was commanding the Western Air Command of the Air Force. He was commissioned in the fighter stream of the IAF on December 31, 1963. He is said to have "actively participated" in the 1965 and 1971 wars.

Air Chief Marshal Shashindra Pal Tyagi took over as the 20th Chief of Air Staff of the Indian Air Force from 31 December 2004. Popularly known as "Bundle", Tyagi was born at Indore on March 14, 1945. He is an alumnus of St Xavier School in Jaipur. He was commissioned in the IAF on 31 December 1963 in the fighter stream.

The initial years of his career in the air force, Tyagi flew Gnats with No.23 Squadron and later served with Hunters of No.27 Squadron. A veteran of both the 1965 and the 1971 Wars, he was one of the pioneer batch of eight pilots selected for conversion on the Jaguar Interdiction aircraft when it was inducted in 1980s. Whilst training at Lossie mouth, he was one of the two Indian pilots chosen for a Photo Recce Course at Coltishall with No.41 Squadron RAF.

Tyagi commanded No.14 Squadron "Bulls" later after coming back to India. A Graduate of the TACDE with a Fighter Combat Leader and Pilot Attack Instructor qualifications, he had also attended the Junior Commanders Course, the National Defence College and finally the Defence Services Staff College at Wellington. He received the Vayu Sena Medal (VM) for distinguished service in 1985.

In his mid career, Tyagi had several other appointments under his belt. He was an instructor at TACDE. As an Air Commodore, Tyagi commanded 33 Wing at Jamnagar. Later he was also posted as the Defence Attache at the Indian Consulate in Saudi Arabia. Air Commodore Tyagi was awarded the Ati Vishist Seva Medal (AVSM) in 1994.

He also held the appointments of Director Operations (Air Defence), ACAS (Intelligence), ACAS (Ops). He has had a stint as a senior fellow at the IDSA and was also a senior Instructor and Directing Staff at the DSSC Wellington. In the rank of Air Marshal, Tyagi was appointed as the SASO of Central Air Command for some time. He took over as the AOC-in-C of Central Air Command not soon after. he is one of the few officers to have the distinction of commanding three Air Commands, Central, South Western and Western Air Command.

Air Marshal Tyagi was awarded the Param Vishist Seva Medal (PVSM) in 2003, and was appointed as one of the honorary ADCs of the President of India. Air Chief Marshal SP Tyagi is married to Mrs. Vandana Tyagi and has one son and a daughter.

SHASHINDRA PAL TYAGI

Air Chief Marshal Shashindra Pal Tyagi, PVSM AVSM VM ADC

Air Chief Marshal Shashindra Pal Tyagi took over as the 20th Chief of Air Staff of the Indian Air Force from 31 December 2004. Popularly known as "Bundle", Tyagi was born at Indore on March 14, 1945. He is an alumnus of St Xavier School in Jaipur. He was commissioned in the IAF on 31st December 1963 in the fighter stream.

The initial years of his career in the air force, Tyagi flew Gnats with No.23 Squadron and later served with Hunters of No.27 Squadron. A veteran of both the 1965 and the 1971 Wars, he was one of the pioneer batch of eight pilots selected for conversion on the Jaguar Interdiction aircraft when it was inducted in 1980s. Whilst training at Lossie mouth, he was one of the two Indian pilots chosen for a Photo Recce Course at Coltishall with No.41 Squadron RAF.

Tyagi commanded No.14 Squadron *"Bulls"* later after coming back to India. A Graduate of the TACDE with a Fighter Combat Leader and Pilot Attack Instructor qualifications, he had also attended the Junior Commanders Course, the National Defence College and finally the Defence Services Staff College at Wellington. He received the Vayu Sena Medal (VM) for distinguished service in 1985.

In his mid career, Tyagi had several other appointments under his belt. He was an instructor at TACDE. As an Air

Commodore, Tyagi commanded 33 Wing at Jamnagar. Later he was also posted as the Defence Attache at the Indian Consulate in Saudi Arabia. Air Commodore Tyagi was awarded the Ati Vishist Seva Medal (AVSM) in 1994.

He also held the appointments of Director Operations (Air Defence), ACAS (Intelligence), ACAS (Ops). He has had a stint as a senior fellow at the IDSA and was also a senior Instructor and Directing Staff at the DSSC Wellington.

In the rank of Air Marshal, Tyagi was appointed as the SASO of Central Air Command for some time. He took over as the AOC-in-C of Central Air Command not soon after. he is one of the few officers to have the distinction of commanding three Air Commands, Central, South Western and Western Air Command.

Air Marshal Tyagi was awarded the Param Vishist Seva Medal (PVSM) in 2003, and was appointed as one of the Honarary ADCs of the President of India. Air Chief Marshal SP Tyagi is married to Mrs. Vandana Tyagi and has one son and a daughter. He retired from the IAF on 31st March 2007.

FALI HOMI MAJOR

Air Chief Marshal Fali Homi Major served as the eighteenth Chief of the Air Staff of the Indian Air Force taking office on April 1, 2007, and becoming the first helicopter pilot in the service to be promoted to the office of Chief. He retired on May 31, 2009, and was succeeded in office by Air Chief Marshal Pradeep Vasant Naik, a fighter pilot.

Major was born on May 29, 1947 in Secunderabad, Andhra Pradesh. A student of Wesley High School, Secunderabad, Air Chief Marshal Major was commissioned into the Indian Air Force on December 31, 1967 as a helicopter pilot. During his long and distinguished service spanning little over 39 years, he has worked in a variety of Command, Staff and Instructional appointments. Besides being a Fellow of the National Defence College, New Delhi, and the Army War College, Mhow, he attended a variety of courses like Junior Commanders' Course, Jungle and Snow Survival Course and Higher Command Courses. He was appointed Joint Director (Helicopter Operations) and Director Operations (Transport & Helicopter).

In 1999, he took over as the Air Officer Commanding Leh (Ladakh), in the aftermath of the Kargil conflict. For his leadership, successful accomplishment of tasks and distinguished service of a very high order, he was awarded the 'Ati Vishist Seva Medal' in Jan 2002. He was promoted to the rank of Air Vice Marshal in Feb 2002 and appointed as Assistant Chief of the Air Staff (Personnel Airmen & Civilians) at Air Headquarters. On promotion to the rank of Air Marshal in Jan 2004 he moved to HQ Integrated Defence Staff as the Deputy Chief of Integrated Defence Staff (Operations) and directed the relief, rescue and rehabilitation operations of the Indian Armed Forces, in India and abroad, in the aftermath of the Tsunami. On 05 Sep 2005, he was appointed as the Air Officer Commanding-in-Chief, Eastern Air Command. That tenure saw the successful conduct of three major international air exercises with the United States Air Force, Republic of Singapore Air Force and the French Air Force. He was awarded the 'Param Vishisht Seva Medal' by the President of India on 26 Jan 2006.

He has the distinction of having 7765 hours of flying experience to his credit. He commanded a helicopter unit, which took part in operations in Siachen (world's highest battlefield) and commanded a Mi-17 squadron during the IPKF operations in Sri Lanka, for which he was decorated with the Vayu Sena Medal(Gallantry).

While serving as a Group Captain, FH Major was awarded Shaurya Chakra for undertaking a very dangerous and exacting rescue mission on October 14, 1992 at Timber Trail in Parwanoo, Himachal Pradesh, where he along with his crew, winched eleven stranded tourists out from a cable car, by hovering precariously close to the set of cables that ran above it.

Air Chief Marshal FH Major is married to Mrs Zareen Major and has one son and one daughter. He also belongs to the distinguished 'Parsi Zoroastrian' community. The Air Chief Marshal is an avid golfer and a cricket fan. Air Chief Marshal Fali Homi Major was born on 29 May 1947 in Secunderabad. He studied at Wesley High School, Secunderabad and was commissioned in the Indian Air Force on 31 Dec 1967.

The Air Chief Marshal has flown over 7000 hours on the Sentinel, T-6G, Mi-4, Mi-8 and Mi-17 helicopters. As a Wing

Commander, he commanded the IAF's first Mi-17 Squadron, which operated at the Siachen Glacier – the World's highest battlefield. As a Group Captain, he commanded another Mi-17 Squadron, leading it into battle during the operations of the Indian Peace Keeping Force in Sri Lanka. For his leadership and courage during this tenure, he was awarded the Vayu Sena Medal (Gallantry). Later, as Station Commander of Air Force Station Sarsawa, he led the daring rescue of eleven passengers from a stranded cable car in the middle of a valley at a resort in Himachal Pradesh. For this act of gallantry, he was awarded the 'Shaurya Chakra'.

He has held a number of other important staff and field appointments – Joint Director (Helicopter Operations) and Director Operations (Transport & Helicopter). In 1999, he took over as the Air Officer Commanding Leh (Ladakh), in the aftermath of the Kargil conflict. For his leadership, successful accomplishment of tasks and distinguished service of a very high order, he was awarded the 'Ati Vishist Seva Medal' in Jan 2002.

He was promoted to the rank of Air Vice Marshal in Feb 2002 and appointed as Assistant Chief of the Air Staff (Personnel Airmen & Civilians) at Air Headquarters. On promotion to the rank of Air Marshal in Jan 04 he moved to HQ Integrated Defence Staff as the Deputy Chief of Integrated Defence Staff (Operations) and directed the relief, rescue and rehabilitation operations of the Indian Armed Forces, in India and abroad, in the aftermath of the Tsunami. On 05 Sep 05, he was appointed as the Air Officer Commanding-in-Chief, Eastern Air Command. That tenure saw the successful conduct of three major international air exercises with the United States Air Force, Royal Singapore Air Force and the French Air Force. He was awarded the 'Param Vishisht Seva Medal' by the President of India on 26 Jan 2006. He took over as the Chief of the Air Staff on 31 Mar 07.

He is a graduate of the National Defence College and Army War College. He is married to Zareen and they have two children. His son is a pilot with Jet Airways. His daughter is married and a homemaker. The Air Chief Marshal is an avid golfer and a cricket fan.

PRADEEP VASANT NAIK

Air Chief Marshal Pradeep Vasant Naik is the current Chief of the Air Staff of the Indian Air Force. He took office on May 31, 2009, becoming the nineteenth Chief of Air Staff following the retirement of Air Chief Marshal Fali Homi Major.

Air Chief Marshal Naik was born on July 22, 1949 at Nagpur and was commissioned into the Indian Air Force on June 21, 1969 as a fighter pilot. He is an alumnus of Sainik School, Satara and National Defence Academy, Khadakvasla in Maharashtra. During his long service spanning nearly 40 years he has served in a variety of command staff and instructional appointments. He has over 3,000 hrs of flying on his log. The Air Chief also took part in 1971 war air actions in the Western sector. Before taking over as Chief of Air Staff, he was the Vice Chief of Air Staff of the Indian Air Force. He has also served as the Air Officer Commanding-in-Chief of the Allahabad-based, Central Air Command.

Besides being a fellow of the National Defence College, New Delhi, College of Defence Management, Secunderabad and Defence Services Staff College, Wellington, he has attended a variety of courses like Flying Instructor's Course, Jungle & Snow Survival Course and Junior Commander's Course. Air Chief Marshal Naik is decorated with the Param Vishisht Seva Medal (PVSM) and Vishisht Seva Medal (VSM). He is also one of the Honorary Aides-de-Camp (ADC) to the President of India.

Air Chief Marshal Naik and his wife Madhubala Naik have two sons; the elder is a fighter pilot with the Indian Air Force, and the younger, a Chief Officer in the Indian Merchant Navy.

Pradeep Vasant Naik was born on 22 July 1949 and commissioned into the Indian Air Force on 21 June 1969. After initial schooling in Sainik School Satara, he graduated with the 33 Course from the National Defence Academy.

In a distinguished career spanning forty years, the CAS has flown a wide variety of combat and trainer aircraft. After initial training on the HT-2, he has flown the Vampire and the Hunter, and has had extensive operational experience on all variants of the MiG-21. He is a Qualified Flying Instructor with vast instructional experience and a Fighter Combat Leader from the prestigious Tactics and Air Combat Development Establishment (TACDE). He was selected as one of the first eight pilots to convert on to the MiG-23 BN in the erstwhile USSR, and was responsible for its induction into the IAF. Besides commanding a front line fighter squadron, he has commanded an important fighter base and Air Force Station Bidar. He has been Directing Staff at TACDE and the Defence Services Staff College.

During his career, the Air Chief Marshal has held numerous important staff appointments at different Headquarters. He has been the Senior Air Staff Officer at HQ Western Air Command, the Air Officer Commanding-in-Chief of Central Air Command and the Vice Chief of Air Staff, prior to his appointment as the Chief of the Air Staff.

The Air Chief Marshal is a graduate of the Defence Services Staff College, and an alumnus of the National Defence College. He is a recipient of the Param Vishisht Seva Medal and Vishisht Seva Medal. He has been appointed Honorary ADC to the Honourable President of India.

He is married to Madhubaala and they have two sons. The elder son is a pilot in the IAF and the younger is a Chief Officer in the Merchant Navy. The Air Chief Marshal is fond of Cricket, Golf, Volleyball and Indian Classical music.

2

Indian Chief of Air Staffs

PHILIP GAME

Air Vice-Marshal Sir Philip Woolcott Game GCB, GCVO, GBE, KCMG, DSO (30 March 1876 – 4 February 1961) was a British Royal Air Force commander, who later served as Governor of New South Wales, Australia. He was Governor during a time of political instability and dismissed the Government of Premier Jack Lang in 1932, following illegal activity on his part. Upon returning to Britain, he was appointed as Commissioner of the Metropolitan Police in London and held it during the tumultuous 1930s and the Second World War.

Early life and career

Game was born in Streatham, Surrey, England on 30 March 1876 to George Beale Game, a merchant from Broadway, Worcestershire. Before entering the Army, he was educated at Charterhouse School. Following officer training at the Royal Military Academy Woolwich, Game was commissioned as a Second Lieutenant on 2 November 1895 into the Royal Artillery. Promoted to Lieutenant on 2 November 1898 and further promoted to Captain on 20 June 1901, he served in the Second Boer War and was Mentioned in Dispatches. As a young Artillery Captain he was made officer in charge of the gun carriage bearing the coffin of Queen Victoria at her funeral in 1901. Following brief postings in India and Ireland, Game attended the Staff College, Camberley in 1910 and was posted as a GSO at the War Office. He later won the Royal United Services Institute Gold Medal Essay. On 11 August 1908 he married

Gwendolen Hughes-Gibb. He was promoted as a Major on 15 February 1912.

Following the outbreak of the First World War in 1914, Game served on the front in France, including at the Battle of Neuve Chapelle. In the war he was awarded the Distinguished Service Order, the Légion d'honneur and the Order of the Crown of Italy and was five times Mentioned in Dispatches. In early 1916 Game transferred to the Royal Flying Corps as a result of Hugh Trenchard's request for an experienced staff officer to serve in his headquarters. Game transferred to the Royal Air Force on its creation in 1918. At the end of the war, game continued to work under Trenchard, but as Director of Training and Organisation in the RAF. In 1922 he was promoted to the rank of Air Vice-Marshal and appointed Air Officer Commanding RAF India. The next year he took up the post of Air Member for Personnel and was appointed as a Knight Commander of the Order of the Bath (KCB) a year later. Game retired suddenly on 1 January 1929, at the age of 52, allegedly due to the rumours of him being appointed as Chief of the Air Staff. On 1 March 1929 he was appointed as a Knight Grand Cross of the Order of the British Empire in the military division (GBE).

Governor of New South Wales

At the height of the Great Depression, Game was appointed Governor of New South Wales in March 1930. He arrived in Sydney with his family in May 1930. On 30 June 1930, Game was appointed by King George V as a Knight of Grace of the Venerable Order of St John (KStJ). At the October 1930 State elections the Bavin Nationalist Government was defeated and the Labor Party leader, Jack Lang, became Premier. Lang's previous term of office from 1925 to 1927 had brought him into conflict with Game's predecessor, Sir Dudley de Chair, over the proposed appointment of additional members to the Legislative Council, in order to enable the abolition of the house, using the same techniques used to abolish the Queensland Legislative Council in 1922. His inability to gain control in the Upper House presented possible obstruction to Lang's legislative programme and in November 1930, claiming a mandate to abolish the Council, Lang requested the necessary additional appointments. However, these requests were met with Game's refusal.

In March and June 1931 Game again refused. Even though in November Game eventually assented to twenty five appointments, Lang's plans for abolition ultimately failed. Reflecting his status as a representative of the British Government, Game at all times informed the Dominions Office of political developments. In hard financial times, NSW soon came into conflict with the federal government as Lang's unorthodox financial policy opposed the economic orthodoxy advocated by Sir Otto Niemeyer who was the main financial advisor to the Federal Scullin Labor Government and later the Lyons United Australia Party Government. In July 1931, in a personal contribution towards economic recovery, Game notified Treasury to make a 25% deduction from his own monthly salary. From April 1931 Lang defaulted on payments of overseas debts to British bondholders in an attempt to negotiate the interest rate.

In March 1932, in anticipation of the opening of the Sydney Harbour Bridge, when Lang decided that he would cut the ribbon and incurred the displeasure of the King, Game reassured the King that Lang had the right to cut the ribbon. Game and his family found much amusement in the controversy thrown up over the matter and the question of whether Game, as Governor, should have a 17 gun salute. The far-right New Guard were nevertheless enraged over Lang's decision, culminating in Francis de Groot's pre-ceremony cutting of the ribbon. The ribbon was hastily re-attached and on 20 March 1932, Lang opened the bridge with Game looking on, and he later gave a speech commemorating the occasion.

When the United Australia Party Government of Joseph Lyons came to power in January 1932, it passed the *Financial Agreement Enforcement Act*, thereby forcing the NSW government to adhere to its debt commitments and to cut government spending. In response, Lang withdrew all the state's funds from government bank accounts so that the federal government could not gain access to the money. Game advised Lang that in his view this action was illegal, and that if Lang did not reverse it he would dismiss the government. Lang stood firm, and issued a leaflet in defiance of Game. Game then reluctantly decided to exercise his reserve powers and called Lang to Government House to dismiss him. However, Lang was not the first to hear of his dismissal. The pianist Isador Goodman, who had been befriended by Sir Philip and Lady Game, was at Government House for dinner that night. There were a number of interruptions, and Goodman asked if he perhaps ought to leave.

On 13 May 1932 Game dismissed Lang's government and appointed the UAP leader, Bertram Stevens, as Premier. Stevens formed a Coalition with Michael Bruxner's Country Party and immediately called an election, at which Lang's NSW Labor Party was heavily defeated. This was the first case of an Australian government with the confidence of the lower house of Parliament being dismissed by a Vice-Regal representative, the second case being when Governor-General Sir John Kerr dismissed Gough Whitlam's government on 11 November 1975. Game himself felt his decision was the right one, despite his personal liking of Lang. He wrote to his mother-in-law on 2 July 1932: "Still with all his faults of ommission and commission I had and still have a personal liking for Lang and a great deal of sympathy for his ideals and I did not at all relish being forced to dismiss him. But I felt faced with the alternative of doing so or reducing the job of Governor all over the Empire to a farce." Lang himself, despite objecting to his dismissal conceded that he too liked Game, regarding him as fair and polite, and having had good relations with him.

During his governorship Game was the patron of several organizations including the District and Bush Nursing Associations, the Royal Agricultural Society of New South Wales and was Chief Scout of the NSW Boy Scouts Association. Lady Game was President of the District and Bush Nursing Associations and the Girl Guides Association. The rest of his term was fairly uneventful and he returned to Britain following the expiration of his term on 15 January 1935. Before he left Sydney he was appointed a Knight Commander of the Order of St Michael and St George (KCMG), on the recommendation of Premier Stevens, for his service as Governor. In honour of their service to the state, Ku-ring-gai Municipal Council named a major road in Lindfield as the 'Lady Game Drive' and a nearby park as the 'Sir Phillip Game Reserve'. In memory of Games' time as Governor, a portrait was commissioned by public subscription and painted by R.G. Eves. It was then displayed at the National Art Gallery of New South Wales before being presented to Government House.

Metropolitan Police Commissioner

Upon his return to Britain, Game served as Metropolitan Police Commissioner from 1935 until 1945. Not long after his appointment in November 1935, Game was responsible for the policing of the funeral of King George V and subsequently, the abdication crisis of King Edward VIII and the 1937 coronation of King George VI. For his work in the 1937 coronation, Game was appointed by King George VI as a Knight Grand Cross of the Royal Victorian Order (GCVO) on 11 May 1937.

Serving as Commissioner during very tumultuous times, Game had to deal with Fascist and Communist demonstrations, an Irish Republican Army bombing campaign, and, during the Second World War, the organization of the police role in air-raid precautions and relief. He dealt effectively with those problems and the consequent improvement in police morale was an important factor in the survival of London during the concentrated German air attack of 1940-1941. In 1943, in an attempt to prevent burglaries, Game urged householders not to keep furs, adapting a verse from Chapter 9 of Ecclesiastes saying, "they are no doubt warmer, and look nicer than a tweed coat, but a live dog is better than a dead lion."

Towards the end of his time as Metropolitan Police Commissioner, Game worked to establish a boys' club. The Sir Philip Game Boys' Club, situated in Croydon, was opened in 1946.

The Club was officially opened on 19th July, 1947, by the then Home Secretary, James Chuter Ede, in the presence of Game. New premises were built and completed in 1964 and were officially opened on the 8 May 1966 by the then Home Secretary, Sir Frank Soskice, in the presence of Lady Game who unveiled a plaque in the memory of her husband. Game was the last senior Armed Forces officer to be appointed

Metropolitan Police Commissioner as since his retirement all successive commissioners have been career police officers. Game was appointed a Knight Grand Cross of the Order of the Bath (GCB) on 2 May 1945 and retired soon after on 1 June 1945.

He died at his home, Blackenhall, Sevenoaks, Kent, on 4 February 1961, survived by his wife, daughter and by his elder son, who had married Vera, daughter of Sir Charles Bickerton Blackburn. His second son had been killed in action at Taranto, Italy, in 1943.

Titles, styles and honours

Titles

- 30 March 1876 – 2 November 1895: Philip Game, Esq
- 2 November 1895 – 2 November 1898: *2nd Lieutenant* Philip Game
- 2 November 1898 – 20 June 1901: *Lieutenant* Philip Game
- 20 June 1901 – 15 February 1912: *Captain* Philip Game
- 15 February 1912 – 23 June 1915: *Major* Philip Game
- 23 Jun 1915 – 18 July 1915: *Major* Philip Game DSO
- 18 July 1915 – 20 May 1917: *Lieutenant Colonel* Philip Game DSO
- 20 May 1917 – 16 October 1916: *Colonel* Philip Game DSO
- 16 October 1916 – 1 April 1918: *Brevet Colonel (Temporary Brigadier-General)* Philip Game DSO
- 1 April 1918 – 14 October 1918: *Brevet Colonel (Temporary Brigadier-General)* Philip Game DSO, RAF
- 14 October 1918 – 1 January 1919: *Brevet Colonel (Temporary Brigadier-General)* Philip Game CB, DSO, RAF
- 1 January 1919 – 31 March 1919: *Colonel (Acting Major-General)* Philip Game CB, DSO, RAF
- 31 March 1919 – 1 August 1919: *Colonel (Acting Brigadier-General)* Philip Game CB, DSO, RAF
- 1 August 1919 – 1 January 1922: *Air Commodore* Philip Game CB, DSO, RAF

- 1 January 1922 – 3 June 1924: *Air Vice-Marshal* Philip Game CB, DSO, RAF
- 3 June 1924 – 1 January 1929: *Air Vice-Marshal* Sir Philip Game KCB, DSO, RAF
- 1 January 1929 – 29 May 1930: *Air Vice-Marshal* Sir Philip Game GBE, KCB, DSO
- 29 May 1930 – 15 January 1935: *His Excellency Air Vice-Marshal* Sir Philip Game GBE, KCB, DSO, Governor of New South Wales
- 15 January 1935 – 3 June 1935: *Air Vice-Marshal* Sir Philip Game GBE, KCB, DSO
- 3 June 1935 – 1 November 1935: *Air Vice-Marshal* Sir Philip Game GBE, KCB, KCMG, DSO
- 1 November 1935 – 11 May 1937: *Air Vice-Marshal* Sir Philip Game GBE, KCB, KCMG, DSO, Commissioner of Police of the Metropolis
- 11 May 1937 – 2 May 1945: *Air Vice-Marshal* Sir Philip Game GCVO, GBE, KCB, KCMG, DSO, Commissioner of Police of the Metropolis
- 2 May 1945 – 1 June 1945: *Air Vice-Marshal* Sir Philip Game GCB, GCVO, GBE, KCMG, DSO, Commissioner of Police of the Metropolis
- 1 June 1945 – 4 February 1961: *Air Vice-Marshal* Sir Philip Game GCB, GCVO, GBE, KCMG, DSO

EDWARD LEONARD ELLINGTON

Marshal of the Royal Air Force Sir Edward Leonard Ellington GCB, CMG, CBE (30 December 1877 – 13 June 1967) was a senior officer in the Royal Air Force. He served as Chief of the Air Staff from 1933 to 1937, then as Inspector General of the RAF until his retirement in 1940.

Early career

After attending the Royal Military Academy Woolwich, Ellington was commissioned into the Royal Field Artillery on 1 September 1897. He was promoted Lieutenant on 1 September 1900 and Captain on 27 April 1904. He learned to fly in 1912 and was awarded Royal Aero Club certificate No. 305 on 1 October 1912.

World War I

When the First World War started, Ellington was under training at the Central Flying School. A few months later, he was sent, not to a flying post but to be the Deputy Assistant Quartermaster-General at the headquarters of the British Expeditionary Force in France. In early 1915 he was granted a brevet promotion to lieutenant-colonel and posted as the Assistant Adjutant and Quartermaster-General of the 2nd Cavalry Division.

From July 1915 onwards, Ellington served as a staff officer first with the 2nd Army, then with the Department of the Chief of the Imperial General Staff and on the General Staff of the VIII Corps after that. In November 1917 he was made the Deputy Director-General of Military Aeronautics under John Salmond at the War Office. When Salmond's time as director came to an end, Ellington succeeded him as Director-General.

In April 1918 Ellington transferred to the Royal Air Force on its creation, with the temporary rank of brigadier-general. However only days later he was promoted to major-general (again temporarily) and appointed Acting Controller-General of Equipment. He became substantive in the post in August 1918.

Inter-war years

Ellington was Air Officer Commanding RAF Middle East from 1922 to 1923, Air Officer Commanding RAF India from 1923 to 1926 and Air Officer Commanding RAF Iraq from 1926 to 1928. He became Air Officer Commanding-in-Chief Air Defence of Great Britain in February 1929 and was promoted air marshal in July that year. The Air Member for Personnel from September 1931, he was promoted air chief marshal on 1 January 1933. In May 1933 Ellington was appointed Chief of the Air Staff (CAS). He succeeded Air Chief Marshal Sir John Salmond, who was acting in the role following the sudden death of his brother Air Chief Marshal Sir Geoffrey Salmond, who had become CAS in April. Ellington was promoted marshal of the Royal Air Force on 1 January 1937.

Following completion of his term as CAS in August 1937, Ellington became Inspector-General of the RAF. It was in his capacity as Inspector-General that in 1938 Ellington visited Australia to investigate standards in the Royal Australian Air Force. His report strongly criticized the RAAF's operational capability and safety standards. Following the publication of the report in July 1938, the Australian Government dismissed Air Vice Marshal Richard Williams from his post as RAAF Chief of the Air Staff. In July 1939 Ellington was augmented in his post as Inspector-General by Air Marshal Sir Charles Burnett, who would become the RAAF's Chief of the Air Staff in 1940.

Ellington retired shortly after the start of World War II, on 4 April 1940, and died on 13 June 1967.

GEOFFREY SALMOND

Air Chief Marshal Sir William Geoffrey Hanson Salmond KCB, KCMG, DSO (19 August 1878-27 April 1933), commonly known as Sir Geoffrey Salmond, was a senior commander in the Royal Flying Corps during World War I. Remaining in the Royal Air Force after the War, he held senior appointments in the Middle East, Great Britain and India. In 1933 Salmond served as Chief of the Air Staff for several weeks before his death from cancer.

Early life and family background

Geoffrey Salmond was born on 19 August 1878 in village of Hougham near Dover in the English county of Kent. His father was Major-General Sir William Salmond, Royal Engineers (1840-1932) who was descended from Major-General J. H. Salmond (1766-1837), military secretary to the Court of Governors of the old East India Company, and author of *The Mysore War*. Geoffrey Salmond was educated at Wellington College in Berkshire before joining the Army.

Royal Artillery service

Salmond joined the British Army, undertaking his officer training at Royal Military Academy Woolwich around 1897. He was commissioned into the Royal Artillery on 23 June 1898 and saw active service during the Second Boer War. He took part in the relief of Ladysmith and the operations on the Tugela Heights. He received he Queen's Medal and seven clasps, then in 1900 he was sent to China and gained a medal for the operations during the Boxer Rebellion there. In 1905, Salmond was seconded to study Japanese. He married Margaret Carr, daughter of William Carr in 1910.

Royal Flying Corps service

On 18 February 1913 Salmond was awarded Royal Aero Club Aviator's Certificate no. 421, after which. on 17 April 1913, he joined the reserve of the Royal Flying Corps (RFC), although he continued to serve in the regular army. Following staff work in military aeronautics, he went on to take up the post of Officer Commanding, No. 1 Squadron RFC. In the First World War the squadron operated over the Western Front and Salmond and his squadron took part in the Battle of Neuve Chapelle, including the Battle of Hill 60 and the Battle of Aubers Ridge.

In 1916 he was sent to command the 5th Wing, RFC, in Egypt, and in July, 1916, he was promoted to temporary Brigadier-General and given command of the RFC in the Middle East, a post which he held with brief intervals, until the end of 1921. The DSO was conferred on him in the *London Gazette* of 3 March 1917, "for conspicuous ability and devotion to duty when personally directing the work of the Royal Flying Corps during the action. The striking success attained was largely due to his magnificent personal example." The action referred to was during the operations in Sinai at the end of 1916. In this command he was responsible for providing air cooperation for General Jan Smuts's force in East Africa, for the forces in Salonika and Mesopotamia, for Allenby's conquest of Palestine, and for the RFC in India.

While holding the command of the Middle East, he had laid out an airway from Cairo to South Africa, clearing a chain of aerodromes in Central Africa. His idea was to send a demonstration flight or flights of RAF aircraft across Africa, thus providing the link of which Cecil Rhodes had dreamed in a Cape-to-Cairo railway. Salmond contemplated flights by both landplane and flying-boat. He was not destined to put his idea into execution, though his airway was used by Sir Pierre van Ryneveld and Sir Christopher Brand on their first flight to South Africa.

Royal Air Force service

On 1 August 1919 Salmond was awarded a permanent commission in the RAF, with the rank of air vice-marshal and he continued to serve as the middle east air commander. In 1922 Salmond returned to Great Britain to take up the post of Director-General of Supply and Research at the Air Ministry. The following year, his post was renamed Air Member for Supply and Research and he remained as the head of Supply and Research for the RAF until late 1926.

Salmond next appointment was in India as the air officer commanding. He travelled to India by aircraft, making him the first officer to travel to an overseas command by air. In 1931, Salmond returned from India to take up command of the Air Defence of Great Britain organization which was responsible for British air defences, including both fighters and bombers. He was promoted to air chief marshal several months later on 1 January 1933. On 1 April 1933, Air Chief Marshal Salmond took over from his brother John as Chief of the Air Staff. At this stage he was already suffering from incurable cancer although it is unclear whether Salmond or his brother knew this at the time. Days later (5 April) arrangements were announced for Sir John Salmond to resume the RAF's senior post temporarily. However, Geoffrey Salmond never recovered and he died on 27 April. Sir John Salmond continued as Chief of the Air Staff for several more weeks after Sir Geoffrey Salmond's death.

Salmond was survived by his wife Margaret and their four children.

JOHN MILES STEEL

Air Chief Marshal Sir John Miles Steel GCB, KBE, CMG, RAF (11 September 1877 – 2 December 1965) was a senior Royal Air Force commander.

Steel attended Britannia Naval College in 1892 and subsequently served in the Royal Navy. In 1917 Steel was transferred from fleet duties to the Royal Naval Air Service and was appointed Officer Commanding RNAS Eastchurch. In early 1918 Steel was appointed Officer Commanding No. 58 Wing which was based at Eastchurch and in March, at the age of 40, Steel learned to fly. On 1 April the Royal Naval Air Service merged with the Royal Flying Corps to form the Royal Air Force. Steel, like other RNAS personnel transferred to the RAF and was promoted to the temporary rank of Brigadier-General. On 1 August 1935, Steel was appointed Air Officer Commander-in-Chief (AOC-in-C), Air Defence of Great Britain. When Bomber Command was created from the Air Defence of Great Britain command, Steel became its first AOC-in-C.

World War II

In August 1939 Steel came back from retirement to serve as Air Officer Commanding Reserve Command. In April 1940 he was succeeded as AOC by William Welsh and Steel returned to retirement.

The following year in April once again returned to active service, this time as the Controller-General of Economy at the Air Ministry. He retired for the last time on 26 September 1945.

Promotions

- Midshipman, RN-1892
- Acting Sub-Lieutenant, RN-1896
- Sub-Lieutenant, RN-1897
- Lieutenant, RN-30 June 1900
- Commander, RN-30 June 1912
- Captain, RN-31 December 1916
- Colonel (Temp. Brigadier), RAF-1 April 1918
- Colonel (Actg. Brigadier), RAF-1 May 1919
- Group Captain, RAF-1 August 1919
- Air Commodore, RAF-5 August 1919
- Air Vice-Marshal, RAF-1 January 1925
- Air Marshal, RAF-1 January 1932
- Air Chief Marshal, RAF-1 July 1936, *retired 1937, returned to service in 1939*

Honours

- Mentioned in Dispatches-10 September 1901
- Mentioned in Dispatches (2)-15 September 1916

- Companion of the Order of St Michael and St George (CMG)-3 June 1919
- Knight Commander of the Order of the British Empire (KBE)-3 July 1926 (CBE-1 January 1919)
- Knight Grand Cross of the Order of the Bath (GCB)-11 May 1937 (KCB-1 January 1935; CB-3 June 1922)

EDGAR LUDLOW-HEWITT

Air Chief Marshal Sir Edgar Rainey Ludlow-Hewitt GCB, GBE, CMG, DSO, MC, DL (9 June 1886 – 15 August 1973) was a senior Royal Air Force commander.

World War I

Ludlow-Hewitt was originally commissioned into the Royal Irish Rifles, but transferred to the Royal Flying Corps before the First World War, where he qualified for the Royal Aero Club's Aviator's Certificate no. 886 on 11 Sept. 1914. During the war he served first as a pilot in No 1 Squadron Royal Flying Corps and then later as the Officer Commanding No 15 Squadron and No 3 Squadron on the Western Front. In 1916 Ludlow-Hewitt took up command of the 3rd (Corps) Wing as a temporary lieutenant colonel. Late in the following year he was promoted to brigadier-general and made the Inspector of Training at the headquarters of the Royal Flying Corps' Training Division. Like other members of the Flying Corps, he transferred to the Royal Air Force on its creation on 1 April 1918. It was also on that date that he became General Officer Commanding (GOC) the Training Division. Less than two months later he was appointed GOC the 10th Brigade.

Later career

In 1937 Ludlow-Hewitt was promoted to air chief marshal and appointed Air Officer Commanding-in-Chief of Bomber Command. However Ludlow-Hewitt was replaced by Portal in April 1940 as he was not considered to be sufficiently ruthless to lead Bomber Command during the Second World War. He spent the remainder of the war as Inspector General of the RAF and did not retire until November 1945, making him the RAF officer with the longest time in the rank of air chief marshal throughout the history of the RAF.

PHILIP JOUBERT DE LA FERTÉ

Air Chief Marshal Sir Philip Bennet Joubert de la Ferté KCB, CMG, DSO (21 May 1887 – 21 January 1965) was a senior commander in the Royal Air Force during the 1930s and the Second World War.

Joubert de la Ferté joined the British Army attending the Royal Military Academy Woolwich and gaining his commission in 1907. From 1907 to 1913 he served in the Royal Field Artillery, rising to the rank of Lieutenant. In 1913 he attended the Central Flying School and went on to serve in the Royal Flying Corps. With the outbreak of war in 1914, he joined the British Expeditionary Force flying one of the first two operational sorties of the war. In 1915 Joubert de la Ferté was appointed Officer Commanding, No. 15 Squadron RFC. Later that year he took up command of No. 1 Squadron. As the war progressed, Joubert de la Ferté commanded several different wings. On the 1 April 1918 Joubert de la Ferté transferred to the Royal Air Force in the rank of Lieutenant Colonel and by the end of hostilities in 1918 he had command of the Royal Air Force in Italy.

During the inter-war years, Joubert de la Ferté occupied several staff and command posts, rising through the ranks. Notably, he served as Air Officer Commanding-in-Chief Coastal Command.At the start of the Second World War, Joubert de la Ferté was Air Officer Commanding Air Forces in India. On his return to Great Britain he occupied a number of senior staff appointments and returned to his former post as Air Officer Commanding-in-Chief Coastal Command. It was there that he pioneered several innovations. These included Planned Flying and Maintenance and the introduction of a torpedo version of the Beaufighter.

On 23 November 1943, Joubert de la Ferté was appointed as the Deputy Chief of Staff (Information and Civil Affairs) at the South East Asia Command. Two years later on 14 November 1945, Joubert de la Ferté retired from the RAF.

JOHN FREDERICK ANDREWS HIGGINS

Air Marshal Sir John Frederick Andrews Higgins KCB, KBE, DSO, AFC, RAF (1 September 1875 – 1 June 1948) was a senior officer in the Royal Flying Corps and a senior commander in the Royal Air Force in the first half of the 20th century. In 1939, Higgins was appointed AOC in C of the Air Forces in India.

PATRICK PLAYFAIR

Air Marshal Sir Patrick Henry Lyon Playfair KBE CB CVO MC RAF (22 November 1889 – 23 November 1974) was a commander in the Royal Flying Corps during World War I and a senior commander in the Royal Air Force until his retirement during World War II.

RICHARD PEIRSE

Air Chief Marshal Sir Richard Edmund Charles Peirse KCB DSO AFC (30 September 1892-5 August 1970), was a senior Royal Air Force commander.

The son of Admiral Sir Richard Peirse, Peirse was educated at Monkton Combe School and at King's College London. He became a Midshipman in the Royal Navy Volunteer Reserve and later served as a pilot with the Royal Naval Air Service until 1 April 1918 when it became the Royal Air Force. With the formation of the RAF, Peirse became Officer Commanding 222 Squadron RAF. By 1933 he was an Air Commodore, and by 1936 he was an Air Vice-Marshal. On the 30 April 1940 as an acting Air Marshal he was appointed Vice Chief of the Air Staff. In 1940, Peirse was made Air Officer Commander-in-Chief Bomber Command. During early 1942, he was overall commander of Allied air forces in the American-British-Dutch-Australian Command, a short-lived, supreme command for all Allied forces in South East Asia.

In March 1942, Peirse was appointed commander of British Air Forces in India and on November 16, 1943 he was made Commander in Chief, Allied Air Command South-East Asia. However his career came to an abrupt halt in 1944, when he eloped with the wife of General Sir Claude Auchinleck.

Awards and decorations

- 10 April 1915 Peirse was awarded the Distinguished Service Order for services rendered in the aerial attack on Dunkirk on the 23 January 1915.

- 1 January 1919 he was awarded the Air Force Cross
- 1 April 1919 he was awarded The Croce di Guerra by the King of Italy for services rendered in the Mediterranean area.
- 6 November 1936 he was appointed to the Most Honourable Order of the Bath (as an Ordinary Member of the Military Division of the Third Class, or Companions of the Most Honourable Order (CB). He was promoted to Knight Commander of the Order of the Bath (KCB) in 1940.
- 15 March 1946 he became a Commander of the United States Legion of Merit.
- 29 July 1947 he was awarded the Cloud and Banner Decoration (Third Grade) by the President of the National Government of the Republic of China.

GUY GARROD

Air Chief Marshal Sir Alfred Guy Roland Garrod GBE, KCB, MC, DFC (13 April 1891 – 3 January 1965) was a senior UK Royal Air Force officer. Originally commissioned in The Leicestershire Regiment of the British Army in 1914, he transferred to the Royal Flying Corps in 1915. After various appointments of increasing seniority during the 1920s and 1930s, he served as the Air Member for Training at the Air Council from 1940 to 1943, was Allied Air Commander in South East Asia between 1944 and 1945, and served on the Military Staff Committee of the United Nations from 1945 to 1948.

MEREDITH THOMAS

Air Vice-Marshal Meredith Thomas CSI, CBE, DFC, AFC RAF (6 July 1892 – 20 May 1984) was a senior commander in the Royal Air Force during World War II. He began his career as a flying ace during World War I, credited with five aerial victories.

World War I service

Meredith joined the Queen's Westminsters in August 1914. He went to France in January 1915, and served as an infantryman on the Western Front until December 1915, and was then commissioned. He transferred to the Royal Flying

Corps in October 1916 and was trained as a pilot, being assigned in 1917 to 41 Squadron to fly a Royal Aircraft Factory FE.8, and later an Airco DH.5. He claimed his first two victories in September 1917, destroying an Albatros D.III on the 25th near Cambrai, and another on the 28th at Bugnicourt. After transferring to a Royal Aircraft Factory SE.5a, he claimed three wins over Albatros D.Vs. He was then returned to instructor duty in England.

Post World War I

In 1919 he was stationed in Germany, and from 1920 to 1923 he served in Iraq, winning the Distinguished Flying Cross in 1922 while a Flight Lieutenant.

RODERICK CARR

Air Marshal Sir Charles Roderick Carr KBE, CB, DFC, AFC (31 August 1891 – 15 December 1971) was a distinguished airman and military leader of New Zealand and India.

Military career

Born in Feilding, New Zealand, he served as an airman in the Royal Navy and Royal Air Force during World War I. In 1919 he went to Russia to fight on the anti-Bolshevist side in the civil war, where he won his DFC for action against the enemy. The citation was as follows:

On the 17th June, 1919, this officer flew a scout machine over the enemy aerodrome at Puchega, at an average height of only 50 feet, for thirty minutes. During this time he succeeded in setting fire to a Nieuport enemy machine, to a hangar which contained three aeroplanes (all of which were destroyed), drove all the personnel off the aerodrome, and killed some of the mechanics.

In 1921 he was a part of Ernest Shackleton's final Antarctic expedition. On his return he was granted an RAF short service commission in the rank of Flying Officer.

In 1927, Carr and Flight Lieutenant L.E.M. Gillmann attempted a non-stop flight to India, in a specially modified Hawker Horsley aircraft carrying much extra fuel and taking off at a weight of over 14,000 lb (6,350 kg). Carr and Gillmann took off from RAF Cranwell on 20 May 1927, but ran out of fuel *en route*, ditching in the Persian Gulf near Bandar Abbas, Iran. Despite this they had covered a distance of 3,420 mi (5,506 km), which was sufficient to set a new world distance record, but which was beaten in turn within a few hours by Charles Lindbergh's solo Atlantic flight between New York and Paris in the *Spirit of St. Louis*, covering 3,590 mi (5,780 km).

During World War II Sir Roderick served in RAF Bomber Command and later became Air Officer Commanding, India Command ("Chief of the Indian Air Force").

Sir Roderick died at Bampton, Oxfordshire, aged 80.

HUGH WALMSLEY

Air Marshal Sir Hugh Sidney Porter Walmsley KCB KCIE CBE MC DFC (6 June 1898 – 2 September 1985) was a senior commander in the Royal Air Force during and after World War II.

AOC 91 (OTU) Group 1942-4, AOC 4 Group 1945 Awarded the MC in 1918, the DFC in 1922, and mentioned in dispatches five times during the Second World War, Hugh Walmsley was born in 1898 and educated at Dover College. During the First World War he was commissioned into the Loyal North Lancashire Regiment before being seconded to the Royal Flying Corps in 1916. Walmsley received a permanent commission in the RAF in 1922 and as a group captain became AOC 91 (OTU) Group in 1942. He took over as AOC 4 Group from AVM John Whitley on 7 May 1945 before moving on to become Air Officer, Transport Command, SE Asia (1945-6) and then AOC Air HQ, India (1946-7). A succession of senior command appointments followed with Deputy Chief of the Air Staff in 1948, and then in 1950 AOC Flying Training Command. Walmsley retired from the RAF in 1952 and became managing director of Air Service Training Ltd and later principal of the College of Air Training until he retired again in 1960. He died at Lymington in August 1985, aged eighty-seven.

THOMAS ELMHIRST

Air Marshal Sir Thomas Walker Elmhirst KBE, CB, AFC, DL, RAF (15 December 1895 – 6 November 1982) was a senior commander in the Royal Air Force in the first half of the 20th century and the first commander-in-chief of the newly independent Indian Air Force where he organised the funeral of Mahatma Gandhi following his assassination in 1948. He later became the Lieutenant-Governor and Commander-in-Chief of Guernsey from 1953 to 1958.

Military career

He was commissioned as a midshipman in the Royal Navy in 1913 and was posted to HMS Indomitable in the British 1st Battlecruiser Squadron under David Beatty, 1st Earl Beatty. When war came he served on HMS Indomitable as she took part in the initial bombardment of the Turkish Dardanelles forts and the Battle of Dogger Bank (1915) where he commanded 'X Gun Turret', the last one to fire at the German ship SMS *Blücher* before she sank.

In 1915 he was selected to be in the first draft of the Royal Naval Air Service where he served until the end of the World War I. He celebrated the armistice by flying an airship (SSZ73) under the Menai Bridge with his friend Gordon Campbell (VC) as his passenger. He then became part of the newly formed Royal Air Force in 1919.

Between the wars he trialled the first gyroscopic compass for aircraft in the RAF and became Air attaché to Turkey in the run up to the World War II.

During World War II he ran the operations room at RAF Uxbridge during the Battle of Britain. He then commanded the Egypt Command Group under Air Marshal Tedder before becoming Second-in-Command of the Desert Air Force. He continued in this role through the battle of Alamein until after the Allied invasion of Sicily. He was then Second-in Command of British Air Forces in NW Europe until the end of the war, serving in D-Day, Normandy, the Ardennes and the advance across the France and Germany.

After the war he was appointed as the Commander of the RAF in India. As independence approached Pandit Nehru asked him to be the first Commander-in-Chief of the new Royal Indian Air Force upon its inception.

In 1953 he ran Operation Totem, the first British nuclear bomb land tests in Emu Field, Australia.

Family

Thomas Elmhirst was born into a landed gentry family in Yorkshire, where the family seat is Houndhill. He was the 4th of eight boys and one youngest sister. His eldest brother William Elmhirst was killed on the Somme and the 3rd son Christopher Elmhirst was killed at Gallipoli. One of his brothers (the 2nd son) Leonard Knight Elmhirst became a noted philanthropist and educational reformer.

He married firstly Katherine Gordon Black, daughter of William Black, on Tuesday, December 16, 1930, and had a son, Roger and a daughter, Jane. Katherine died in 1965.

He married secondly Marian Ferguson (née Montagu Douglas Scott), widow of the late Colonel Andrew Henry Ferguson, on Wednesday, October 30, 1968. Marian was the paternal grandmother of Sarah, Duchess of York, and maternal great grandmother of HRH Princess Beatrice of York and HRH Princess Eugenie of York. Thomas Elmhirst died at Dummer, Hampshire, on Saturday, November 6, 1982, in his 87th year. He was survived by his second wife, Marian Elmhirst (née Montagu Douglas Scott), and his children and grandchildren from his first marriage.

RONALD IVELAW-CHAPMAN

Air Chief Marshal Sir Ronald Ivelaw-Chapman GCB, KBE, DFC, AFC, RAF (17 January 1899 – 28 April 1978) was a senior commander in the Royal Air Force in the middle of the 20th century and the penultimate RAF commander-in-chief of the Indian Air Force. Ronald Ivelaw-Chapman was born in British Guiana to a successful merchant. He came to England with his parents in 1903 and attended Cheltenham College.

First World War

He joined the Royal Flying Corps in 1917 and served as a Bristol Fighter pilot on the western front with 10 Squadron in the last eleven months of the war.

Between the Wars

In January 1929 history was made by Ivelaw-Chapman, then a flight-lieutenant in the RAF. A successful rescue of the

British Legation in Kabul, took place via the Himalayas. Passage was made in a series of troop carrying Vickers Victoria bombers. The evacuation took place under extreme circumstances, for both aircraft, pilots, and passengers, nonetheless rescuing Ambassador Sir Francis and Lady Humphrys.

For this "Chaps" Ivelaw-Chapman received the Air Force Cross.

Second World War

At the outbreak of the Second World War Ivelaw-Chapman now a Wing Commander was part of the operations staff of RAF Bomber Command headquarters. In June 1940 he was promoted to Group Captain and was appointed station commander at RAF Linton-on-Ouse, a 4 Group bomber station near York. In 1941 he returned to a staff job at the Air Ministry involved in D-Day planning. In 1943 he was again appointed a station commander at RAF Elsham Wolds, a 1 Group bomber station.

On the night of the 6/7 May 1943 Ivelaw-Chapman was flying as second pilot of a 576 Squadron Avro Lancaster on a mission to bomb an ammunition dump at Aubigne in France. His aircraft was shot down by a night fighter and Ivelaw-Chapman went on the run.

Because of his experience and knowledge Churchill ordered the French resistance to do all they could to help him return to England, he was to be killed if he was in danger of being captured by the Germans. He was captured by the Gestapo on 8 June 1944, the most senior Bomber Command officer to have been captured by the Germans. Churchill's fear was unfounded as the Germans did not realise his importance and he was treated as an ordinary prisoner of war.

Post war

After the war he was promoted to Air Vice Marshal and took command of No. 38 Group RAF at Marks Hall, Earls Colne, Essex. In 1950 he became an Air Chief Marshal and accepted the post of Commander-in-Chief of the newly formed Indian Air Force.On his return to the UK became Vice-Chief of the Air Staff in 1952 before he retired in 1957.

GERALD GIBBS (RAF OFFICER)

Air Marshal Sir Gerald Ernest Gibbs KBE, CIE, MC & Two Bars, RAF (Born South Norwood, 3 September 1896; died Kingston upon Thames, 13 October 1992) was a senior commander in the Royal Air Force in the first half of the 20th century and the last RAF commander-in-chief of the Indian Air Force. During WWI he scored 10 victories (all in the S.E.5), becoming a double ace. Educated at Kingston Grammar School.

SUBROTO MUKERJEE

Air Marshal Subroto Mukerjee, OBE (5 March 1911 – 8 November 1960) was the first Chief of the Air Staff of the Indian Air Force (IAF). Born in a Bengali family of repute, he was educated in India as well as England. He joined the Royal Air Force and later was one of the first recruits of the Indian Air Force. He had an illustrious career and had been awarded with many honours until his accidental death in 1960. He has been called the "Father of the Indian Air Force".

Early life

Subroto Mukerjee was born in Kolkata (then Calcutta) on 5 March 1911. His paternal grandfather, Nibaran Chandra Mukherjee, a Brahmo, was a pioneer in social and educational reforms in the country and a member of the Brahmo Samaj while his maternal grandfather, Dr. PK Roy of the Indian Education Service, was the first Indian Principal of the Presidency College, Calcutta. His maternal grandmother Sarala Roy was the founder of the Gokhale Memorial School. His father was Satish Chandra Mukherjee, an early Indian ICS officer. Youngest of four children, Subroto was taken to England when he was three months old. However, he spent his childhood in Krishnanagar and Chinsura of Bengal. From his very early days Subroto had shown an aptitude for a military career – probably infused by his uncle, Indra Lal Roy, who had joined the Royal Flying Corps in the First World War. Roy was the first Indian to be awarded the Distinguished Flying Cross and the only Indian flying ace.

Subroto was educated in Diocesan School and Loreto Convent in Calcutta and also in a school in Hampstead in England. Later Subroto joined Howrah Zila School and passed matriculation examination in 1927. He studied in Presidency College, Calcutta for one year and then went to Cambridge University.

Joining the Air Force

About this time the Government of India (under British rule) decided to take some Indians in the Royal Air Force. Subroto wrote the Cranwell entrance examination and London Matriculation in 1929 and was one of the first six Indian males selected to undergo two years of flying training at the Royal Air Force College, Cranwell. The other five were H.C. Sirkar, A.B. Awan, Bhupendra Singh, Amarjeet Singh and J.N. Tandon.

On 8 October 1932, the six Indians cadets were commissioned in the Royal Air Force. On the same day, the Indian Air Force Act was passed by the Indian Legislative Assembly, and the Indian Air Force was born. Subroto was commissioned as a pilot. After completing their training at Cranwell, the Indian pilots passed through the Army Cooperation School at Old Sarum in Wiltshire.

They served in RAF squadrons before coming back to India to serve Indian Air Force. On 1 April 1933, "A" Flight of the No 1 Squadron, Indian Air Force, was formed at Karachi. Subroto was one of the five Indian pilots who made up the flight. The flight was equipped with four Westland Wapiti biplanes.

Subroto Mukherjee's elder sister Renuka Ray (1903–1995) was a prominent personality. She was a parliamentarian, cabinet minister and an ambassador. She studied in Cambridge University and London School of Economics.

Operations at North West Frontier

A rebellion took place in North West Frontier region (India–Afghanistan border) in 1936, led by the Pukhtoon tribes. The Indian Air Force would play a major role in controlling the rebellion in the harsh terrains of the region. Subroto Mukerjee was awarded India General Service Medal with clasps "North West Frontier 1936-37", and "North West Frontier 1937-39" and "Mentioned-in-Despatches" in 1942 for service during the operations in North West Frontier Province.

During WW2

Subroto Mukerjee was one of the three flying officers of the three flights of No. 1 Squadron of IAF in 1938. Coastal Defence Flights (CDFs) of the Indian Air Force Volunteer Reserve were formed with the outbreak of World War II. In 1939, Subroto Mukerjee was promoted to Squadron Leader and took over command of No 1 Squadron, IAF. Subroto Mukerjee had many "first"s to his credit — the first Indian to command a Flight, a Squadron, a Station (Kohat), and finally, the Service itself. He was also the first IAF pilot to carry out an airdrop over a beleaguered army picket. He commanded RAF Station Kohat from August 1943 till December 1944. In June 1945 he was awarded the Order of the British Empire (Military Division).

After Independence

India became independent from the British rule on 15 August 1947. However, due to partition of India, assets of the Indian Air Force (like other branches of the military) had to be divided between the two new countries of India and Pakistan. The first three Air Chiefs of independent India, Air Marshals Sir Thomas Elmhirst KBE, CB, AFC, Sir Ronald Ivelaw Chapman, KBE, CBE, DFC, AFC, and Sir Gerald Ernest Gibbs, KBE, CIE, MC, were from the RAF. The IAF had to reorganise itself after the partition. Subroto assisted the Air Chiefs in reorganising the IAF. He went to the Imperial Defence College in England for further training in 1952.

On returning to India in 1954, Subroto Mukerjee took over as the Commander-in-Chief of the Indian Air Force on 1 April 1954, in the rank of Air Marshal. When the Change in Designation Act, 1955, was passed, the title of "Commander-in-Chief" was replaced by Chief of the Air Staff, IAF. Thus Mukerjee became the first Indian Commander-in-Chief as well as Chief of Air Staff of the Indian Air Force.

Death and commemoration

Subroto Mukerjee was one of the passengers in Air India's first ever flight – to Tokyo – in November 1960. On 8 November 1960, Mukerjee was having a meal with a friend of his, an officer in the Indian Navy, in a restaurant in Tokyo. A piece of food lodged in his windpipe, choking him to death. His body was flown to Palam Airport, New Delhi on 9 November 1960, and on 10 November 1960 he was cremated with full military honours. He was paid the final tribute in the form of a fly-past of forty nine aircraft, one for each of his forty nine years.

Aspy Engineer, a close associate of Mukerjee, assumed the role of Chief of Air Staff of IAF from 1 December 1960. He issued a Special Order of the Day paying tribute to Subroto Mukerjee and called him as the "Father of the Indian Air Force".

Subroto Mukerjee conceived the idea of an inter-school all-India football tournament which was implemented after his death. The tournament, known as Subroto Cup Football Tournament still helps to find talented players from schools.

Subroto Mukherjee married Sharda Pandit from a prominent Maharashtrian family in 1939.

They have one son. Mrs. Sharda Mukherjee was active in social work and after her husband's death, took active part in public affairs. She was later appointed as the Governor of Gujarat.

Rank Promotions

- Pilot Officer, RAF-1932
- Flying Officer-1936
- Flight Lieutenant-1938
- Squadron Leader-1939
- Wing Commander-1942
- Wing Commander, RIAF-1945
- Group Captain-1946
- Air Commodore-1947
- Air Vice-Marshal-1949
- Air Marshal, IAF-1954

Honours

- King George VI Coronation Medal-1937
- India General Service Medal (w/Clasps)-1939

- Mentioned in Despatches (MID)-1942
- Officer of the Order of the British Empire (OBE)-1945
- 1939-1945 Star-1945
- India Service Medal-1945
- War Medal 1939-1945-1945
- Indian Independence Medal-1948
- Queen Elizabeth II Coronation Medal-1953
- Yugoslavian People's Army Medal, 1st Class-1954

3

Historical Background of the Indian Air Force

INTRODUCTION

The Indian Air Force is the air arm of the armed forces of India. Its primary responsibility is to secure Indian airspace and to conduct aerial warfare during a conflict. It was officially established on October 8, 1932 as an auxiliary air force of the Indian Empire and the prefix *Royal* was added in 1945 in recognition of its services during the World War II. After India achieved independence from the United Kingdom in 1947, the Royal Indian Air Force served the Union of India, with the prefix being dropped when India became a republic in 1950.

Since independence, the IAF has been involved in four wars with neighboring Pakistan and one with the People's Republic of China. Other major operations undertaken by the IAF include Operation *Vijay*, Operation *Meghdoot* and Operation *Cactus*. Apart from conflicts, the IAF has been an active participant in United Nations peacekeeping missions.

The President of India serves as the Commander-in-Chief of the IAF. The Chief of Air Staff, an Air Chief Marshal (ACM), is a four star commander and commands the Air Force. There is never more than one serving ACM at any given time in the IAF. One officer has been conferred the rank of Marshal of the Air Force, a 5-star rank and the officer serves as the ceremonial chief. With strength of approximately 170,000 personnel and 1,700 aircraft, including 852 combat aircraft in active service, the Indian Air Force is the world's fourth largest. In recent years, the IAF has undertaken an ambitious expansion and modernisation program to replace its aging Soviet-era fighter jets. Among the various expansion plans is the MRCA program under which the IAF plans to induct 126 fighter jets at a cost of US$12 billion.

Mission

The IAF's mission is defined by the Armed Forces Act of 1947, Constitution of India and the Air Force Act of 1950, in the aerial battlespace, as: *Defence of India and every part thereof including preparation for defence and all such acts as may be conducive in times of war to its prosecution and after its termination to effective demobilisation.* Moreover, the air force, along with the other branches of the Indian armed forces, can assist local and state governments; if assistance is sought by such government during natural disasters and for maintaining internal security.

History

The Indian Air Force was established as an auxiliary air force of the RAF with the enactment of the Indian Air Force Act of 1932 on October 8 that year. On April 1, 1933, the IAF commissioned its first squadron, No.1 Squadron, with four Westland Wapiti biplanes and five Indian pilots. The Indian pilots were led by Flight Lieutenant (later Air Vice Marshal) Cecil Bouchier. Until 1938, No. 1 Squadron remained the only squadron of the IAF, though two more flights were added. During the Second World War, the Air Force had grown to seven squadrons in 1943 and to nine squadrons in 1945. In recognition of the crucial role played by the IAF, King George VI conferred it the prefix *Royal* in 1945. Indian National Army youth cadets were trained by Imperial Japanese Army Air Force Academy in 1944. After Indian independence in 1947, Royal Indian Air Force (RIAF) was bifurcated. Three of the ten operational squadrons and facilities located within the borders of Pakistan were transferred to Royal Pakistan Air Force.

In 1947, when a conflict broke out over the control of erstwhile principality of Jammu & Kashmir, the Maharaja of the state decided to accede India in order to receive military help. The day after instrument of accession was signed, the RIAF was called upon to mobilise armed troops into the war-zone. This led to the eruption of full scale war between India and Pakistan without a formal declaration. During the war, the RIAF did not engage Pakistan Air Force in air-to-air combat; however, it did provide effective transport and close air support to the Indian troops. When India became a Republic in 1950, the *Royal* title was dropped to become the Indian Air Force.

In 1960, when Belgium's 75-year colonial rule of the Congo ended abruptly, widespread violence and rebellion engulfed the nation. IAF aircraft arrived in Congo to support United Nations Operation in the Congo and started undertaking operational missions in November. The unit remained there until 1966, when the UN mission ended.

During the Sino-Indian War of 1962, India's military planners failed to deploy and effectively use the IAF against the invading Chinese forces. Three years after the Sino-Indian conflict, in 1965, India went to war with Pakistan again over Kashmir. Learning from the experiences of the Sino-Indian war, India decided to use its air force extensively during the war. This was the first time the IAF actively engaged an enemy air force. However, instead of providing close air support to the Indian Army, the IAF carried out independent raids against Pakistani Air Force (PAF) bases. These bases were situated deep inside Pakistani territory, making IAF fighters vulnerable to anti-aircraft fire. During the course of the conflict, the PAF enjoyed qualitative superiority over the IAF because most of the jets in IAF's fleet were of World War II vintage. Despite this, the IAF was able to prevent the PAF from gaining air superiority over conflict zones. By the time the conflict had ended, Pakistan claimed to have shot down 113 IAF aircraft while the Indians claimed that 73 PAF aircraft were downed. More than 60% of IAF's air combat losses took place during the disastrous battles over Kalaikunda and Pathankot; where most of the losses were on the ground.

After the 1965 war, the IAF underwent a series of changes. In 1966, the Para Commandos regiment was created. With an intention of increasing its logistics supply and rescue operations ability, the IAF inducted 72 Avro 748s which were built by

Hindustan Aeronautics (HAL) under license from Avro. India started to lay more stress on indigenous manufacture of fighter aircraft. HAL HF-24 Marut, designed by the famed German aerospace engineer Kurt Tank, were inducted into the air force. HAL also started working on a new improved version of the Folland Gnat, known as HAL Ajeet. At the same time, the IAF also started inducting Mach 2 capable Soviet MiG-21 and Sukhoi Su-7 fighters.

By late 1971, another war between India and Pakistan seemed inevitable because of the intensification of the independence movement in erstwhile East Pakistan. On November 22, 1971, 10 days before the start of a full-scale war, four Pakistani Air Force (PAF) F-86 Sabre jets attacked Indian and Mukti Bahini positions near the international border. Three of the four PAF Sabres were shot down by IAF's Folland Gnats. On December 3, India formally declared war against Pakistan following massive preemptive strikes by the PAF against Indian Air Force installations in Srinagar, Ambala, Sirsa, Halwara and Jodhpur.

However the plan failed as the IAF had anticipated such a move and no major losses were suffered. The Indian Air Force was quick to respond to Pakistani air strikes, following which the PAF carried out mostly defensive sorties. Within the first two weeks, the IAF had carried out almost 2,000 sorties over East Pakistan and also provided close air support to the advancing Indian Army.

IAF also assisted the Indian Navy in its operations against the Pakistani Navy and Maritime Security Agency in the Bay of Bengal and Arabian Sea. On the western front, the IAF destroyed more than 29 Pakistani tanks, 40 APCs and a railway train during the Battle of Longewala. The IAF undertook strategic bombing of West Pakistan by carring out raids on oil installations in Karachi, the Mangla Dam and a gas plant in Sindh. Similar strategy was also deployed in East Pakistan and as the IAF achieved complete air superiority on the eastern front, the ordnance factories, runways, and other vital areas of East Pakistan were severely damaged. By the time Pakistani forces surrendered, the IAF claimed that 94 PAF aircraft, including 54 F-86 Sabres. The IAF had flown over 6,000 sorties on both East and West fronts; including sorties by transport aircraft and helicopters. Towards the end of the war, IAF's transport planes dropped leaflets over Dhaka urging the Pakistani forces to surrender, demoralising Pakistani troops in East Pakistan.

In 1984, India launched Operation Meghdoot to capture the Siachen Glacier in the contested Kashmir region. IAF's Mi-8, Chetak and Cheetah helicopters airlifted hundreds of Indian troops to Siachen. Launched on April 13, 1984, this military operation was unique because of Siachen's inhospitable terrain and climate. The military action was successful, given the fact that under a previous agreement, neither Pakistan nor India had stationed any personnel in the area. The Indian forces, facing no opposition, took control over most of the heights on the glacier.

On May 20, 1999, the Indian Air Force was called in to provide close air support to the Indian Army at the height of the ongoing Kargil conflict. Because of Kashmir's high altitude and rigid terrain, the IAF initially expressed its reservations to deploy the slow-moving Mil Mi-8/17 helicopters which had a service ceiling of 10,000 feet. These concerns materialised when the Pakistani forces shot down an IAF Mi-8 helicopter and two fighter jets, MiG-21 and MiG-27, that had reportedly strayed into Pakistan's airspace.

After the initial setbacks, the IAF deployed the Mirage 2000 which not only had better defence equipment compared to the MiGs, but also gave IAF the ability to carry out aerial raids at night. The Mirages successfully targeted enemy camps and logistic bases in Kargil and within days, their supply lines were severely disrupted.

The IAF also deployed its radars and the MiG-29 fighter jets in vast numbers to keep check on Pakistani military movements across the border. The MiG-29s were also used extensively to provide fighter escort to the Mirage 2000. At the height of the conflict, the IAF was conducting over forty sorties daily over the Kargil region. The IAF's operations in Kargil not only boosted the morale of the Indian Army, but also paved the way for the early recapture of Muntho Dhalo and Tiger Hill. By July 26, the Indian forces had successfully liberated Kargil from Pakistani forces and Islamist militants. On August 10, 1999, IAF MiG-21s intercepted a Pakistan Navy Breguet Atlantic which was flying over the disputed region of Sir Creek. The aircraft was shot down killing all 16 Pakistani Navy personnel on board. India claimed that the Atlantic was on a mission to gather information on IAF air defence, a charge emphatically rejected by Pakistan which argued that the unarmed aircraft was on a training mission.

Since late 1990s, the Indian Air Force has been modernising its fleet to counter challenges in the new century. The fleet size of the IAF has decreased during this period because of the retirement of older aircraft. Still, India maintains the fourth largest air force. As new aircraft enter service and numbers recover, the IAF plans to have a fleet of 42 squadrons.

Structure of the IAF

The President of India is the Supreme Commander of all Indian armed forces and by virtue of that fact is the notional Commander of the Air Force. India's Ministry of Defence under the Defence Minister oversees the Air Force, by way of direct civilian leadership. The Prime Minister and the National Security Council provide indirect leadership by shaping government security policy. A Chief of the Air Staff with the rank of Air Chief Marshal commands Air Headquarters and provides military leadership. He is assisted by six officers: a Vice Chief of the Air Staff, a Deputy Chief of the Air Staff, the Air Officer in Charge of Administration, the Air Officer in Charge of Personnel, the Air Officer in Charge of Maintenance, and the Inspector General of Flight Safety. In January 2002, the government conferred the rank of Marshal of the Air Force on Arjan Singh making him the first and only *Five Star* rank officer with the Indian Air Force and ceremonial chief of the air force.

Commands and Structure

The Indian Air Force is divided into five operational and two functional commands. Each Command is headed by an Air Officer Commanding-in-Chief with the rank of Air Marshal. The purpose of an operational command is to conduct military operations using aircraft within its area of responsibility, whereas the responsibility of functional commands is to maintain combat readiness. Aside from the Training Command at Bangalore, the center for primary flight training is located at the Air Force Academy in Hyderabad, Andhra Pradesh, followed by operational training at various other schools. Advanced officer training for command positions is also conducted at the Defence Services Staff College; specialised advanced flight training schools are located at Bidar, Karnataka, and Hakimpet, Andhra Pradesh (also the location for helicopter training). Technical schools are found at a number of other locations.

Bases

The IAF operates over sixty air bases, with more being built or planned. Western Air Command is the largest Air Command. It operates sixteen air bases from Punjab to Uttar Pradesh. Eastern Air Command operates fifteen Air bases in Eastern and North-eastern India. Central Air Command operates seven Air Bases in Madhya Pradesh and surrounding states of central India. Southern Air Command, a strategically important Air command, in line with India's latest doctrine of protecting the vital shipping routes. It operates nine Air bases in Southern India and two in the Andaman and Nicobar Islands. South Western Air Command is the front line of defence against Pakistan, this important Command operates twelve air bases in Gujarat, Maharashtra and Rajasthan. India also operates the Farkhor Air Base in Tajikistan

Wings

A Wing is a formation intermediate between a Command and a Squadron. It generally consists of two or three IAF Squadrons and Helicopter Units, along with Forward Base Support Units (FBSU). FBSUs do not have or host any Squadrons or Helicopter units but act as transit airbases for routine operations. In times of war, they can become fully fledged air bases playing host to various Squadrons. In all, about 47 Wings and 19 FBSUs make up the IAF.

Squadrons

Squadrons are the field units and formations attached to static locations. Thus, a Flying Squadron is a sub-unit of an air force station which carries out the primary task of the IAF. All fighter squadrons are headed by a Commanding Officer with the rank of Wing Commander. Some Transport squadrons and Helicopter Units are headed by a Commanding Officer with the rank of Group Captain. Within this formation structure, IAF has several service branches for day-to-day operations. They are:

IAF Personnel

The IAF has a strength of 170,000 personnel. Its rank structure is based on that of the Royal Air Force. The highest rank attainable in the IAF is Marshal of the Indian Air Force, conferred by the President of India after exceptional service during wartime. MIAF Arjan Singh is the only officer to have achieved this rank. The head of the Indian Air Force is the Chief of the Air Staff, who holds the rank of Air Chief Marshal. The current Chief of the Air Staff is Air Chief Marshal P.V.Naik, appointed on May 1, 2009, following the retirement of Air Chief Marshal Fali Homi Major.

Officers

Anyone holding Indian citizenship can apply to be an officer in the Air Force as long as they satisfy the eligibility criteria. There are four entry points to become an officer. Male applicants, who are between the ages of 16½ and 19 and have passed high school graduation, can apply at the *Intermediate* level. Men and women applicants, who have graduated from college (three year course) and are between the ages of 18 and 28, can apply at the *Graduate* level entry. Graduates of engineering colleges can apply at the *Engineer* level if they are between the ages of 18 and 28 years. The age limit for the flying and ground duty branch is 23 years of age and for technical branch is 28 years of age. After completing a master's degree, men and women between the ages of 18 and 28 years can apply at the *Post Graduate* level. Post graduate applicants do not qualify for the flying branch. For the technical branch the age limit is 28 years and for the ground duty branch it is 25. At the time of application, all applicants must be single. The IAF selects candidates for officer training from these applicants. After completion of training, candidate are commissioned as Flying Officers.

Airmen

The duty of an airman in the Indian Air Force is to make sure that all the air and ground operations run smoothly. From operating Air Defence systems to fitting missiles, they are involved in all activities of an air base and give support to various technical and non-technical jobs.

The recruitment of personnel below officer rank is conducted through All India Selection Tests and Recruitment Rallies. All India Selection Tests are conducted among 14 Airmen Selection Centres (ASCs) located all over India.

These centres are under the direct functional control of Central Airmen Selection Board (CASB), with administrative control and support by respective commands. The role of CASB is to carry out selection and enrolment of airmen from the Airmen Selection Centers for their respective commands.

Candidates initially take a written test at the time of application. Those passing the written test undergo a physical fitness test, an interview conducted in English, and medical examination.

Candidates for training are selected from individuals passing the battery of tests, on the basis of their performance. Upon completion of training, an individual becomes an Airman. Some MWOs and WOs are granted honorary commission in the last year of their service as an honorary Flying Officer or Flight Lieutenant before retiring from the service.

Garud Commando Force

The Garud Commando Force is the Special Forces unit of the Indian Air Force. It was formed in September 2004 and has a strength of approximately 1500 personnel.

The unit derives its name from *Garuda*, a divine bird-like creature of Hindu Mythology, but more commonly the word for eagle in Sanskrit.

Garud is tasked with the protection of critical Air Force bases and installations; search and rescue during peace and hostilities and disaster relief during calamities. Presently, the GARUDs are deployed in Congo as part of the UN peace keeping operations.

Non Combatants Enrolled and civilians

Non Combatants Enrolled (NCs(E)) were established in British India as personal assistants to the officer class, and are equivalent to the *orderly* or *sahayak* of the Indian Army. Almost all the commands have some percentage of civilian strength which are central government employees. These are regular ranks which are prevalent in ministries. They are usually not posted outside their stations and are employed in administrative and technical work. More than 250 different designations exist.

Land-Based Air Defence

- Isayev SA-3 Goa: The Indian Air Force is considering upgrading its Pechora SA-3 missiles with Polish help whilst it waits for the Akash. According to Janes Missiles and Rockets (December 2005), the IAF would like to conduct the Newa-SCM upgrade package upgrade to 20 S-125M Pechora-CC systems, using primarily the Tatra 8x8 chassis, which is licence-built in India. Installation on specially adapted heavy equipment trailers or Tatra 8x8 vehicles was studied at the request of the Indian Air Force. It incorporates a new ZNO-X digital transmitter/receiver block developed by the Przemyslowy Instytut Telekomunikacji (PIT) to replace the original magnetron-based hardware. The unit uses digital technology, including digital frequency synthesis, and has automatic built-in test facilities. While the ZNO-X is an expensive upgrade, it significantly improves system performance. Most of the upgrade work would be done in India, although the core elements of the upgrade would be delivered from Poland.Pechora SAM will be phased out by 2012. As of 2009, no firm SA-3 upgrade program has been signed for.
- SA-8 Gecko
- SA-10 Grumble/S-300. Reportedly 6 batteries were purchased in August 1995
- SA-16 Gimlet-MANPAD.

Aircraft Inventory

The Indian Air Force has a strength of over 1,915 (combat

and non-combat) aircraft. Most are of Soviet/Russian origin. The Air Force also operates some aircraft from Britain and France. Hindustan Aeronautics Limited produces some of the Russian and British aircraft in India under licence. The exact number of aircraft in service with the Indian Air Force cannot be determined with precision from open sources. Various reliable sources provide notably divergent estimates for a variety of high-visibility aircraft.

Fighter and Multi-role Combat Aircraft

These aircraft are primarily for air defence and air superiority purposes. However, most of them have significant strike and close air support capabilities. The Sukhoi Su-30MKI is the IAF's prime air superiority fighter. The Su-30K variant was first acquired in 1996. That year, the IAF signed a US$1.6 billion contract with Russia for the supply of 50 Su-30MKIs and the technology transfer and license to manufacture 140 Su-30MKIs by Hindustan Aeronautics Limited. The two-seat, multi-role fighter has a maximum speed of 2500 km/h (Mach 2.35) and a service ceiling of 20,000 meters. With one mid-air refueling, it can travel as far as 8000 km, making it a suitable platform to deliver strategic weapons..In 2007, the IAF spent US$700 million to upgrade its remaining 10 Su-30Ks and 8 SU-30MKs to MKI Std variant and signed a contract for the supply of 40 additional MKIs with Russia.

The MiG-29 (NATO: *Fulcrum*) is the IAF's dedicated air superiority fighter. It has a top speed of 2,445 km/h (Mach 2.3) and is armed with a 30 mm cannon along with R-60 & R-27 R missiles. The IAF began deploying MiG-29s in 1984, becoming the second air force to do so.. Since their induction, the IAF's MiG-29s have undergone a series of upgrades including more efficient and powerful radar (Zhuk-ME), weapons system, and engines. Mirage 2000s, capable of flying at 2,500 km/h (Mach 2.35), are the IAF's premier multirole fighter jet. These aircraft can carry a wide range of weaponry including two 30 mm integral cannon, two *Matra Super 530D* medium-range missiles, two *R550 Magic* close combat missiles and various ground attack munitions.

Since 1963, over 450 MiG-21 combat aircraft have served in the IAF. Most of these MiGs have been upgraded since induction. In 1996, India signed a US$300 million deal with Russia to upgrade 125 MiG-21 *Bis*, and a multi-million dollar deal was awarded to Israel's Elta for upgrading the avionics of the MiGs. Because of their frequent crashes, the MiG-21s have been dubbed *flying coffins* by the media. As of 2007, about 250 MiG-21s remain in service with the Indian Air Force and are planned to be replaced by the indigenously built HAL Tejas starting 2010. IAF has had problems in aircraft maintenance with many crashes in recent years. During the 2005-09 period, 32 MiG series fighters in service with the IAF crashed, resulting in the death of five pilots.

Strike, Attack and Close Support Aircraft

Squadrons of Jaguar (known as the *Shamsher* in Indian service) and MiG-27 aircraft serve as the IAF's primary ground attack force. The twin-engine Jaguar IB, with a top speed of Mach 1.6, is capable of carrying nuclear weapons. The IAF has 100 Jaguar IS and 8 maritime strike Jaguar IM aircraft. The single-seat MiG-27 carries one GSh-6-30 six-barreled 30 mm cannon, 4000 kg of general-purpose ordnance, SPPU-22 and SPPU-6 gun pods, and various guided air-to-surface missiles. In January 2009, India successfully completed the upgrade programs on the Air Force's MiG-27 ground attack variants. DRDO carried out the avionics upgrades on the fighter aircraft. In the upgraded MiG-27s, the avionics system is built around a modular mission computer termed Core Avionics Computer (CAC). The upgraded ground attack fighters are equipped with Inertial Navigation and Global Positioning System (INGPS) providing accurate navigation during aircraft sorties. To provide more accuracy to the aircraft's weapon systems, accurate ranging sensors such as Laser Designator Pod (LDP) and Laser Ranger and Marked Target Seeker (LRMTS) have been integrated in it also. To improve situational awareness of the pilot during air combat, a digital map generator has been integrated along with a digital video recording system, which helps in mission analysis and debrief support.

Airborne Early Warning Aircraft

In 2004, the IAF ordered 3 IAI Phalcon Airborne Early Warning radar system from Israel Aerospace Industries, which is considered to be the most advanced AEW&C system in the world. The air force will use 3 newly acquired Ilyushin Il-76 Phalcons as the platform for this radar. In May 2008, India appears to have ordered an additional three Phalcon radar-equipped IL-76s from Israel, pushing up the value of the deal from US$1.1 to 1.5 billion. An Indian defence delegation headed by Defence Secretary Vijay Singh, visited Israel in November 2008 to discuss the purchase of the planes and missiles from Israel Aerospace Industries (IAI). It has been reported that India has placed a follow-up order for 3 more Phalcon radar equipped IL-76 from Israel at a cost of $1.5 billion, pushing the total number to be acquired up to 6. The first Phalcons arrived in India on May 25, 2009 and are expected to be commissioned into service by 2010. IAF Air Chief said that it would take a year and a half to get each and every combat plane in IAF to link with Phalcon.

Transport Aircraft

The IAF operates 25 Ilyushin Il-76s for military transport duties such as heavy lift at all operational levels. The Il-76 MD is a strategic air-lifter with a payload of 95,000 lb and a range of over 5,000 km (2,700 nm; 3,100 statute miles). In 2003, the IAF orderd 6 IL-78MKI aircraft from Uzbekistan and are fitted with aerial refueling pods from Israel. India took delivery of the tankers in 2004.

IAF has a fleet of 64 Avro 748 which has a payload of 5,136 kg (11,323 lb) and has a range of 1,715 km (926 nm; 1,066 mi). The air force also operates a fleet of 94 twin-engined turboprop Antonov An-32 and 73 Dornier Do 228 utility aircraft. In an effort to infuse fresh life into its transport fleet, the Indian Air Force will begin an upgrade programme for its Antonov An-32s and Dornier Do 228s in 2009.

Training Aircraft

The HPT-32 Deepak is IAF's basic flight training aircraft for cadets. Developed during the late 1970s, it has been in service with the IAF since 1984. The IAF uses the HAL HJT-16 Kiran mk.I for intermediate flight training of cadets, while the HJT-16 Kiran mk.II provides Stage II flight training. In 2004, the IAF placed an order for 66 BAE Hawk Mk 132

Advanced Jet Trainers in a deal worth over 1 billion GBP. Deliveries began in November, 2007 and induction in February, 2008. Pilot instructors and engineers were trained in the UK, and the aircraft is scheduled to replace the mk.II. HAL is developing the HJT-36 *Sitara* to replace the Kiran mk.I.

Helicopters

An important objective of the IAF is to support ground troops by providing air cover and by transporting men and essential commodities across the battlefield. For this purpose the Air Force maintains a fleet of helicopters. Helicopters in service with the IAF are:

Unmanned Aerial Vehicles

The primary role of unmanned aerial vehicles (UAVs) is to provide aerial surveillance and reconnaissance. The IAF operates IAI Malat built Searcher II and Heron UAVs. Israel Aircraft Industries and Aeronautical Development Establishment (ADE). India's leading unmanned aerial vehicle research agency are also jointly developing three new UAVs.

UAVs can also be used as a *pilot-less target aircraft*. HAL *Lakshya*, indigenously developed pilotless target aircraft, was inducted into the IAF in July 2005. Another UAV, the HAL *Nishant* Remote Piloted Vehicle (RPV) has also been developed, with an endurance of over 3 hours. The UAV can be used to carry out ground attacks and aerial surveillance.

Ongoing Expansion

Future Aircraft

As of 2008, the Indian Air Force plans to induct 126 multi-role combat aircraft (with an option for an additional 74 aircraft), 280 Su-30MKI air superiority fighters (Ordered at cost of US$8.4 billion, 120 are already in service with the IAF), 220 HAL Tejas, 47 SEPECAT Jaguar combat aircraft. Additionally, the Indian Air Force has signed contracts for 66 BAE Hawk Mk.132 trainers (deliveries underway), 80+40 combat helicopters, 3 new Long Range UAVs, 6 mid-air refueling planes, 225+ HJT-36 Sitara Intermediate Jet Trainer aircraft and some additional medium-range transport aircraft. The Indian Air Force began the upgradation of its MiG-29 fleet in 2007. India awarded

Russia a US$965 million contract to upgrade its multi-role MiG-29 into MiG-29SMT warplanes, on Monday March 10, 2008. According to the deal, Russia will re-arm the twin-engined MiG-29s with air-to-air missiles, and the upgraded MiGs will feature increased fuel capacity and state-of-the-art avionics.

Confirmed Sales

In early 2008, the IAF signed a deal to acquire 6 C-130J Super Hercules, modified for special mission roles, for US$1.06 billion. Lockheed Martin is expected to deliver the planes in 2011. In December 2008, India and Russia inked a deal for the supply of 80 Mi-17V-5 (also known as Mi-171) medium lift helicopters at a cost of US$1.2 billion. The two countries had earlier negotiated a price of $650 million, but early in 2008 Russia asked for a revision of the contract price. Russia is expected to deliver the Mi-171 to the IAF in 2010. The deal also envisages a US$405 million "offset" obligation by Russia. The new choppers, which have an 18,000 ft operational ceiling, will replace 50 Mi-8s currently in service with the IAF, some of which are over 35 years old, and boost IAF's capability to support high-altitude posts in Siachen and Ladakh sectors. The helicopter will come with the circuitry and hard points to carry weapons.

Under procurement

Because of delays in inducting the indigenous HAL Tejas, the IAF issued an Request of Intent (RoI) for the procurement of 126 multi-role combat aircraft to replace around 250 Cold War-era MiG-21 it operates. Contenders for the $10 Billion contract are the MiG-35 from Mikoyan of Russia, the Rafale from Dassault Aviation of France, the Eurofighter Typhoon, JAS 39 Gripen from Saab of Sweden, the F-16IN from Lockheed Martin and F/A-18E/F Super Hornet from Boeing. In May 2009, the IAF picked Airbus A330 multi-role tanker transport (MRTT) over Russia's Ilyushin Il-78 as the future tanker for the air force. The deal is worth approximately US$1 billion.

On May 26, 2009, the Indian Ministry of Defence invited bids for 22 combat helicopters and 15 heavy-lift helicopters in a deal worth US$2 billion. Companies which have expressed their interest in the tender include — Russia's Kamov and Mil

Moscow Helicopter Plant, Europe's AgustaWestland and Eurocopter and United States' Bell Helicopter and Boeing. Boeing submitted its initial bid on Oct 23, 2009 offering the AH-64D Apache Longbow attack helicopter and the CH-47F Chinook heavy-lift, twin-rotor helicopters. On June 15, 2009, the IAF announced that it was interested in purchasing about 10 C-17 Globemaster III tactical military transport aircraft. The IAF will be sending a proposal to the Indian Defence Ministry to acquire these aircraft through US Government's Foreign Military Sales (FMS) route.

A tender for supply of 317 light helicopters will be floated by Ministry of Defence combining the requirements of Indian Air force (125) and Indian Army (197). Unnamed government official stated that Letters of Interest (LOI) have been sent to Kamov, Bell, Augusta Westland and Eurocopter. In February 2008, Bell withdrew from the race, citing differences in offset clause with the Government of India. HAL has also recently joined the race with its Light Observation Helicopter (LOH). Although it is still on the drawing board, HAL officials seem to be confident to deliver in time.

Under Development

HAL initiated the Light Combat Aircraft (LCA) programme in 1983 to develop a replacement aircraft for IAF's ageing MiG-21. After development during the 80s and 90s the first flight occurred in 2001. The aircraft has since been christened HAL Tejas. The IAF plans to induct 220 Tejas aircraft. It has ordered 28 limited production aircraft. These aircraft are expected to enter service in 2010.

In October 2007, India and Russia signed a pact to develop a Fifth Generation Fighter Aircraft. The Indian version will be a two-seater, air superiority fighter. Another agreement was signed between India's Hindustan Aeronautics and Russia's United Aircraft Corporation (UAC) in December 2008 which detailed the joint development and production the aircraft. Work on the program will start by mid-2009 and the program is expected to be completed by 2017. During this period, these companies will form a joint-venture for the development of a Multirole Transport Aircraft, which will replace the IAF's ageing fleet of Antonov An-32s. Both HAL and UAC will invest US$300 million each on the program.

HAL has also started design work on Medium Combat Aircraft (MCA) is a twin-engined 5th generation stealth multirole fighter. It will complement the HAL Tejas and the Sukhoi/HAL FGFA in the Indian Air Force. The main purpose of this aircraft is to replace the aging SEPECAT Jaguar & MiG-27.

In 2004, Defence Research and Development Organisation revived the Airavat Project, which was India's first attempt in developing an indigenous AEW aircraft. A $210 million deal signed with Brazil's Embraer in 2008 for the supply of three Embraer EMB-145 regional jets. India has sent a request for proposal to six vendors for the supply of Active Array Antenna Unit (AAAU) and various other sub-systems. These vendors include Israel's Elta, the European consortium EADS, France's Thales, Sweden's SAAB Erikson and the United State's Raytheon and Northrop Grumman.

HAL has developed HAL HJT-36 Sitara for the IAF which carried out its maiden test flight in 2003. These aircraft are scheduled to replace the aging HJT-16 Kiran mk.I as intermediate jet trainer. The company is developing an Light Combat Helicopter for the IAF based on HAL Dhruv. It is being designed to fit into an anti-infantry and anti-armour role and will be capable to operate from altitudes an 6,500 metre. First flight of HAL LCH (Light Combat Helicopter) is expected in 2009.

Aerospace Command

The IAF is setting up an aerospace command. This command will leverage space technology including satellites. The command will be utilised by all the three services of the Indian armed forces and also for civilian purposes by ISRO. On October 22, 2001, ISRO launched the Technology Experiment Satellite (TES). Its onboard 1-metre resolution camera was the testbed for Indian space based imagery intelligence. ISRO launched follow-up military satellite CARTOSAT-2A on 28 April, 2008. It carries a panchromatic camera (PAN) with a resolution less than 1-metre but lacks night time and cloudy weather observation capability. ISRO launched a sophisticated radar-imaging satellite on 20 April 2009 called RISAT-2. It is capable of imaging in all-weather conditions and has a resolution of one metre. ISRO has denied that the spacecraft is spy satellite; however, experts believe that the satellite will allow India's security agencies to monitor military activities and movements of suspected terrorists in neighboring countries as well as enable the IAF to carry out precise strikes against targets like terrorist training camps.

Surface to Air Missile Systems

- Barak SAM-India and Israel have agreed to expand their missile development cooperation with a longer-range version of their extended-range Barak ship defence system for the Indian Air Force.
- Trishul(Trident): Development of Trishul is complete. It has met the IAF requirements during its various developmental flight trials. DRDO is presently in dialogue with IAF for possible induction. Frontier India reports that Indian Air force is considering to induct small quantity to meet partial requirement of LLQRM (Low Level Quick Reaction Missile) System.. However it is not known if IAF has placed a formal order of Trishul SAM System.
- SPYDER (*S*urface-to-air *PY*thon and *DER*by): In June 2007, India signed a $250 million to purchase SPYDER mobile air defence missiles from Israel. The two countries signed an additional $4 billion deal for the joint-development of a medium range surface-to-air missiles. However, the procurement of SPYDER missiles was delayed because of an ongoing investigation against Israel Aerospace Industries and RAFAEL by Indian intelligence agencies for its alleged kickbacks in the Barak-I deal with the Indian Navy. In August 2008, a $2.5 billion deal was signed by India and Israel to develop an advanced version of the SPYDER.
- Maitri LLQRM (Low Level Quick Reaction Missile): DRDO is in talks with MBDA to develop Maitri LLQRM for Army, Air force and Navy. Sources said that DRDL

is preparing feasibility report and is awaiting formal clearance from defence ministry.

- Akash: Indian Air force has approved the induction of Akash Missile System and had initiated the process of inducting the system. Akash has successfully demonstrated its performance through number of flight tests. DRDO and IAF jointly began a ten day intensive trial of Akash on December 13, 2007 aimed at making IAF familiar with the system.

IAF currently operates two squadrons of Akash. It is happy with the missile and is in the process of acquiring more squadrons for deployment in the North East.

Surface to Surface Missiles

- Prithvi II: 250 km Prithvi-II Ballistic Missile is under IAF service which could be used to target airfields, command and control centers etc.

Air to Surface Missiles

- DRDO-NPO Mashinostroeyenia Brahmos-Air launched version under Development

LIST OF REGIMENTS OF THE INDIAN ARMY

Indian Army Regiments

Infantry Regiments (29)

- Brigade of the Guards
- The Parachute Regiment
- Mechanised Infantry Regiment
- Punjab Regiment
- Madras Regiment
- The Grenadiers
- Maratha Light Infantry
- Rajputana Rifles
- Rajput Regiment
- Jat Regiment
- Sikh Regiment
- Sikh Light Infantry

- Dogra Regiment
- Garhwal Rifles
- Kumaon Regiment
- Assam Regiment
- Bihar Regiment
- Mahar Regiment
- Jammu & Kashmir Rifles
- Jammu & Kashmir Light Infantry
- Naga Regiment
- 1 Gorkha Rifles
- 3 Gorkha Rifles
- 4 Gorkha Rifles
- 5 Gorkha Rifles (Frontier Force)
- 8 Gorkha Rifles
- 9 Gorkha Rifles
- 11 Gorkha Rifles
- Ladakh Scouts.

Armoured Regiments (62)

- President's Bodyguard
- 1 Horse or Skinner's Horse
- 2 Lancers
- 3rd Cavalry
- 4 Horse or 'Hodson's Horse'
- 5 Armoured Regiment
- 6 Lancers
- 7 Cavalry
- 8 Cavalry
- 9 Horse or 'The Deccan Horse'
- 10 Armoured Regiment
- 11 Armoured Regiment
- 12 Armoured Regiment
- 13 Armoured Regiment
- 14 Horse or 'The Scinde Horse'

- 15 Armoured Regiment
- 16 Cavalry
- 17 Horse (The Poona Horse)
- 18 Cavalry
- 19 Armoured Regiment
- 20 Lancers
- Central India Horse (in 21st position)
- 40 Armoured Regiment
- 41 Armoured Regiment (India)
- 42 Armoured Regiment
- 43 Armoured Regiment-The only regiment in the Armoured Corps to hold the MBT Arjun as part of its standard weapons platform.
- 44 Armoured Regiment
- 45 Cavalry
- 46 Armoured Regiment
- 47 Armoured Regiment
- 48 Armoured Regiment
- 49 Armoured Regiment
- 50 Armoured Regiment
- 51 Armoured Regiment
- 52 Armoured Regiment
- 53 Armoured Regiment
- 61 Cavalry
- 62 Cavalry
- 63 Cavalry
- 64 Cavalry
- 65 Armoured Regiment
- 66 Armoured Regiment
- 67 Armoured Regiment
- 68 Armoured Regiment
- 69 Armoured Regiment
- 70 Armoured Regiment
- 71 Armoured Regiment

- 72 Armoured Regiment
- 73 Armoured Regiment
- 74 Armoured Regiment
- 75 Armoured Regiment-the only Indian armoured regiment to have been raised on foreign soil during the 1971 Indo-Pak war at Gadra Road (now in Pakistan)on 12 March 1972.
- 76 Armoured Regiment
- 81 Armoured Regiment
- 82 Armoured Regiment
- 83 Armoured Regiment
- 84 Armoured Regiment
- 85 Armoured Regiment
- 86 Armoured Regiment
- 87 Armoured Regiment
- 88 Armoured Regiment
- 89 Armoured Regiment
- 90 Armoured Regiment.

Units of the Regiment of Artillery

A few of the units of artillery are listed below:

- 37 (Coorg) Anti-Tank Regiment RIA
- 40 Field Regiment (Asal Uttar)
- 61 Medium Regiment
- 76 Field Regiment
- 216 Medium Regiment
- 163 Medium Regiment
- 168 Field Regiment
- 169 Field Regiment (Longewala)
- 195 Field Regiment (Banwat)
- 255 Field Regiment
- 286 Medium Regiment
- 311 Field Regiment
- 92 Medium Regiment
- 15 Medium Regiment

- 3342 msl regt
- 175 med regt=175 field regt
- [[70 Fd Regt(SAVIOURS)].

STARTING PERIOD OF INDIAN AIR FORCE

The history of the Indian Air Force began with its establishment in 1932 and continues up to the present day.

Formation and early pilots

The Indian Air Force was established in British India as an auxiliary air force of the Royal Air Force with the enactment of the Indian Air Force Act 1932 on 8 October that year. with four Westland Wapiti biplanes and five Indian pilots. The Indian pilots were led by RAF Commanding officer Flight Lieutenant (later Air Vice Marshal) Cecil Bouchier.

The first five pilots commissioned into the IAF were Harish Chandra Sircar, Subroto Mukerjee, Bhupendra Singh, Aizad Baksh Awan and Amarjeet Singh. A sixth officer, S N Tandon had to revert to ground duties as he was too short. All of them were commissioned as Pilot Officers in 1932 from RAF Cranwell. Subroto Mukerjee later went on to become the IAF's first Chief of the Air Staff. Subsequent batches inducted before World War II included Aspy Engineer, K K Majumdar, Narendra, Daljit Singh, Henry Runganadhan, R H D Singh, Baba Mehar Singh, S N Goyal, Prithpal Singh and Arjan Singh. "The Indian Air Force is what it is today because of one thing only-the imagination, courage, loyalty and great quality of the first little pioneer band of Indian officers and airmen, for they were the salt of the earth. They have built up a great fighting service and I am proud to have been associated with this wonderful achievement, if only for a little while." —Air Vice Marshal Sir Cecil Bouchier, First Commanding Officer of the Indian Air Force.

World War II (1939-1945)

During World War II, the IAF played an instrumental role in blocking the advance of the Japanese army in Burma, where its first air strike was on the Japanese military base in Arakan. It also carried out strike missions against the Japanese airbases at Mae Hong Son, Chiang Mai and Chiang Rai in northern

Thailand. During the war, the IAF went through a phase of steady expansion. New aircraft, including the U.S. built Vultee Vengeance and the British Hawker Hurricane and Westland Lysander, were added to its fleet.

Subhas Chandra Bose sent Indian National Army youth cadets to Japan to train as pilots. They went on to attend the Imperial Japanese Army Air Force Academy in 1944. In recognition of the services rendered by the IAF, King George VI conferred the prefix "Royal" in 1945. Thereafter the IAF was referred to as Royal Indian Air Force. In 1950, when India became a republic, the prefix was dropped and it reverted back to Indian Air Force.

Partition of India (1947)

With the partition of the Indian sub-continent into two separate nations, the Union of India and the Dominion of Pakistan, the military forces were also partitioned. This gave a reduced Royal Indian Air Force and a new Royal Pakistan Air Force in 1947.

First Kashmir War 1947

In a bid to gain control of the erstwhile princely state of Jammu and Kashmir, Pathan tribesmen poured into Kashmir on October 20, 1947, aided by the Pakistani Army. Incapable of withstanding the armed assault in his province, the *Maharaja* of Kashmir, Hari Singh, asked India for help. The Government of India made its assistance conditional upon Kashmir's accession to India. The Instrument of accession was signed on October 26, 1947 and the next day Indian troops were airlifted into Srinagar. The agreement was later ratified by the British.

Taking off from Safdarjang, then known as *Willingdon Airfield*, the IAF landed Indian troops at Srinagar airfield at 09:30 hours IST on October 27. This was the most instrumental action of the war as the troops saved the city from the invaders. Apart from the airlifting operations and supplying essential commodities to the ground troops, the Indian Air Force had no other major role to play in the conflict. On December 31, 1948, both nations agreed to a UN mediated cease-fire proposal marking the end of hostilities. A Line of Control has since separated Indian-held Kashmir from Pakistani-held Kashmir.

Congo Crisis (1961)

Belgium's 75-year colonial rule of the Democratic Republic of the Congo Congo ended abruptly on June 30, 1960. Unable to control the deteriorating situation in its former African colony, Belgium asked for UN assistance. In India, Prime Minister Jawaharlal Nehru was quick to respond to the initial appeal for help and sent IAF Canberra aircraft as a part of the UN-led mission in Congo.

Sino-Indian War (1962)

In 1962, border disputes escalated into full-scale war between India and China. Indian military and civilian leadership failed to organise and co-ordinate the air assaults efficiently and eventually the Indian Air Force was never used during the conflict apart from occasional supply missions.

Second Kashmir War 1965

Three years after the Sino-Indian conflict, India went to war with Pakistan again over Kashmir. Learning from the experiences of the Sino-Indian war, India decided to use its air force extensively during the war. This was the first time the IAF actively engaged an enemy air force. However, instead of providing close air support to the Indian Army, the IAF carried out independent raid missions against Pakistani Air Force (PAF) bases. These bases were situated deep inside the Pakistani territory, making IAF fighters vulnerable to anti-aircraft fire. conflict.

On September 1, 1965, the IAF fighters intervened in an on-going battle between Indian and Pakistani forces in Chhamb. However, it was inadequate in close air support role. Initially, IAF had sent the obsolete Vampires and later Mystères to stop Pakistani advance. But after incidents of friendly fire, they were not called again for close air support. Two days later, IAF Folland Gnat fighters shot down a PAF F-86 Sabre over Chhamb area. The Gnats were effective against the F-86 and earned the nickname *Sabre Slayer*. According to one Western source, the Gnats accounted for at least 6 Sabre kills.

During the course of the conflict, the PAF enjoyed qualitative superiority over the IAF because most of the jets in IAF's fleet were of World War II-vintage. Despite this, the IAF was able to prevent the PAF from gaining air superiority over conflict zones. By the time the conflict had ended, Pakistan claimed to have shot down 113 IAF aircraft while the Indians claimed that 73 PAF aircraft were downed. More than 60% of IAF's air combat losses took place during the disastrous battles over Kalaikunda and Pathankot. However, the IAF lost most of its aircraft on ground and the attrition rate (losses per 100 sorties) of the IAF stood at 1.49 while PAF's attrition rate was 2.16, because the IAF has larger number of aircrafts with higher number of take off and landing sorties.

Bangladesh Liberation War 1971

After the 1965 War, the Indian Air Force went through an intense phase of modernisation and consolidation. With newly acquired HF-24, MiG-21 and Sukhoi Su-7BM (though the versions of these acquired between 1965 and 1971 did not have night-fight capability) aircraft, the IAF was able to measure up to the most powerful air forces in the world.

The professional standards, capability and flexibility were soon put to the test in December 1971 when India and Pakistan went to war over (then) East Pakistan. At the time, the IAF was under the command of Air Chief Marshal Pratap Chandra Lal. On November 22, 10 days before the start of a full-scale war, four PAF F-86 Sabre jets attacked Indian and Mukti Bahini positions near the Indo-Bangla border in the Battle of Garibpur. In what became the first ever Dogfight over East Pakistan skies (present day Bangladesh), three of the 4 PAF Sabres were shot down by IAF Gnats, and hostilities commenced. December 3 saw the formal declaration of war following massive, but failed preemptive strikes by the Pakistan Air Force against Indian Air Force installations in the west. The PAF targets were against Indian bases in Srinagar, Ambala, Sirsa, Halwara and Jodhpur on the lines of Operation Focus. But the plan failed miserably as Indians had anticipated such a move and no major losses were suffered. The Indian response over Pakistan skies however produced severe blows to the PAF.

Within the first two weeks, the IAF had carried out more than 4,000 sorties in East Pakistan and provided successful air cover for the advancing Indian army in East Pakistan. IAF also assisted the Indian Navy in sinking several Pakistani naval vessels in the Bay of Bengal. In the west, the air Force demolished scores of tanks and armoured vehicles in a single battle-the Battle of Longewala. The IAF pursued strategic bombing by destroying oil installations in Karachi, the Mangla Dam and gas plant in Sindh. As the IAF achieved complete air superiority over the eastern wing of Pakistan within a few days, the ordnance factories, runways, and other vital areas in East Pakistan were severely crippled. In the end, the IAF played a pivotal role in the victory for the Allied Forces leading to the liberation of Bangladesh. In addition to the overall strategic victory, the IAF had also claimed 94 Pakistani aircraft destroyed, with some 45 of their own aircraft admitted lost. The IAF had however, flown over 7000 combat sorties on both East and West fronts and its overall sortie rate numbered over 15000. Comparatively the PAF was flowing fewer sorties (though PAF had qualitative advantage; its Mirage III fighter/bombers could fly at night, where no IAF fighter had that capability—the only aircraft in IAF with this capability was the Canberra bomber) by the day fearing loss of planes. Towards the end of the war, IAF's transport planes dropped leaflets over Dhaka urging the Pak forces to surrender; East Pakistani sources note that as the leaflets floated down, the morale of the Pakistani troops sunk.

Operation Meghdoot 1984

Operation Meghdoot was the name given to the preemptive strike launched by the Indian Military to capture most of the Siachen Glacier, in the disputed Kashmir region. Launched on April 13, 1984, this military operation was unique as it was the first assault launched in the world's highest battlefield. The military action was quite successful as Indian troops managed to gain two-thirds of the glacier with the rest remaining under Pakistani control.

Operation Poomalai (1987)

Failing to negotiate an end to the Sri Lankan Civil War, India sent a convoy of unarmed ships to northern Sri Lanka to provide more than 1000 tonnes of humanitarian aid, but it was intercepted by the Sri Lankan Navy and sent back. Following this, the Indian Government decided to carry out an airdrop of the humanitarian supplies on the evening of 4 June 1987 designated Operation Poomalai (Tamil: Garland) or Eagle Mission 4 as a show of force to the Sri Lankan government, of symbolic support to the Tamil rebel and to preserve the credibility of the then Indian Prime Minister Rajiv Gandhi. Five An-32s of the Paratroop Training School in Agra, escorted by five Mirage 2000s of the No.7 Squadron were to carry out the supply drop. The message was conveyed to the Sri Lankan Ambassador to New Delhi that Indian Air Force would be flying a mission at 1600 Hours to drop supplies over Jaffna. The ambassador was told that the aircraft were expected to complete their mission unhindered and any opposition by the Sri Lankan Air Force 'would be met by force' by the escorting Mirage 2000s. The air drop was a success and the IAF was unopposed by the Sri Lankan forces. Sri Lanka accused India of "blatant violation of sovereignty". India insisted that it was acting only on humanitarian grounds.

Operation Pawan (1987)

The IAF supported the Indian Peace Keeping Force (IPKF) in northern and eastern Sri Lanka. About 70,000 sorties were flown by the IAF's transport and helicopter force in support of nearly 100,000 troops and paramilitary forces without a single aircraft lost or mission aborted. IAF An-32s maintained a continuous air link between air bases in South India and Northern Sri Lanka transporting men, equipment, rations and evacuating casualties. Mi-8s supported the ground forces and also provided air transportation to the Sri Lankan civil administration during the elections. Mi-25s of No. 125 H.U. were utilised to provide suppressive fire against militant strong points and to interdict coastal and clandestine riverine traffic.

Kargil 1999

During the Kargil War with Pakistan, the Indian Air Force is said to have proved the decisive force in accelerating the end of the conflict. It successfully provided considerable air-cover for Indian troops fighting against Pakistani soldiers and also carried out air assaults against enemy forces in Kashmir. Most notable were the IAF's Mirage 2000 aircraft, which carried out surgical operations to assist ground troops in securing the strategically crucial *Tiger Hill* from its Pakistani captors. The IAF also carried out several operations to provide essential supplies to the ground troops. During the conflict, one IAF MiG-27 and an IAF MiG-21 were claimed shot down by Pakistani air defence missiles However the Indian Air Force had stated that the MiG-27 had an engine flameout in the initial stages of attacking the mountain top targets with its cannon. This is confirmed by an Unofficial Pakistan Air Force Website-PAF Combat.com, maintained by a serving Air Commodore of the PAF. The MiG-21M was on a search operation to find the MiG-27s crash site, when it was shot down. Later, a Mi-17 helicopter was shot down by a shoulder-held missile with the loss of all its crew.

Atlantique Incident

On August 10, 1999, a Pakistan Navy French-built naval Breguet Atlantic was flying over the Rann of Kutch area and was shot down by two IAF MiG-21 jets killing all 16 aboard.

AIR FORCE HISTORY

The Indian Air Force (IAF) has come a long way from its modest beginning to become one of the finest air forces in the world, renowned for its professionalism and competence. The Royal Indian Air Force had its origins in the recommendation of the Skeene Committee in 1926. Six years later the Indian Legislature passed the Indian Air Force Act. The IAF came into being on October 8, 1932, and the first flight was formed in 1933. At that time, there were only six officers-five pilots and one equipment officer apart from 19 Havai Sepoys (air soldiers) and its aircraft inventory comprised four Westland Wapiti biplanes at Drigh Road (now in Pakistan).

The outbreak of second world war resulted in the expansion of IAF. By the end of 1941, the IAF had three squadrons and five coastal defence flights. The Japanese attack on Pearl Harbour brought the war to India's doorstep and in December 1942, the IAF was inducted into Burma for the first Burma Campaign. In recognition of the services rendered by the Indian Air Force during the war, the service was bestowed with the prefix "Royal" on 12 March 1945 and was then known as the Royal Indian Air Force (RIAF). In 1946 it consisted of 8 fighter and 2 transport squadrons with modern aircraft.

On the division of the country into the two Dominions of India and Pakistan, the Dominion of India ieceived 7 fighter squadrons and 1 transport squadron as its share. The principal components of RIAF at the time of partition in 1947 were Nos 3,4,7,8 and 10 Squadrons with Tempest II, No 2 Squadron with Spitfires, and No 12 Squadron with C-47s and No 1 Air Observation Flight. The RIAF lost many permanent bases and other establishments as a result of the division of the country. It had virtually no breathing space to recover from the surgery that had accompanied the partition. Tribal raiders-clothed, fed and armed by Pakistani military commanders-raided Kashmir in October 1947. On October 26, the same year, the Maharaja of Kashmir signed the Instrument of Accession as per the requirements of the partition process and asked for military help. The next day, RIAF flew to Srinagar carrying the first contingent of the Indian Army in three DC-3 Dakotas of 12 Squadron. A couple of days later, the Spitfires from Ambala reached Srinagar and were soon engaged in strafing the raiders beyond Pattan. Within a week, the Tempests of No 7 Squadron were playing a decisive role in the battle of Shelatang and had halted the movement of the insurgents. The fighting continued for 15 months and the RIAF was involved throughout the operations.

In January 1950, India became a Republic within the British Commonwealth and the Indian Air Force dropped its "Royal" prefix. At this time, it possessed six fighter squadrons of Spitfires, Vampires and Tempests operating from Kanpur, Poona, Ambala and Palam, one B-24 bomber squadron, one C-47 Dakota transport squadron, one AOP flight, a communication squadron at Palam and a growing training organisation.

The real test of IAF's airlift capability came in October 1962 when an open warfare erupted on the Sino-Indian border. During the period, October 20–November 20, pressure on the transport and helicopter units was intense, troops and supplies having to be flown to the support of the border posts virtually round-the-clock and at high altitudes. The helicopters had to constantly run the gauntlet of Chinese small arms and anti-aircraft fire, while operating on tricky helipads in the mountains. Many notable feats were performed by the IAF during this conflict, including the operation of C-119 Gs from airstrips 17,000 ft AMSL in the Karakoram Himalayas and the airlifting by AN-12Bs of two troops of AMX-13 light tanks to Chushul, in Ladakh, where the small airstrip was 15,000 ft AMSL.

An unusual task given to the IAF was to support United Nations in Congo (now Zaire) in 1961-62 for dealing with the Katanga rebellion. Following an appeal by the UN troops to restore law and order in Congo six Canberra B(1) 58s of No 5 Squadron were flown from Agra to Central Africa. Operating from Leopoldville and Kamina, the Canberras soon destroyed the rebel Air Force, raided Katangan targets and provided the UN ground forces with its only long-range air support force.

On September 1, 1965 Pakistan launched a massive attack in the Chhamb sector. In response to the urgent requests for air strikes against Pakistani armour advancing in the Chhamb-Jaurian sector, IAF fighters went into action.

Vampires of No 45 Squadron undergoing operational training at a forward base, mounted their first sorties at 1745 hrs on the first day of the conflict and on their heels came the Mystere of Nos 3 and 31 Squadrons operating from Pathankot. IAF Gnats proved their mettle in shooting down several PAF F-6 Sabres in this sector, the first aerial victories being notched up by Nos 23 and 9 Squadrons.

Full-scale war broke out on September 6 all along the international border between West Pakistan and India. Pakistan attempted a pre-emptive strike on the same day, attacking IAF bases at Adampur, Halwara, Pathankot, Srinagar, Jamnagar and Kalaikunda. On the following day, IAF retaliated with air raids and shot down a PAF star fighter in air combat in Sargodha. The IAF provided close air support to the Indian Army in the famous battle of 'Assal Uttar' in Khemkaran sector. In this battle, the thrust of Pakistani Armoured Division was beaten back. The IAF also interdicted Pakistan's railway network, successfully hitting at the Pakistani forces as well as their stores of necessary war-material and also their lines of communication and supply by blowing up trains carrying these goods. With the assistance of IAF, India's ground forces advanced to the outskirts of Lahore. A cease-fire was shortly declared.

As the political situation in the sub-continent deteriorated, the load of 10 million Bangladeshi refugees in India was too much for a weak Indian economy. The IAF was alerted to the possibility of another armed conflict.

For some weeks in November, both Indian and Pakistan governments protested violations of national airspace along the western border, but aerial conflict between the respective air arms began in earnest on 22 November, preceding full-scale warfare between India and Pakistan by 12 days.

At 1449 hours, four Pakistani Sabres strafed Indian and Mukti Bahini positions in the Chowgacha Mor area, and 10 minutes later, while engaged on a third strafing run, the Sabres were intercepted by four Gnats from No. 22 Sqn, a detachment of which was operating from Dum Dum Airport, Calcutta. During the ensuing melee, three of the Sabres were shot down, all Gnats returning to base unscathed. The first blood of a new Indo-Pakistan air war had been drawn. Other encounters were to follow over the next 10 days, within both Indian and Pakistani airspace, before full-scale war began on 3 December.

On December 3, 1971, pre-emptive strikes were launched by the Pakistani Air Force against IAF bases at Srinagar, Amritsar and Pathankot followed by attacks on Ambala, Agra, Jodhpur, Uttarlai, Awantipur, Faridkot, Halwara and Sirsa. In response to these strikes, the IAF carried out some 4000 sorties in the west from major and forward bases in Jammu, Kashmir, Punjab and Rajasthan while, in the east, a further 1978 sorties were flown.

It was in the western theatre that the MiG-21 was employed in Pathankot in the north to Jamnagar in the southwestern area. The MiG-21 mounted combat air patrol missions over vital points and vital areas, flew escort missions for bombers and strike-fighters and was continuously scrambled to intercept hostile intruders. The first aerial victory was on December 12, 1971, when MiG-21s of No 47 Squadron shot down a PAF F-104 over the Gulf of Kutch. This was followed by three more victories in quick succession on December 17 when MiG-21s of No 29 Squadron escorting Maruts, shot down intercepting F-104s near Uttarlai in Rajasthan desert in gun-missile encounters while a third F-104, on an intruding mission, was shot down by another MiG-21 of No 29 Squadron. This singular contribution by IAF resulted in a decisive victory for India that resulted in the birth of an independent state of Bangladesh with the unconditional surrender of 90,000 soldiers of Pakistan's armed forces.

By the mid '70s, the IAF was clearly in need of urgent re-equipment decisions and various requirements, better known by their acronyms DPSA, TASA, METAC and HETAC, were pursued and decisions were forthcoming at last. The period, the IAF was to benefit from a crest in the eighties, the period 1978-88 witnessing a major modernisation programme which replaced most of the earlier generation and obsolete equipment with spanking new aircraft types and weapon systems. No less than twenty new aircraft types and sub-types entered the IAF's service over these years, including various strike fighters, third-generation supersonic interceptors, tri-sonic reconnaissance aircraft, strategic heavy lift transports, medium tactical transports, light transport aircraft, heavy lift and medium-assault helicopters, basic trainers, surface-to-air missiles and an array of sophisticated weaponry.

The IAF has been strenuously involved in many other major operations that have extended the capacity of its transport and helicopter fleet. With the support of the Indian Army and para-military forces in Northern Ladakh, IAF launched operation Meghadoot to control the heights predominating the Siachen glacier. The IL-76, AN-32, Mi-17 IV and Chetak/Cheetah helicopters of the IAF still continue with their untiring zeal ferrying men and material to the dizzy heights under the most inhospitable conditions.

To support the mission of the Indian Peace Keeping Force (IPKF) in northern and eastern Sri Lanka, IAF launched operation Pawan which lasted almost some thirty months. Some 70,000 sorties were flown by the IAF's transport and helicopter fleet to and within Sri Lanka without a single aircraft lost or mission aborted.

In November 1988, in response to the Maldives government's appeal for military help against a mercenary invasion, IAF launched operation Cactus to airlift a parachute battalion group from Agra to Maldives. IL-76 aircraft of No 44 Squadron landed at Hulule with in short time. The Indian paratroopers secured the airfield and restored the government's rule at Male within hours. IAF Mirage-2000 and AN-32 aircraft also supported the operation.

The IAF took part in the UN peace-keeping duties in Somalia in 1993-94 and once again in Sierra Leone in 2000-2001 sending its helicopters including Mi-8, Mi-17 and Mi-25s.

Operation Safed Sagar, as the air operation in the Kargil area was called, was indeed a milestone in the history of military aviation. This was the first time that air power was employed in such an environment. Fighters as well as armed helicopters carried out many hundreds of sorties against the armed intruders who had infiltrated into the Indian territory. The use of air power in this theatre was instrumental in accelerating the end of the conflict to India's advantage. IAF's air strikes against enemy supply camps and other targets yielded rich dividends. A noteworthy fact is that there was not a single operation on ground that was not preceded by air strikes, each and every action was a result of coordinated planning between 15 Corps and AOC, J&K. The enemy was kept off the back of the Indian Army. In the area of interdiction of enemy supplies, the successful and incessant attacks on the enemy's logistic machines, over the weeks, culminated in a serious degradation of the enemy's ability to sustain them.

THE INDIAN AIR FORCE OF THE 1980S

THE Indian Air Force (IAF), the largest air arm in non-Communist Asia, is engaged in an extensive modernization effort. For example, advanced combat aircraft, including the Soviet MiG-23 and 27 Flogger, Anglo-French Jaguar, and French Mirage 2000 are being assimilated by the IAF or soon will be added to its inventory. As a consequence, India will have the capability to overwhelm the Pakistani Air Force (PAF), despite the PAF's acquisition of forty F-16s; gain local air superiority in a conflict with China along their common border; and inflict significant damage on the navies of extraregional powers operating in waters adjacent to the subcontinent.

Command Structure

The IAF headquarters, located in New Delhi, consists of four principal branches: Air Staff (led by an air chief marshal designated as Chief of the Air Staff), Administration, Plans and Policy, and Maintenance.

Operational and support elements are organized into four geographic commands (Southwestern, Western, Central, and Eastern) and two functional commands (Training and Maintenance). The area commands direct some forty-five fixed-wing squadrons, fourteen helicopter units, and more than thirty SA-2/SA-3 squadrons. The IAF's fixed-and rotary-wing aircraft inventory numbers 1400, of which approximately 635 are combat aircraft. Indian Air Force personnel strength is 113,000.

Missions

The IAF has been tasked with the following responsibilities: air defense, long-range interdiction/counterair operations, close air support, reconnaissance, transport, and heliborne support.

Air defense

The Soviet MiG-21 is the numerically predominant interceptor in the IAF. Currently, India is replacing its MiG-21 FL Fishbed-D assets with the more advanced MiG-2 1bis Fishbed-N. The IAF has integrated the Matra 550 Magic close-combat missile with the "bis" variant and is endeavoring to upgrade this aircraft's radar, avionics, and vertical acceleration. India now is manufacturing the MiG-21bis under license; the production run of 150 units will be completed in the mid-1980s.

The MiG-21 fleet is being supplemented by variable-geometry MiG-23MF Flogger air superiority fighters. These aircraft are armed with the AA-7 Apex AAM, the AA-8 Aphid, and 23-mm cannon. Reportedly, the IAF will employ Floggers and Fishbeds in groups of six: two MiG-23MFs will attempt to down incoming aircraft with air-to-air missiles; and intruders eluding these Floggers will be met by four MiG-21s.

Air defense resources will be augmented materially by the impending acquisition of forty Mirage 2000 multirole fighters.

Early in 1985, IAF pilots will start ferrying the forty aircraft from France to India, with the last delivery scheduled for December 1986. New Delhi retains the option to assemble/coproduce an additional 110 aircraft, although it is unlikely that this option will be exercised.

The Indian Mirage will be fitted with internally mounted electronic support measures (ESM) and electronic countermeasures (ECM) equipment. The aircraft will carry two 30-mm Defa cannon, along with two Matra 550 short-range and two Matra Super 530-D medium-range air-to-air missiles (AAMs). Alternatively, it can be loaded with 11,000 pounds of ordnance on nine external stations.

The Mirage 2000 will be powered initially by the SNECMA M53-5 engine rated at 20,000-pound thrust, but later it will be retrofitted with the 22,000-pound-thrust M53-P2. Similarly, the Thomson-CSF RDM (multifunction Doppler) radar will be superseded in 1985 by the Thomson-CSF/Electronique Serge Dassault pulse-Doppler radar designated RDI. The RDI radar, mated with the Matra 530-D AAM, gives the Mirage 2000 a look down/shoot down capability.

In endeavoring to justify Mirage 2000 expenditures, government spokesmen have argued that Pakistan's acquisition of sophisticated American aircraft alters the balance of air power in the subcontinent. Therefore, it is necessary to procure the Mirage 2000 to serve as a counterpoise to the F-16. However, it is doubtful that the IAF leadership fully embraces this proposition.

The IAF is aware that, among air forces in the region, it enjoys an overwhelming superiority (both qualitative and quantitative) in virtually all categories of air weaponry and equipment. Indeed, this marked power asymmetry allowed the IAF to advocate conclusion of the Mirage 2000 agreement (while the aircraft still was under development) in the face of a late 1982-early 1983 F-16 delivery date. If F-16 deployment had been perceived as affecting Indo-Pakistani power relationships significantly in the near term, then the IAF probably would have supported one or more of the following policy alternatives: prompt off-the-shelf acquisition of an existing interceptor capable of carrying long-range AAMs and guns with a high rate of fire, significant expansion of the MiG-23MF procurement program, immediate purchase of advanced AAMS, and/or greatly accelerated upgrading of ground-based air defense systems.

Manned interceptors, in conjunction with SA-2/SA-3 squadrons, form one component of India's Air Defense Ground Environment system (ADGES). Other constituent elements include static and mobile radars, tropospheric scatter and microwave communication links, and regional air defense centers tasked with threat assessment and determination of appropriate responses. The ADGES, to be completed by the end of this decade, suffers from a number of shortcomings. First, the system may prove vulnerable to low-flying aircraft, especially those employing ECM. Second, terrain masking may prevent radar detection of intruding aircraft in hilly areas along the northern border. Third, there is insufficient redundancy in the ADGES communications network. Nevertheless, the ADGES will furnish an air defense capability far exceeding that of any neighboring state.

Long-range interdiction/counterair operations

In the event of hostilities with Pakistan, the IAF reportedly plans to attack command and control centers, all Pakistani Air Force main bases, and segments of the communication/transportation infrastructure. The resulting immobilization of Pakistan's armed forces would be followed by strikes against major ground units. The Jaguar, India's principal deep-penetration/all-weather interdiction aircraft, would perform many of these missions. Two Jaguar squadrons now are operational; this force will expand to five squadrons by 1987.

Approximately 60 percent of the Jaguars to enter IAF service will be assembled in India. These aircraft will incorporate Adour Mk811 turbofan engines (affording 15-25 percent greater thrust than the original power plant), the Sagem Uliss 82 second-generation navigation/attack system, and two Matra 550 Magic AAMs carried on overwing pylons (thereby freeing the one fuselage and four underwing stations for a variety of ordnance options, including bombs of up to 1000 pounds, cluster munitions, and rocket pods). The Jaguar also may be fitted with the French Agave radar in order to increase its maritime interdiction capabilities.

Close air support

Indian planners anticipate that any future war with Pakistan will be a high-intensity, short-duration affair (partly because of likely diplomatic intervention by third parties). Consequently, the IAF is developing a powerful tactical strike force to facilitate rapid advances by ground elements. Offensive air support will be furnished by at least three MiG-23BN and eight MiG-27 squadrons, augmented by the MiG-21M Fishbed-J and Ajeet (an upgraded version of the British Gnat). Aging Hawker Hunter Mk 56, Sukhoi Su-7, and Hindustan Aeronautics Limited HF-24 Marut fighter-bombers are being removed from the inventory.

The MiG-23BN, already operational in the IAF, has a centerline GSh-23 cannon and six fuselage and underwing hardpoints, which can be loaded with a variety of ordnance ranking from iron bombs to ASMS. The MiG-27 Flogger-D, a dedicated ground-attack variant of the MiG-23, will be assembled (and, eventually, produced under license) in India. April 1984 is the target date for the assembly of the first MiG-27 by Hindustan Aeronautics Limited (HAL), a public-sector firm. In addition to a 23-mm cannon, the MiG-27 can carry up to 7716 pounds of external ordnance, including a mix of air-to-air and air-to-surface missiles.

Reconnaissance

New Delhi's desire to enhance its information-gathering capabilities (especially concerning Pakistani and Chinese military installations and troop disposition in border areas) led to the 1981 purchase of Soviet MiG-25R Foxbat reconnaissance aircraft. Reconnaissance tasks also are discharged by Jaguars fitted with photoreconnaissance pods, Canberra PR Mk 57s, and camera and sensor-equipped HS-748 Avros. Maritime reconnaissance responsibilities were transferred to the Indian Navy in the mid-1970s.

Transport

The multiplicity and obsolescence of transport aircraft types, along with concomitant difficulties in spare parts procurement, have served to degrade IAF operational readiness in the airlift area. The IAF transport fleet in the main consists of 1940s-vintage C-47 Dakotas; Fairchild C119Gs (nicknamed "flying coffins" by Indian aircrews), which entered service in 1952 and were to have been retired in 1967; An-12 Cubs, scheduled for retirement in 1975, but which will remain in the inventory until the late 1980s; Caribous; and Otters. Serviceability rates of these aircraft are quite low. For example, in 1982 all C-19s and many C-47s were grounded because of metal fatigue and wing spur cracks. Few Caribous are airworthy at any time. These circumstances, in turn, have placed a considerable burden on the two An-12 squadrons. Intensive use of the IAF's thirty-odd Cubs (e.g., transporting supplies to troops in Ladakh and lifting paramilitary forces to assist in suppression of domestic violence) has resulted in availability levels as low as 20 percent.

The IAF is attempting to remedy this situation by procuring appreciable numbers of modern transport aircraft. The Air Force has ordered approximately 100 Soviet An-32 Cline medium transports to replace the C-119s and Caribous. The An-32 is a rear-loading STOL aircraft able to paradrop men and equipment. The An-12is to be superseded by the Soviet I1-76 Candid heavy transport. Finally, a defense committee has selected the Dornier Do 228-200 light transport to assume communication, liaison, and utility duties presently handled by C-47s and Otters.

Heliborne support

Some airlift support is provided by IAF rotary-wing aircraft, such as the Soviet Mi-8 Hip. The Mi-8, which can lift twenty-eight troops or as much freight as the C-47, plays an important logistic support role in northern and northeastern India. Further, many of the more than sixty Hips in service are armed with 57-mm rocket pods to provide close air support for army units.

The IAF helicopter inventory also includes the SA 316B Alouette III (renamed Chetak) and the SA 315B Lama (renamed Cheetah)—French helicopters manufactured under license in India. A number of the approximately 150 IAF Chetaks are fittedwithAS-11 antitank guided missiles. In addition to its antitank responsibilities, the Chetak is tasked with communication and liaison missions. The Cheetah performs a variety of activities in mountainous areas and, organized into airborne observation post flights, assists in directing Indian Army artillery fire.

The IAF has a requirement for a multipurpose advanced light helicopter (ALH). Such a helicopter was to be designed and produced by Hindustan Aeronautics Limited; however, changes in IAF design parameters, inadequacies of HAL's engineering staff, and a generally dilatory approach to project decisionmaking have slowed ALH development for a decade. Consequently, India is purchasing Soviet Mi-24 Hind gunships as an interim step. However, rather than being an interim step, the Hind purchase may indicate termination of indigenous helicopter design/fabrication efforts.

RELATIONSHIP WITH OTHER SERVICES

Indian Air Force interaction with the Indian Navy and Army is marked by both conflict and cooperation. Protracted jurisdictional battles have been fought with the Navy over maritime patrol and interdiction. In the mid-1970s, the following compromise was reached: the Navy assumed responsibility for reconnaissance missions, while maritime interdiction remained under IAF control. However, IAF control of this interdiction mission may prove nominal at best, as the Navy's air arm rapidly is augmenting its inventory of advanced antishipping weaponry by procuring such systems as the Sea Eagle longrange missile (to be carried by Westland Sea King helicopters). In addition to this clash with the Navy, the IAF is engaged in a dispute with the Army about helicopters. The Indian Army is endeavoring to bring IAF helicopter assets within its organizational purview, arguing that most rotary-wing aircraft perform ground force support functions. Furthermore, its leaders suggest that their service's combat effectiveness would be enhanced greatly by integration of attack helicopters with mechanized infantry, armor, and heliborne troops. The IAF rejects the "major user" principle, asserting that all air activity must be coordinated by one service.

Despite these policy disharmonies, the military leadership recognizes that India's strategic environment demands increased interservice cooperation. As a result, the number of joint service exercises has increased dramatically. For example, a large amphibious warfare exercise was held in the Nicobar Islands during April 1983. Indian Air Force participation included preinvasion strikes by Canberra medium bombers, evaluation of damage levels by photoreconnaissance, and rocket attacks against enemy positions by Mi-8 helicopters. More significantly, the first triservice command has been established in the Andaman and Nicobar Island chain. Headed by a naval officer reporting to Eastern Naval Command, this organization has been assigned several ships, an army brigade, and, in the future, a fighter squadron.

IAF Capabilities

Traditionally, Indian defense planning has focused on the threats presented by Pakistan and China. The IAF appears capable of fulfilling its combat missions against either of these potential adversaries.

In an Indian-Pakistani conflict, there would be a pronounced disparity in IAF-PAF strength levels. For example, India enjoys a substantial numerical advantage in sophisticated fighters and fighter-bombers. In contrast, the obsolescent F-6, a Chinese version of the MiG-19, forms the major part of Islamabad's interceptor/ground attack force. Beyond this, the IAF surpasses the PAF in virtually all operational and support areas, ranging from command, control, and communications (C) and electronic warfare (EW) to logistics. If India and Pakistan engage in a fourth war, it is likely that the IAF would defeat the PAF in short order.

Indian Air Force weapon systems and equipment also are qualitatively superior to those of the People's Republic of China, but China's combat aircraft far outnumber those of the IAF. Nevertheless, in a Sino-Indian conflict, China probably would not be able to apply all her air resources against the IAF. First, few Chinese airfields are close enough to the Indian border to permit effective operations. Second, those bases that are near India have not been upgraded in terms of support facilities, and this deficiency would impede Chinese efforts to reposition units. Finally, aircraft deployed to Tibet would be hampered by high-altitude takeoffs, which would decrease munitions loads and increase fuel consumption. In contrast, New Delhi has been assiduous in concentrating air and ground forces against China. Thus, many IAF squadrons are located within striking distance of the China-India frontier. Assuming meteorological conditions in the Himalayas do not preclude flight operations, the IAF should prove able to gain local air superiority in an Indian-Chinese conflict.

In addition to security concerns generated by Pakistan and China, New Delhi is disquieted both by the presence of extraregional powers in waters contiguous to India and by the vulnerability of its island possessions. While the Navy must assume primary responsibility for defense of offshore areas, the Air Force will perform significant duties as well. Thus, a fighter squadron is to be stationed in the Andamans, and a squadron also may be placed in the Lakshadweep chain. Island-based units probably will consist of Jaguars fitted with advanced antishipping weaponry. IAF maritime interdiction resources, along with the Indian Navy's Sea Harriers and Sea Kings armed with third-generation Sea Eagle missiles, will constitute a formidable threat to forces operating in the Indian Ocean.

Future Procurement Activity

If India's civilian leadership maintains or increases present IAF funding levels, Air Headquarters is likely to seek further force modernization, including acquisition of the following systems: an airborne early-warning system to provide look down acquisition and integrated battle management capabilities; precision and standoff munitions to ensure high kill ratios and minimize exposure of costly strike aircraft; sophisticated ECM equipment; a "Wild-Weasel"-type electronic defense suppression system; a state-of-the-art air superiority fighter, such as the Soviet MiG-29 Fulcrum (reportedly, New Delhi has purchased a number of MiG-29s, which may enter the IAF inventory by the end of 1984); a domestically manufactured light combat aircraft to replace the Ajeet and Hunter; and an advanced remotely piloted vehicle to deliver ordnance in hostile air defense environments.

THE IAF has become one of the world's strongest air forces, a fact that must be appreciated by any of India's potential military adversaries. India's increased air power, in conjunction with the ambitious modernization programs of her Army and Navy, not only will reinforce India's national security but enhance her ability to attain foreign policy goals.

For example, it affords New Delhi the means to impose stability on island-states in the Indian Ocean-an important option for India, given the recent communal violence in Sri Lanka. It also permits New Delhi to assist threatened Indian nationals, or citizens of Indian descent, in countries along the Indian Ocean littoral. Further, as part of India's overall arms buildup, IAF modernization provides a military underpinning for Indian claims of middle-power status in the context of global interaction.

4

The Indian Air Force: Flying into the 21st Century

The Indian Air Force (IAF) enters the 21st century bloodied by a brief, but educational conflict. Air strikes over Kargil provided the IAF a unique opportunity to evaluate its own strengths and limitations. It afforded the IAF a chance to acquire expertise in the operation of Precision Guided Munitions (PGM) and Beyond Visual Range (BVR) missiles under combat conditions. It also put the service's transport and logistics capability to the test. The tragic loss of aircraft in combat exposed the dangers of operating in today's Man Portable Air Defense System (MANPADS) rich environment. The purpose of this article is two-fold. First, it considers how the IAF has evolved through the 1990s and where it is headed in the first decade, or so, of the 21st century. Second, it offers some recommendations on how the IAF might deal with specific challenges in the future.

The 1990s

The 1990s started on a very inauspicious note for the Indian armed forces in general, and for the IAF in particular. Economic difficulties in the early 1990s, along with the collapse of the Soviet Union severely affected future expansion and modernization plans. Various modernization programs were pushed back by at least half a decade. Major problems with the availability of spares and support from the ex-USSR affected operations severely during the period 1991-1994. Peacetime daily serviceability rates declined from an average 70-72% in the preceding decade to as low as 60% for some types. The MiG-29 and An-32 fleets were particularly hard hit. In case of the former, serviceability had declined to as low as 55%. It should be noted that daily serviceability rates during peacetime represent the number of armed and operational combat aircraft that the IAF can put into the air at immediate notice. While wartime serviceability has been historically much higher (in 1971 it was 96%), reduced peacetime availability does affect routine operations. This was evident from the near stagnation in flying hours during the early 1990s. Pilots averaged a mere 120 hours/year in 1992/93, compared to 180-200 hours in 1988/89 and today. Total annual flying hours declined from 256,200 hours in 1991/92 to 239,000 hours in 1993/94. A recovery began only in 1994/95 and in 1997/98, the IAF crossed the 300,000 hours mark.

These tense times offered the IAF several lessons, namely the need to establish local overhaul facilities and the conservation, where possible, of equipment and spares. An increase in simulator availability has gone a long way allowing for the latter. These lessons seem to have been learnt well and have benefited the force immensely. Sensationalism in the media notwithstanding, the 1990s have been the safest decade in the IAF's history even as flying hours soared post-1994. Indeed 1997/98 saw the IAF's lowest ever accident rate. Moreover, between 1991 and 1998, IAF attrition (1.07 per 10,000 hours) has remained well below that of its principal adversary (PAF: 1.37 per 10,000 hours). India's economic revival since the mid-1990s together with changed geopolitical circumstances has allowed the IAF to take up its long overdue upgrade and reorganization programs with vigor.

Stepping into the new

Two events in the early 1990s laid the groundwork for the transformation of the IAF. The Allied air campaign over Iraq was closely studied and its lessons incorporated, as far as possible, into the IAF's own operational doctrines. During the same period, the IAF emerged as India's strategic service – the only leg of India's nuclear deterrent. The formulation in 1997 of its first ever Air Power Doctrine (APD) is a culmination of the IAF's research into the changed nature of air warfare, its implications for the force, and the challenges of operating nuclear weapons. The APD lays emphasis on four fundamental issues:

1. The need to accord offensive air operations the same priority as air defense.
2. The acceptance of a reduction in force levels, compensated by an increase in technology levels.
3. Emphasis on the acquisition of force multipliers.
4. Improvements in C4I structures and a revamped, modernized air defense and communication network.

The preceding points provide the "macro" map to modernization and are aimed at ensuring that the IAF remains a viable deterrent against both of its principal adversaries (PAF and PLAAF). The four issues also provide useful headings around which to base further discussion of the IAF's combat fleet. It should be noted that the four are connected and there are many areas of overlap.

AIR DEFENSE AND OFFENSIVE AIR OPERATIONS

Air defense was the primary function of the IAF until offensive air operations were also accorded the same priority. It remains an important component of the air power doctrine and the IAF has invested heavily in upgrading it. The air defense set up has three components – namely-armed interceptors, surface to air missiles and an extensive sensor network.

The backbone of the IAF's air defense fleet comprises of MiG-21s. Almost 16 operational squadrons fly in the air defense role. The oldest MiG-21 sub-types are being progressively retired, but both the MiG-21M and MiG-21bis continue to carry the IAF's primary air defense mantle. They continue to pull all the routine alerts along the border and form an important component of the air force's tactical reconnaissance force. The Gulf War and conflicts since have highlighted the need for aircraft with sensors that are more advanced and the ability to engage targets at increasing ranges. The baseline MiG-21M and MiG-21bis, given the vintage of their designs, are sorely lacking in these capabilities. However, the sheer size of the IAF's MiG-21 fleet has meant that any modernization plans would have to include these aircraft. While the MiG-21FL/Ms are now over 25 years old, the oldest MiG-21bis airframe is only 18 years old and the latter type is eminently upgradable. In the 1980s, the IAF did carry out a limited upgrade to configure the MiG-21Ms and MiG-21bis to carry the Matra Magic II air-air missile (AAM), and later for the R-60 AAM. A number of MiG-21bis were also fitted with head-up displays (HUD), but the aircraft remained sorely lacking in sensor ability.

Until the mid-1990s, a comprehensive upgrade of the MiG-21 had to be repeatedly postponed for either a lack of funds, or a dearth of suitable upgrade packages. However, a comprehensive upgrade of 125 "new" MiG-21bis is now underway. The program is almost two years behind schedule. The delay has been caused primarily due to re-design problems. The replacement of the MiG-21's original avionics by newer generation lightweight systems had altered the aircraft's center-of-gravity.

These have now been overcome and the first 36 upgrade kits arrived in India during the last quarter of 1999. Under this program, the MiG-21 will be fitted with new avionics, the lightweight Super Kopyo multi-mode radar, IRST, and a comprehensive self-defense suite. While endurance and payload restrictions will remain, the MiG-21s will now be able to deploy almost as wide a range of air-air and air-surface ordnance as the most modern aircraft – including the R-77 AAM (AA-12 "Amraamski") and the Kh-31 ASM. One can expect to see this potent point defense fighter remain in service well into the second decade of the 21st century. Indeed the MiG-21s proposed replacement – the LCA – is not expected to begin entering service until 2010.

The move to make the MiG-21 fleet BVR capable, underscores the importance that the IAF accords staying on the cutting edge. The benefits of a BVR capable air defense force was much appreciated during operations over Kargil, where offensive air operations went unchallenged by the Pakistan Air Force. By all accounts, R-77 and R-27 armed MiG-29s on escort duty and CAP, ensured that PAF fighters stayed well over 40 km away from the border.

Even more modern types are undergoing comprehensive upgrades as well. The MiG-23MF, however, is an exception, with the sole remaining unit, filling an important role as a BVR training unit. Both the IAF's second-generation BVR types – the MiG-29 and Mirage 2000 – are also being upgraded with sensors that are more modern. In case of the former, it is expected that all aircraft will have their N-109 radar replaced by an electronically scanned Phazatron system. The older "A" versions are also being upgraded to fire the R-77s, like the newer "SE" variant. While the latter has more capable radar (NO-19M), it too will be the subject of an avionics upgrade. The MiG-29 is also being equipped for air-air refueling to increase endurance.

A major component of upgrade programs for air-superiority fighters across the board will eventually see them equipped with the HMS/R-73 combination. Both squadrons of Mirage 2000s will undergo an avionics upgrade, although the exact nature of the upgrades remains unclear. The Mirage 2000 was India's first second-generation BVR capable aircraft and its multi-role capabilities came in very handy during PGM strikes over Kargil in 1999. The aircraft has consistently maintained the highest serviceability of any type in IAF service (>90%) and has a superb safety record. The flexibility offered by the type has led the IAF to consider "topping up" existing units with a purchase of ten additional Mirage 2000Hs. Also under consideration is the purchase of the up to two squadrons of Mirage 2000Ds. Whether the latter deal comes through will depend as much on finances as on a successful completion of the Su-30MKI development program. Russia is currently filling an order for 50 Su-30MKIs. Eighteen Su-30MKs are already in service with No.24 squadron and a second squadron (No.20) has been earmarked for conversion.

In an effort to simplify logistics, the IAF has successfully integrated western missiles with its Soviet designed aircraft and vice versa. Under the first such program, MiG-21s were retrofitted with a capability to launch the Magic II AAM. More recently, MiG-29s have been adapted to carry the Super-530D. Integrating Soviet missiles with the Mirage 2000s proved more of a challenge, but was overcome by the mid-1990s. Indeed Mirage 2000s on missions over Kargil in the summer of 1999 were carrying R-73 AAM. The Mirage 2000 is also capable of deploying the R-27 AAM. It is more than likely that once the R-77 enters service in quantity, it will be integrated with the Mirage 2000.

As noted earlier, the IAF's APD now puts offensive air operations on par with air defense. Allied air campaigns since the Gulf War have been very closely studied by the Indian Air Force. A series of studies from the College of Air Warfare (CAW) have acknowledged that the quickest way to bring a military campaign to a successful conclusion is to destroy the enemy's war making potential. Not surprisingly, the IAF's attack fleet is increasingly being equipped with enhanced standoff attack capabilities. Since the early 1990s, the IAF has made a determined effort to build up stocks of PGMs. There has been an increase in the number of armed helicopters within both the IAF and the Army Aviation Corps (AAC). This has allowed the IAF to reorient its attack away from the role of "flying artillery" that has been demanded of it in the past. Indeed as the air campaign over Kargil demonstrated, the IAF achieved the best results only when it was able to persuade the Indian Army that it's fighters were better utilized in closing enemy supply lines and taking out C3I nodes, rather than providing support to company and battalion sized operations. It should be recognized that the situation in Kargil was unique, and that close air support still has some applicability in the plains. Joint exercises since Kargil have convincingly demonstrated the merits of the IAF's re-orientation of its air support doctrine.

Kargil provided the air force with unique environment to hone its attack skills. The IAF launched PGMs in anger for the first time. Mirage 2000s, MiG-27s, and MiG-23BNs carried out devastating attacks against enemy command nodes and logistics in the area. In what became a much-celebrated event, Litening equipped Mirage 2000s took out the Pakistani battalion HQ atop Tiger Hill with pinpoint accuracy. 1000 lb. bombs fitted with IR seekers were used extensively against vital C3I facilities. The Mirages tracked ground targets from 15 km out and then released their weapons at about 6km and holding the lasers onto target at the closest of about 3-4 km. This allowed them to remain well outside the envelope of enemy air defenses. As mentioned earlier, the conflict also exposed some of the limitations of the attack fleet and tactics. In particular, battlefield interdiction was found to be of greater utility than close air support in the mountains. It also alerted the air force to the ever present dangers of operating in a MANPADS (and indeed SAM) rich environment. The IAF lost two fighters, one MiG-27 and one MiG-21M, and an attack helicopter over Kargil. While the MiG-27 was lost because of an engine flameout due to ingestion of smoke and debris, the MiG-21 was lost to a SAM while searching for the downed MiG-27. It is now appreciated that a lack comprehensive of countermeasures (chaff/flare dispensers) across the MiG-21 fleet contributed significantly to the tragedy. Until Kargil, only the MiG-23BN, few Jaguars, and a handful of MiG-27s were fitted with automated countermeasures (in addition to the air defence types). Upgrading the self-defense and jamming capabilities of the rest of the attack fleet has now assumed a sense of urgency and base repair depots have taken on the task of upgrading chaff/flare dispensers.

The bulk of the IAF's attack fleet is relatively young, most of the aircraft having been procured since the 1980s. The MiG-27 forms the backbone of the IAF's tactical strike aircraft, equipping some eight squadrons and one training establishment. Three squadrons of MiG-23BNs support these. Their sophisticated electronic warfare capability has caused them to be called "most modern" of IAF strike aircraft. Five squadrons of Jaguars form the IAF's deep penetration strike fleet. The IAF expects all of these types to remain viable for the near future. Both the MiG-27 and Jaguar are expected to remain in service until 2020. To this end, a comprehensive sensor and electronic warfare upgrade program has been initiated. The IAF's commitment to keeping the Jaguar in service for many years to come has been re-affirmed by its decision to order two more batches of the type. A 1999 order for 17 two-seaters is currently under production. An additional 20 single-seaters have been ordered this year. Extremely versatile Mirage 2000s and Su-30s complement the dedicated strike fleet.

In addition to fulfilling overland strike duties, the IAF is tasked with the providing tactical air support to the navy. One

Jaguar squadron has been specifically earmarked for this role on the western coast and is equipped with a mix of Sea Eagle armed Jaguar IS and IMs. Additionally, the IAF is in the process converting a MiG-27 squadron to cover the eastern coast. These aircraft operate in conjunction with the Navy's own air assets – including Sea Harriers and Tu-142s.

The 1990s have seen the IAF's strike fleet take on the additional task of delivering nuclear weapons. The Jaguar was the first aircraft evaluated for the role and was found too sluggish with the first generation gravity bombs. Consequently, Antilope equipped Mirage 2000s have taken on the task of providing India with a viable nuclear deterrent. It is now believed that the compactness of the second generation of nuclear warhead has allowed the nuclear delivery role to be taken on a by a larger number of aircraft – namely MiG-27s and Jaguars. It can reasonably be expected that in the future the Su-30 is likely to provide the backbone of India's manned deterrent force. It is also believed that the IAF is entrusted with the operation of India's emerging nuclear missile force. Unspecified numbers of Prithvi SRBMs and Agni IRBMs form the basis of this force. It should be noted that as the size and sophistication of the missile arsenal grows manned delivery platforms will loose a great deal of their importance. As things stand today, the IAF offers adequate deterrence vis-à-vis Pakistan, however the situation vis-à-vis China is less clear. Unfortunately, until the Indian missile arsenal reaches maturity, India's ability to inflict unacceptable damage on China remain restricted. While the IAF is likely to remain the sole strategic service for some time, it is likely to be joined by the navy when the latter deploys cruise missiles and if its lease/ purchase of Tu-22Ms materializes.

Reduction of force levels and increased technology

The IAF has accepted for sometime that the increased costs of maintaining a modern and effective air force in the future would necessitate the need for a reduction in force levels. Consequently, procurement and upgrade programs since the late 1980s have emphasized the need to extract the maximum out of every aircraft. This means two things in practice. First, it means that all existing aircraft will be the subject of upgrades that make them more lethal and enhance survivability. The installation of new radar, avionics, weapons aiming system, electronic warfare suites are all consistent with the IAF's prevailing philosophy. Second, the IAF has decided that all new types of fighters added to inventory will be multi-role-the Su-30MKI and LCA are both designed to meet this requirement.

Where possible, existing platforms are being adapted to multi-role use. Indeed the extensive upgrade package for the MiG-21bis gives it a true multi-role capability. Similarly, trials are in progress to provide upgraded MiG-27s with a secondary air-air capability. The integration of the pod mounted Komar radar will allow the MiG-27 the ability to operate BVR AAMs such as the R-27 and R-77. With the imminent withdrawal of all three of Eastern Air Command's MiG-21FL squadrons, the MiG-27s will have to don the air defense mantle in the east, in the absence of any permanently based air defense units in the region. The quest for additional Mirage 2000s also fits this pattern. It is yet unclear whether the Mig-29 upgrades will bestow the type with multi-role capability.

The IAF's 1990s projection of a leaner meaner force for the beginning of the 21st century is likely to be quite accurate. The force will be meaner and more capable. It is also likely to be smaller. The last remaining MiG-21FL/M squadrons are likely to give up their aircraft in the near future, as is the solitary MiG-23MF squadron. Although the relative age of the latter unit's airframes and the training role that they fill, will likely allow them to outlive the older MiG-21s. If IAF decides to restrict the number of MiG-21bis upgrades to 125 airframes, we could expect to see a more substantial drop in number of operational squadrons. Hypothetically speaking, if procurement and modernization programs remain at present levels, by 2005 we could expect to see total numbers for fighter squadrons decline from the current peak of 39 to 32. The capabilities of newer aircraft ensure that the older MiG-21s need not be replaced one on one (even if cost permitted). For example, a single Su-30 can deliver as much ordnance as a squadron of MiG-21FLs and at greater ranges, and with greater accuracy.

The desire to reduce the multiplicity of combat aircraft types in IAF service is unlikely to produce any significant results for the next decade or so. The retirement of MiG-21 and MiG-23 variants will reduce the number of types in service from 10 to 7. Indeed, as is underscored by the extensive modernization programs, most of these aircraft remain too useful to discard. MiG-21/MiG-23/27/29, Mirage 2000, Jaguars, and Su-30 are likely to fly side by side well into the next decade. And while the multiplicity of types has not adversely affected the IAF's combat performance, it does make logistics more complicated. However, increased commonality between avionics and other sub systems across the fleet is expected to make maintenance and logistics easier than they have ever been. Not only will this fleet be capable of delivering larger amounts ordnance more accurately over greater distances, but can also expect a greater level of survivability thanks to the increasing availability of force multipliers.

Emphasis on force multipliers

The IAF has been slow to induct force multipliers. While quick to deploy sizeable numbers of EW, ECM, and Reconnaissance assets, the IAF lacked an in-flight refueling capability and AWACS for years. Until the arrival of the Su-30s, only two aircraft types came with plumbing for in-flight refueling – Jaguars and Mirage 2000s. However, the IAF had the refueling probes of these aircraft removed in service. Until the early 1990s, the IAF remained a largely tactical force in its outlook. The prevailing view was that in case of a war with Pakistan, all major targets could be reached without the need for in-flight refueling. It was envisioned that any conflict with China would remain largely localized, again putting all targets within easy range of its aircraft. However, nuclearization and an expansion in the size of the IAF supporting aircraft forced a reconsideration of this view. The need to deploy specialized aircraft for duties such as Suppression of Enemy Air Defenses (SEAD) and the lengths of time that such aircraft would have to kept airborne created a pressing need for an in-flight fueling capability. The first in-flight refueling trials were conducted between IAF Jaguars and a RAF VC-10 tanker on loan as recently as 1996. Since then, the IAF has placed orders for a number of IL-78 tankers. It is expected that eventually eight such aircraft will be acquired. In the interim, the IAF has inducted UPAZ buddy refueling system for its Su-30s, Mirages, and Jaguars. The MiG fleet too is being equipped with in-flight refueling capability as part of their upgrades. In the context of nuclearization, the introduction of in-flight refueling provides the IAF with a rudimentary, if somewhat less than secure, deterrent capability against China.

The deployment of MiG-21s as airborne radar pickets in 1971, provided the IAF with an early introduction to the benefits of Airborne Early Warning (AEW). Unfortunately, an initial paucity of funds and an eventual inability to find a suitable platform set the IAF's efforts to acquire an AEW/AWACS back by many years. The IAF evaluated the Soviet A-50 in 1988 and rejected it for being incompatible with the existing air defense grid. Recent efforts to build a such a system indigenously has been hampered by the inadequacy of the trials platform (a Hs.748) and the loss of one prototype (of three) along with the R&D team. The need for an AWACS was sorely felt during the Kargil war in 1999. Consequently, the IAF has resumed its search with much vigor. A pair of A-50s with the new Shmel-2 radar was leased from the Russian AF in May of this year to help familiarize the service with operation of such systems. The IAF is reluctant to purchase the A-50 "as is" because, as in 1988, it would be a challenge to integrate the system with the Indian air defense set up. The IAF is also unhappy that some of the information processing for the A-50 has to be done via ground stations. The IAF would like to customize the system with Indian and non-Russian electronic subsystems so that it can be integrated with the Indian air-defense grid with less difficulty. For this reason, it will still be sometime before the IAF fields a viable AWACS/AEW force. The service has a requirement for up to six such aircraft.

There are two further dimensions to the IAF's quest for force multipliers – namely, EW and Reconnaissance. The IAF has rather extensive ELINT gathering and reconnaissance assets available. The bulk of the ELINT aircraft (B707, An-32, and B737) are operated under the auspices of the Aviation Research Center (ARC) and photographic reconnaissance assets are operated by directly by the IAF. Scores of MiG-21MRs and MiG-23BNs form the backbone of the tactical reconnaissance force. For strategic reconnaissance the IAF deploys squadron each of Canberra PR 57/67 and MiG-25Rs, complemented by a few Gulfstream III SRA-1s fitted with oblique cameras, which can look deep into enemy territory. Additionally several types of combat aircraft can be fitted with reconnaissance pods. It is expected that the MiG-21MRs are will be withdrawn in the near future. However, the IAF is looking at potential upgrade packages for the Canberras (both P 67s and B (I) 58 versions) in order to keep these forty-year old aircraft in service until 2010. Most recently, the IAF has acquired the Viten Vicon reconnaissance pods for use in strike squadrons, in order to give then an autonomous reconnaissance capability. The recent introduction of high altitude unmanned aerial vehicles (UAVs) gave the IAF its first significant experience with real-time reconnaissance capability. It is expected that in the next 5-7 years the defense forces will deploy dedicated satellites to enhance their intelligence gathering capabilities.

The IAF accepts the fact that losses in men and materials are to be expected during the course of combat operations. However, the IAF has invested quite heavily in trying to make sure that such losses are kept to a minimum. Budgetary constraints notwithstanding, the IAF has attempted, with some success, to create a comprehensive countermeasures force. Specialized aircraft have been acquired to support strike packages with ECM and ECCM cover. Stocks of anti-radiation systems – both missiles (ARMAT, Kh-25MP, Kh-59) and drones (Harpy) – have been diligently built up for this purpose. A number of MiG-23 airframes have been modified for SEAD duties with ARMs. It is also understood that the both of two-seat Jaguars currently under production will augment existing SEAD capabilities. The Jaguars greater endurance may have contributed to its selection as the primary EW support aircraft for the future.

Improvements in C4I and land-based air defense

Nuclearization of the Indian subcontinent has important implications for the future of both C4I and land-based air defense. Cognizant of this, the IAF has been working continuously since the early 1990s to shield and harden its communication network/nodes against nuclear attack. This is critical because of the second strike doctrine adopted by India. As the principal operator of India's nuclear weapons, the IAF's C4I network must be able to survive a first strike. In addition to the radiation hardening, it is understood that several levels of redundancy have been built into the network. The IAF has also undertaken the task of incrementally upgrading the strike fleet with EMP shielding.

The IAF already fields a formidable (in a regional context) ground based air defense system. India's air defense network is essentially divided into two parts-the Air Defense Ground Environment System (ADGES) and the Base Air Defense Zones (BADZ). These two components are closely linked and share information relating to air defense tasks. The ADGES and BADZ along with their associated sensor network and SAM units provide India with an extremely potent defense against both Pakistani and Chinese manned aircraft. Additionally, SAMs and fighters of the Navy also defend sensitive nuclear installations along India's western coasts. The ADGES is currently being upgraded with the new Indian and Israeli radar. The Pechora SAMs which form the backbone of the IAF's SAM units are also undergoing upgrades which will see them fitted with more sensitive seeker heads. The IAF is also looking at the Akash to provide it with the next generation SAM.

The emerging challenge to the air defense network is defense against ballistic missile attack. Over the last two years, the Indian press has been awash with reports that the government has sanctioned the building of an ATBM defenses. The IAF feels that the limited ability of the current sensor network to detect and track missile launches needs to be substantially upgraded. Furthermore, the Russian S-300 SAM is being considered to provide the backbone of ATBM defenses. While the system has undergone several trials in India (and may even be deployed in limited numbers), the IAF and the government are wary of relying excessively on the baseline system which has been compromised. Negotiations are underway for Indian to acquire a transfer of technology for the indigenous production of an S-300 derivative with Indian developed electronics and subsystems. It is likely that technology developed for the Akash SAM will be incorporated into any Indian manufactured S-300 derivative. Indeed, it is believed that the Akash SAM and the associated Rajendra phase array radar have some ATBM capability. The creation of an effective ATBM screen is high priority for the IAF but it will be many years before such a screen is operational.

Transports and Helicopters

The IAF has a sizable fixed and rotary winged transport fleet. While not as glamorous as their counterparts in the fighter stream, the IAF transport and helicopter formations contribute more than half of the IAF's annual flying hours. Operating out of some of the world most dangerous and inhospitable airstrips, the IAF's transport and helicopter formations play a crucial role in keeping the Indian Army and Air Force supplied. During last the Kargil operations last year, transport pilots were the unsung heroes of the war-flying day in and day out to maintain an uninterrupted air-bridge to the world's highest battle zone. Indeed post-Kargil the transport squadrons are logging almost 30% more hours than their counterparts in the fighter stream. India's airlift capabilities are significant. The ability to airlift the equivalent of a brigade plus their equipment at a time easily gives the IAF the largest military lift capability in Asia.

Two squadrons of IL-76 provide the IAF with its heavy lift capability, some 1,080,000 kg in all. These aircraft regularly operate out airfields in Ladakh situated at over 10,000 ft above sea level. The IAF is considering replacing the engines of these aircraft with western engines with a view to increasing operating efficiency. Increased logistical commitments in the aftermath of Kargil have caused the IAF to revive plans to add to its IL-76 fleet.

The An-32 from the backbone of the IAF's medium lift capabilities. Originally equipping six operational squadrons and a training unit, several of the type has now been put into storage. The An-32s were hit hard by the chaos in the ex-USSR as spares became harder to obtain. In response to these problems, the IAF successfully fitted several An-32s with An-12 power plants upon the retirement of the latter, and put a number airframes into storage. Although the spares problem is no longer as acute as in the early 1990s, the IAF has seen fit to keep the type flying with four operational squadrons and prevent wear & tear on the rest. The IAF still maintains one and a half squadrons of Hs.748 military freighters. The retirement of these aircraft in the near future is bound to affect the IAF airlift capabilities. It is not yet clear what aircraft the IAF considering as replacements for the type, although a fleeting interest has been shown in the ATR-42. The An-32s will also need replacements by the end of the decade as spares become harder to come by and airframe life will rapidly expire. The IAF Do-228 light transports are relatively new and the type is still in production in-country and one can expect the type to stick around well into the future.

The IAF helicopter fleet has come a long way from its humble beginnings. The IAF currently operates dozens of helicopter units, including three dedicated attack helicopter units. The "Hip" family is the workhorse of the IAF helicopter fleet. Hundreds of Mi-8/17s fly everything from liaison to assault missions. The Mi-17 fleet was quite active over Kargil and one of the type was lost in action. The recent deal to add 40 new Mi-17-1B helicopters to the IAF, is consistent with the IAF policy to replacing the older Mi-8s with its more modern and powerful stable-mate. A number of Mi-17s are also to be upgraded with sensors such as Forward Looking Infra Red (FLIR) in order to help augment the attack helicopter fleet. The IAF's attack helicopter fleet comprises of between two and three Mi-25/35 units. The Mi-35 recently underwent a comprehensive upgrade in Israel. It is also understood that there is solitary Chetak unit for anti-armor operations. Additionally, the "Hip" family can be fitted with a range of guided and unguided weapons. The IAF flies several Cheetahs and Chetaks in the liaison, SAR, and training roles. These types will eventually be replaced by Advanced Light Helicopter from Hindustan Aeronautical Limited, that has recently entered production. The IAF also operates a solitary unit of Mi-26 heavy-lift helicopters. The prohibitive cost of operating the type means that they are usually employed on special duties that are beyond the capabilities of other aircraft in the force. There is an ongoing tussle between the Army and IAF, over control of the attack & assault helicopter fleet. The former argues that the optimal deployment of these aircraft is only possible when ownership rests with the service that is expected to benefit from them.

Training

The IAF offers a very rigorous flying training schedule for its pilots. Before being assigned to operational squadrons, pilots are expected to log over 300 hours of flying at the basic, intermediate and advanced levels. However, maintaining the very high standards of training will pose a challenge for the air force in the new century. The problem is particularly acute at the advanced fighter training level. The problem arises form the age and unsuitability of the MiG Operational Flying Training Unit's (MOFTU) aircraft. As of now fighter pilots are expected to log 125 hours on the unit's MiG-21FL and UM before being assigned to squadrons.

The some of these aircraft are now over 30 years old and in very poor state of repair. The MiG-21FLs were phased out of Indian production in the mid-1970s hence spares for the type are very difficult to come by.

Whatever spares are available are second-hand. Furthermore the early generations of MiG-21s are unforgiving aircraft and pushing over a certain AoA at over 600 knots, sends the aircraft into an uncontrollable spin. Old airframes together with the fact that many IAF pilots go straight from basic training to MiG-21FL/UM explains the high accident rates for the type. In addition to the human cost, this has an unfavorable impact on morale for younger pilots. The IAF has been trying for years to purchase suitable Advanced Jet Trainers (AJT) to ease the transition to high performance aircraft. Both the Hawk and Alpha Jet were evaluated in the 1980s, but funding problems & dithering on the part of the government kept IAF from placing orders.

More recently, the IAF has revised its interest in purchasing the Hawk (the Alpha Jet being long out of production). However, Britain's inability (and reluctance) to refurbish Indian Navy Sea Harriers in the face of a US arms embargo have thrown into doubt the UK's ability to provide support for any Hawks that may be purchased. With the acquisition of AJT hanging in the air, the IAF's training problems are likely to get more acute. It is unfortunate that neither the IAF nor the Ministry of Defence has shown any interest in turning the HJT-36 intermediate trainer, now in development, into an AJT.

After a bad patch in the early 1990s, the IAF has been able to restore training in operational squadrons to their normal levels. Increased use of simulators have made a substantial difference to IAF training programs in recent years by making enhancing safety and preserving airframe life. Advanced fighter training has received a boost with the acquisition of Air Combat Maneuvering Instrumentation (ACMI) systems for the Tactics & Air Combat Development Establishment (TACDE) at Jamnagar. TACDE now offers courses in EW and helicopter combat. It also provides Dissimilar Air Combat Training (DACT) facilities to the Sea Harriers of the Navy.

Manpower Issues

During the 1990s, India has experienced the highest levels of economic growth since independence. For the armed forces, this growth has had positive as well as negative consequences. On the positive side, economic growth has allowed them to benefit from larger budgetary allocations.

On the negative side, an explosion in private sector jobs and salaries, have lured many away from careers in the armed forces. This is not a problem unique to India. Even wealthier countries, such as the United States military, have problems filling vacancies with suitable candidates. According to the Minister of Defence, the IAF was 500 pilots short of its authorized strength of 3347 in 1999. While the IAF still manages to maintain an adequate pilot to cockpit ratio and smaller force levels may yet alleviate some of the problems, the shortages are disturbing.

The IAF will have re-visit its personnel policy not only for pilots, but also for the technical branches as these are also likely to be affected by a greater demand for technical skills in the civilian sector. The recent decision to recruit women into the technical and flying branches has been a step in the right direction. By enlarging the pool of applicants, the IAF is sure to raise the overall quality of entrants.

Some Recommendations

The IAF is a thoroughly professional and increasingly well equipped force. It has emerged stronger through very trying times at the beginning of the 1990s. One should, however, not underestimate the challenges that lie ahead. However, based on emerging trends one can offer a number of macro recommendations that can only benefit the IAF in the future.

The Kargil war demonstrated the importance of joint operations between the services. After some initial setbacks and disagreements, the Army and the Air Force evolved a satisfactory, if somewhat ad hoc, mechanism for joint operations. This, unfortunately, was a temporary arrangement brought on by demands of war. The lack of a more formal mechanism for inter-service co-operation hampers an optimal use of the armed forces. The question of "jointness" and service integration is essentially political and is dealt with in a preceding section.

The biggest challenge facing the armed forces in general, and the IAF in particular, is the recruitment of suitable manpower for future needs. It is inconceivable that the IAF, or any air force, can offer compensation packages on par with private sector in a fast growing economy. Nor should they try. To this end, the IAF should adopt more an imaginative recruitment policy.

Instead of listing amounts for base salary, house rent allowance, flight pay, etc. in its recruitment brochures, as is the case now, the IAF should highlight the intangibles that the private sector could never provide. The promise of adventure, camaraderie, the lure of fast jets and a chance to serve one owns country is something that draws many young people towards the IAF. This is not to say that material benefits do not matter-they do. However, a professional air force can not be built on the size of compensation packets alone. Judging by the number of daily inquires that we at Bharat Rakshak receive, there are many dedicated young men and women who are interested in a career with the IAF – and not just in the flying branch! It is ultimately to the IAF to reach out and encourage such people. And this is only possible if the IAF raises the profile of its recruitment drive. Taking a leaf out of the Army's PR campaign would be step in the right direction. Backseat videos, documentaries and advertising campaigns in the media are the best way for the IAF to reach out to the public.

There are other measures that the IAF can introduce to tide over personnel shortages. These shortages should be expected to remain a perennial feature. The pyramidal structure of any armed force ensures that each year large numbers of qualified individuals are lost through a natural process of attrition.

Many people leaving the service do so with between 10-15 years of service. These individuals retain the physical and mental capacity to carry out a variety of operational tasks. Many of these retirees are often still willing to help out, given the opportunity.

The IAF should consider instituting a reserve system that can exploit this trained pool of manpower. The institution of a reserve system along the lines of the United States National Guard system merits some thought. In addition to helping fill peacetime shortages, a reserve system would enhance the IAF's war making potential. Additional ways in which manpower management can be improved includes the secondment of administrative and facilities officers to oversee the administration of facilities. This would allow the command and operational staff to remain focused on their primary task.

Overt nuclearization of the Indian subcontinent behooves the IAF to take up NBC training with greater urgency. While essential units are well versed with the procedures of dealing with an NBC attack, much more education is required. The air force has an important role to play in helping formulate disaster management policies in the face of unconventional attacks.

Last, but by no means the least, changed geo-political circumstances mean that the IAF should no longer rely on uninterrupted flows of arms and equipment from abroad. The spares crisis of the 1990s and recent Sea Harrier episode highlight the need for greater reliance on in house maintenance and production. More recently, the Israeli decision, under US pressure, to cancel the sale of a Phalcon AWACS to China highlight the dangers of excessive dependence on outside suppliers. While there are no quick fixes to the production dilemma, the IAF can do much by ensuring that it builds up substantial stocks of critical spares and ordnance. The co-production of PGMs, avionics, and engines should be encouraged where possible.

THE STRENGTH OF INDIAN AIR FORCE

The Indian Air Force Today

There are five operational air commands, the Western Air Command with headquarters in Delhi being the prime one and responsible for air operations from Kashmir southwards to Rajasthan and including the capital and the Punjab, with an Operations Group dedicated for Jammu & Kashmir including Ladakh. Central Air Command based at Allahabad, encompasses most of the Indo-Gangetic plain while Eastern Air Command, from Shillong, is responsible for Bengal, Assam, the eastern states of Arunachal Pradesh, Meghalaya, Mizoram and the others bordering area on Tibet, Bangladesh and Burma.

South Western Air Command, at Jodhpur, is responsible for air operations in most of Rajasthan, southwards through Gujrarat to Saurashtra and the Kutch area. Southern Air Command was formed in July 1984 with

headquarters at Trivandrum and has, geographically, the largest territory, from the Deccan plateau area to the southern tip of the peninsula and including the island territories of Lakshwadeep and the Andaman & Nicobar Islands. Training Command has its headquarters at Bangalore, with the majority of flying and ground training establishments located in Southern India. Maintenance Command operates from Nagpur in Central India. The five Operational Commands through administrative Wings, control some 45 fixed-wing squadrons, 20 helicopter units and numerous surface-to-air missile squadrons, with unit establishments varying from 12 to 18 aircraft. This represents a total aircraft strength of nearly 1,700 including training and support types, manned by some 120,000 personnel.

The Indian Air Force is today the world's fourth largest, well-equipped and professionally trained, smartly efficient and with an elan second to none.

Helicopters

The IAF's helicopter fleet has steadily increased in numbers over the past twenty years, blossoming from a handful of U.S. types in the '60s to over 500 French, Indian and Soviet built types. The pride of the force is, undoubtedly, the Mi 26 heavy lift helicopter which has been operated by No. 126 H.U. with outstanding results in the mountains of Northern India. The bulk of rotorcraft are Mi 17s and Mi 8s, well over one hundred of these types serving in Helicopter Units throughout the country, playing a vital logistic support role. Mi 8s are operated for commando assault tasks, for ferrying supplies and personnel to remote mountain helipads and jungle clearings, carrying out SAR (Search and Research Operations) and logistic support tasks in the island territories, employed with the Indian permanent station in the Antarctica and so on.

The smaller Alouette 111, renamed Chetak, is as ubiquitous, being employed for casevac (Casualty Evacuation), communications and liaison duties with the IAF having received over 150 examples of this versatile rotorcraft.

In 1986, however, the Government of India formally constituted the Army's Aviation Corps and most Chetak and Cheetahs operating in AOP Squadrons were transferred from the Air Force on 1st November 1986. The Air Force continues to fly armed Chetaks in the anti-tank role as well as for CASEVAC and general duties while the lighter Cheetah is operated by (FAC) flights.

In May 1984, No. 125 Helicopter Unit was formed with the formidable Mi-25 gunship helicopter, used to much effect in Sri Lanka. The upgraded Mi 35 has followed in April 1990, with No. 104 HU being reequipped with the type. Future requirements for armed helicopters are planned to be met by the indigenous Advanced Light Helicopter (ALH) currently under development by HAL at Bangalore.

Trainer

The IAF replaced its HT 2 primary trainers with the HPT32 (Deepak), the new piston engined trainer being utilised at the Basic Flying Training School at Allahabad since January 1988 and at Air Force Academy at Dundigal. Flight cadets then proceed to the Air Force Academy, Dundigal for instruction on the HJT 16 Kiran, first on the Mk. I/IA and then on the armed Mk II version or the Polish origin Iskra, for tactical flying. After commissioning, pilots are streamed to various conversion units, depending on their selection and proficiency. Future fighter pilots are sent to operational conversion units (now known as the MOFTU or MIG Operational Flying Training Unit) where operational and tactical flyng is conducted on MIG 21

Thus are born the IAF's leaders and even future spacemen, like Sqn Ldr Rakesh Sharma, India's first cosmonaut who participated in a joint space flight with the Soviets in 1984.

DETAILS OF AIRCRAFTS

MiG-29

Country of origin : USSR

Type : Air superiority fighter

Powerplant : Two Tumansky RD-33 turbofans of 8300 kg (18,300 lb.st)reheat thrust each.

Armament : One 30mm cannon plus four R.60 close-combat and two R.27R medium-range radar-guided missiles.

Max. take off wt : 18000 kg (39,683 lb)

Max. speed : 2445 km/hr (1518 mph) at 11,000m (36,100 ft) or Mach = 2.3

Initial climb rate : 330m/sec (64,960 ft/min)

Service ceiling : 17,000m (55,775 ft)

Dassault-Breguet Mirage-2000H

Country of Origin : France

Type : Air defence and multi-role fighter.

Powerplant : One SNECMA M53-P2 turbofan of of 9700 kg reheat thrust.

Armament: Two 30mm DEFA 554 cannon and two Matra Super 530D medium-range plus two R. 550 Magic II close combat missiles; upto 6000 kg (13225 lb) of external ordanance.

Max. take off wt : 16,650 kg.

Max speed : 2495 Km per hour.

Max climb rate : 249 m/sec

Combat radius : 700 km

Sepecat Jaguar International

Country of origin : UK-Frane

Type : Strike fighter

Powerplant : Two Rolls-Royce\Torbomeca Adour Mk. 811 each of 37.4 kn (8400 lb.st) with afterburning

Armament : Two 30 mm Aden cannon plus two R.550 Magic CCMs (overwing), maximum external stores load of 4750 kg

Max. take off wt : 15,700 Kg

Max level Speed : 1350 km per hour

Typical attack radius, with external fuel : 908 km.

MiG-27ML

Country of origin : USSR

Type : Tactical strike fighter

Powerplant : One Tumansky R-29-300 turbojet of 11,500 kg with reheat

Armament : One 23mm six-barrel rotary cannon and upto 4000 kg.

Max take off wt. : 18,000 kg.

Max speed : 1700 km per hour

Combat radius : 390 km.

Sukhoi Su-30

Country of origin : USSR

Type : Twin cockpit Multirole Fighter

Powerplant :2 x AL-31F

Armament : One 30mm GSH-301 gun with 150 rounds; external stations for more than 8000 of stores, including bombs upto 500 kg each; unguided rockets of various calibers; up to medium range air-to-air missiles with active or semi-active radar homing; up to two IR homing medium-range and six IR homing close range air-to-air missile.

Max. take off wt :34,000Kgs

Max.level speed:M2.35(2500 kmph)

Combat Range With internal fuel :1620 nautical miles (3000 Kms)

Take off Run : 550 mts Landing Run : 670 mts

MiG-25

Country of origin : USSR

Type : Strategic reconnaissance aircraft.

Powerplant : Two Tumansky R-31 turbojets each of 107.9 kn with after burning.

Equipment : Optical sensors and SLAR (Side Locking Aperture Radar).

Max level speed : Mach = 3.2 at height.

Service ceiling : 24,400 m.

MiG-23MF

Country of origin : USSR

Type : Air superiority fighter

Powerplant : One Tumansky R-29B of 11500 reheat thrust

Armament : One 23mm twin barrel GSh-23L cannon and two R-23R/T medium range plus two R-60 close combat missiles.

Max take Off wt. : 20,100

Max speed : 2446 km per hour

Combat radius : 850 km

MiG-21bis

Country of origin : USSR

Type :Multi role fighter/ground attack aircraft

Powerplant : One Tumansky R-25 turbojet of 7500 kg with reheat

Armament : Twin barrel 23mm GSh-23 cannon plus four R.60 close combat missiles.

Max. take off wt : 8745 Kg

Max speed : 2230 km per hour

Combat radius : 547 km

BA-Hawker Hunter F.56A

Country of origin : UK

Type : Fighter ground attack aircraft (Now used for target towing)

Powerplant : One Rolls Royce Avon 207 turbojet of 4562 kg

Armament : Four 30 Aden cannon with 150 rpg; two 1000 lb bombs or four 1001 Imp. gallon napalm tanks or 68mm rocket pods.

Max take off wt : 8060 kg

Max Speed : 1009 km per hour

Service ceiling : 15,700m

BAe/English Electric Canberra B(I) 58.

Country of origin : UK

Type : Tactical bomber and interdictor

Powerplant : Two Rolls Royce Avon 109 turbojets ech of 3357 kg

Armament : 4 X 20mm Hispano cannon or 3 X 1000 lb bombs internally plus 2 X 1000 lb underwing or (Bomber) 8000 lb bombload internally & underwing.

Max take off wt : 25,540 kg

Max speed : 933 km per hour

Max range : 1287 km

ILLUSHIN IL-76 MD

Country of origin : USSR

Type : Heavy duty/long haul military transport

Powerplant : Four Soloviev D-30KP 1 turbofans of 12,000 kg each

Capacity : 225 paratroopers or 40 tonnes freight, wheeled or tracked armoured vehicles etc.

Armament : Twin 23mm cannon in tail turret.

Max take off wt : 170,000 kg

Max cruise speed : 850 km per hour

Max Range (with reserves) : 6500 km

Antonov AN-32

Country of origin : USSR

Type : Medium tactical transport

Powerplant : Two Ivchenko AI-20M turboprops of 4195 ehp each.

Capacity : Crew of 5 plus 39 paratroopers on tip-up seats; maximum of 6.7 tonnes payload

Max take off wt : 27,000 kg

Max cruise speed : 530 km

Max Range : 2500 km

HAL-Dornier 228-201

Country of origin : Germany

Type : Logistic air support; staff transport

Powerplant : Two Garrett TPE-331-5-252D turboprops of 715 shp each

Capacity : 19 passengers or 2057 kg freight.

Max. take off wt : 5980 kg

Max cruise speed : 428 km per hour

Max Range : 1112 km

HAL/BAe (Avro) 748M

Country of origin : UK

Type : Military transport and freighter

Powerplant : Two Rolls Royce Dart RDa7Mk. 532-2L turboprops of 1700 KW each

Capacity : Upto 48 paratroops or 6 tonnes freight

Max take off wt : 21,092 kg

Max cruise speed : 452 km per hour

Max Range : 1778 km

Boeing 737-200

Country of origin : USA

Type : VIP passenger transport

Powerplant : Two pratt & Whitney JT8D-17A turbofans of 71.2 KN each.

Capacity : VIP/Executive cabins, total seating for upto 60 passnegers.

Max take off wt : 53,070 kg

Max cruise speed : 943 km per hour

Max range : 4262 km

MiL Mi-26

Country of origin : USSR

Thype : Military heavy lift helicopter

Powerplant : Two Lotarev D-136 turboshafts of 11,240 shp each

Capacity : 70 combat equipped troops or 20,000 kg payload.

Max take off wt : 56,000 kg

Max speed : 295 km per hour

Hovering ceiling : 4500 m

Max range : 800 km

MiL Mi-25

Country of origin : USSR

Type : Assault and anti armour helicopter

Powerplant : Two Isotov TV3-117 turboshafts of 2200 shp each

Capacity : Eight man assault squad.

Armament : Four barrel 12.7 mm rotary gun in nose barbette and upto 1500 kg of external ordnance including Scorpion anti-tank missiles

Max takee off wt : 11,000 kg

Max cruise speed : 310 km per hour

Max range : 750 km

MiL Mi-17

Country of origin : USSR

Type : Medium transport helicopter

Powerplant : Two Isotov TV3-117 7MT turboshafts of 1900 shp each

Capacity : 24 troops or upto 3.3 tonnes of freight

Armament : Six UV-17 57mm rocket pods.

Max take off wt : 13,000 kg

Max cruise speed : 240 km per hour

Max Range : 950 km

HAL/Aerospatiale Alouette III (Chetak)

Country of origin : France

Type : Light utility helicopter

Powerplant : One Turbomeca Artouste IIIB turboshaft of 870 shp

Capacity : Upto six passengers or 500 kg load.

Armament (anti-tank version): Four AS-11 wire guided missiles

Max take off wt : 2250 kg

Max speed : 220 km per hour

Hovering ceiling : 1750 km

HAL/Aerospatiale SA 315B Lama (Cheetah)

Country of origin : Frane

Type : FAC/Casevac helicopter

Powerplant : One Turbomeca Art IIIB turboshaft of 870 shp

Capacity : 3 passengers or external sling loads of 1000 kg

Max take off wt : 2200 kg

Max cruise speed : 121 kms her hour

Rate of climb (S/L) :250m/min

Hovering ceiling : 2400 m

Aircraft Types Operated by the Indian Air Force (1932-1991)

Type	Service Period
Westland WapitiILA	1933-42
Hawker Hart	1939-40
De Havilland D.H. 82A Tiger Moth	1939-57
De Havilland D.H. 89 Dragon Rapide	1941-44
Armstrong Whitworth A.W. 15 Atalanta	1941-42
Hawker Audax	1941-45

Bristol Blenheim Mk. 1	1941-42
Westland Lysander Mk. I1	1941-43
North American T-6G Texan Harvard I	1942-75
Hawker Hurricane Mk IIB/IIC	1942-45
Vultee Vengeance Mk 1/III	1942-44
VickersValentia Avro Anson 1942-45 HAL/MS 748	1942-44
De Havilland D.H. 85 Leopard Moth	1942-43
De Havilland D.H. 94 Minor Moth	1942-43
Fairchild PT-26 Cornell	1943-46
Hawker Hurricane Mk X11	1943-45
Hawker Hurricane MklV SukhoiSu-7BM l	1944-45
Supermarine Spitfire Mk V111	1944-48
Boulton Paul Defiant TT Mk Ill Mil Mi-8	1944-45
Fairey Battle	1944-45
Auster AOP41511619	1945-70
Supermarine Spitfire Mk XIV	1945-50
Hawker Tempest Mk 11	1946-53
Douglas C-47 Dakota	1946-88
Airspeed Oxford SepecatJaguar S/B	1947-49
Percival Prentice T Mk 3	1948-59
Consolidated Vultee B-24 Liberator Boeing 737	1948-68
De Havilland Vampire FB Mk 52	1948-72
De Havilland Devon C Mk 1 MiG-25R/bT	1950-88
Supermarine Spitfire MkXVI11	1951-57
HAL HT-2 Mil Mi-25	1953-88
De Havilland Vampire NFMk. 54	1953-66
De Havilland Vampire TMk. 55 11yushinll-76MD	1953-75
Dassault Ouragan (Toofani)	1953-67
Fairchild C-1 19GL Packet MiG-27M	1953-86
Sikorsky S-55	1954-66
Super Aero AE´45.5 1955-57 MiG-29B I rB llyushin 11:14	1955-77
De Havilland DHC-3 Otter 1956-91 HAL HJT-16 Kiran Mk. II, Vickers Viscount	1956-67
Bell Model 47G Mil Mi-35	1957-72
Dassault Mystere IVA	1957-73
English Electric Canberra B (1) Mk 58 B.Mk.66,B.Mk. 12, PR. Mk.57, PR.Mk.67, T.Mk.54	1957-
Hawker Hunter F Mk.56.F Mk 56 A,T Mk. 66, T Mk. 66D	1957-

HAL/Folland Gnat Mk 1	1958-78
Sikorsky S-62B	1960-64
Mil Mi-4	1960-81
Antonov An-12 B	1961-
Lockheed Super Constellation	1961-84
Aerospatiale HAL Alouette III (Chetak)	1962-
DHC-4 Caribou	1963-87
MiG-21 F-13	1963-68
HAL/HS 748	1964-
HAL HF-24 Marut Mk.1.JT	1964-83
HAL HAOP-27 Krisha'	1965-77
MiG-21 FL/U	1966-
TupolevTu-124	1966-81
SukhoiSu-7BM l:	1968-86
HAL HJT-16 Kiran Mk l/IA	1968-
Mil Mi-8	1971-
Aerospatiale/HAL Cheetah	1973-
MiG-2 1 MF/M	1973-
TS-11 Iskra	1975-
HAL Ajeet (Gnat Mk.II)	1977-91
MiG-21bis	1977-
SepecatJaguar S/B	1979-
MiG-23BNlIJM	1981-
Boeing 737	1981-
MiG-23MF	1982-
MiG-25R/bT	1982-
AntonovAn-32	1984-
Mil Mi-25	1984-
MilMi-17	1985-
11yushinll-76MD	1985-
Dassault Mirage 2000H	1985-
MiG-27M	1984-
Mil Mi-26	1986-
MiG-29B/UB	1987-
HAL HPT-32	1988-
HAL HJT-16 Kiran Mk. II	1988-
HAL Dornier 228-201	1988-
Mil Mi-35	1990-

5

Future of the Indian Air Force

The Indian Air Force started modernising and upgrading its aging and outdated equipment since the late 90's. For that reason it has started procuring and developing aircraft, weapons, associated technologies, and infrastructures. Some of these programmes date back to the late 80's. The primary focus of upgradation are the aircraft procured from the Soviet Union that form the backbone of the Air Force.

Upgrades

The Indian Air Force began an upgrade of its MiG-29 fleet in 2007. India awarded Russia a US$965 million contract to upgrade its Air Superiority MiG-29 into multi role MiG-29SMT warplanes, on Monday 10 March 2008. According to the deal, Russia will re-arm the twin-engined MiG-29s with air-to-air missiles, and the upgraded MiGs will feature increased fuel capacity, will include latest avionics, Zhuk-ME Radar, engine, weapon control systems etc.

Although not initially designed to carry nuclear or strategic weapons, the Indian Air Force will receive 40 upgraded Su-30MKIs capable of carrying the BrahMos cruise missile possibly by 2012. In addition, there are also plans to integrate the nuclear-capable Nirbhay missile with the aircraft as well. In May 2010, India Today reported that Russia had won a large contract to upgrade 40 Su-30MKI fighters with new radars, onboard computers, electronic warfare systems and the ability to carry the BrahMos missile. The first two prototypes with the 'Super-30' upgrade will be delivered to the Indian Air Force in 2012, after which the same upgrades will be performed on the last batch consisting of 40 production aircraft. The exact value of the contract has yet to be disclosed however.

In March 2010, India and France finalized the long delayed deal to upgrade all of India's Mirage 2000H to Mirage 2000-5 Mk 2 variant with new radar systems, a new weapon suite, missiles, electronic warfare system etc. French claim that the combat-proven aircraft will be upgraded to next-generation fighter level. The first four to six Mirages will be upgraded in France, with the rest 50 or so being upgraded in India by Hindustan Aeronautics under transfer of technology. Under the upgrade, the entire airframe will be stripped down to be re-wired and re-equipped with new avionics, mission computers, glass cockpits, helmet-mounted displays, electronic warfare suites and of course weapon systems to extend and enhance the operational life of the multi-role fighters by around 20 years.

UNDER PROCUREMENT

Fighter Aircraft

The IAF has issued a Request of Intent (RoI) for the procurement of 126 multi-role combat aircraft. Contenders for the $10 Billion contract are the MiG-35 from Mikoyan of Russia, the Rafale from Dassault Aviation of France, the Eurofighter Typhoon, from EU, JAS 39 Gripen from Saab of Sweden, the F-16IN from Lockheed Martin and F/A-18E/F Super Hornet from Boeing. Report suggest that the Rafale and Typhoon has been selected for the final stage.

Transport Aircraft

On 15 June 2009, the IAF announced that it was interested in purchasing about 10 C-17 Globemaster III tactical military transport aircraft. The C-17 deal, expected to be worth over $2.5 billion, would be done through Pentagon's Foreign Military Sales (FMS) route under which inter-governmental deal is signed for arms sales. It is possible that the deal might include an option for 10 more aircraft. In early 2008, the IAF signed a deal to acquire 6 C-130J Super Hercules, modified for special mission roles, for US$1.06 billion. Lockheed Martin is expected to deliver the planes in 2011.

Trainer Aircraft

The IAF is planning to acquire 181 basic trainer aircraft. The IAF will select an aircraft from among six contenders-Grob G-120TP, Embraer EMB 314 Super Tucano, Korean Aerospace Industries KT-1, Finmeccanica M-311 and Pilatus PC-7 after flight trials.

Helicopters

On 26 May 2009, the Indian Ministry of Defense invited bids for 22 combat helicopters and 15 heavy-lift helicopters in a deal worth US$2 billion. Companies which have expressed their interest in the tender include — Russia's Kamov and Mil Moscow Helicopter Plant, Europe's AgustaWestland and Eurocopter and United States' Bell Helicopter and Boeing. Boeing submitted its initial bid on 23 Oct 2009 offering the AH-64D Apache Longbow attack helicopter and the CH-47F Chinook heavy-lift, twin-rotor helicopters.

In December 2008, India and Russia inked a deal for the supply of 80 Mi-17V-5 (also known as Mi-171) medium lift helicopters at a cost of US$1.2 billion. The two countries had earlier negotiated a price of $650 million, but early in 2008 Russia asked for a revision of the contract price. Russia is expected to deliver the Mi-171 to the IAF in 2010. The deal also envisages a US$405 million "offset" obligation by Russia. The new choppers, which have an 18,000 ft operational ceiling, will replace 50 Mi-8s currently in service with the IAF, some of which are over 35 years old, and boost IAF's capability to support high-altitude posts in Siachen and Ladakh sectors. The helicopter will come with the circuitry and hard points to carry weapons. In September 2010, the IAF placed an order for 59 more MI-17V5 helicopters in addition to the 80 ordered in 2008, this is to replace its ageing fleet of the older MI-17s and MI-8s; the process would be completed by 2014.

The Indian Air Force has signed a 560 million euro contract with Italy's AgustaWestland for 12 AW101 helicopters. The aircraft will be delivered with self-protection equipment capable of warding off missile threats and will serve as VIP transports the Indian President and Prime Minister. A tender for supply of 317 light helicopters will be floated by Ministry of Defence combining the requirements of Indian Air force (125) and Indian Army (197).

Unmanned Aerial Vehicles

The Indian air force has submitted a request for information to international suppliers for a unmanned combat air vehicle (UCAV) with low radar cross-section, high service ceiling, an expected range of 500nm (925km) and the capability to carry precision-guided weapons in an internal weapons bay.

Surface to Air Missile Systems

In June 2007, India signed a $250 million to purchase SPYDER (*S*urface-to-air *PY*thon and *DER*by) mobile air defense missiles from Israel. The two countries signed an additional $4 billion deal for the joint-development of a medium range surface-to-air missiles. However, the procurement of SPYDER missiles was delayed because of an ongoing investigation against Israel Aerospace Industries and RAFAEL by Indian intelligence agencies for its alleged kickbacks in the Barak-I deal with the Indian Navy. In August 2008, a $2.5 billion deal was signed by India and Israel to develop an advanced version of the SPYDER.

Cruise Missiles

DRDO is developing the air launched version of the Brahmos cruise missile in a joint venture with Russia's NPO Mashinostroeyenia. The air launched version for the Indian Air Force is ready for testing. The IAF has signed a contract with Russia to upgrade 40 Su-30MKIs to give them the capability of carrying the BrahMos cruise missile by 2012. DRDO is also developing the nuclear capable Nirbhay cruise missile.

UNDER DEVELOPMENT

Fighter Aircraft

HAL initiated the Light Combat Aircraft (LCA) programme in 1983 to develop a replacement aircraft for IAF's ageing MiG-21. After development during the 80s and 90s the first flight occurred in 2001. The aircraft has since been named HAL Tejas. The IAF is reported to have a requirement for 200 single-seat and 20 two-seat conversion trainers. It has ordered 48 limited production aircraft. These aircraft are expected to get Initial Operational Clearance (IOC) in December with induction in early 2011.

In October 2007, India and Russia signed a pact to develop a Fifth Generation Fighter Aircraft which is a derivative project from the PAK FA.

The Indian version will be a two-seater, air superiority fighter. Another agreement was signed between India's Hindustan Aeronautics and Russia's United Aircraft Corporation (UAC) in December 2008 which detailed the joint development and production the aircraft.

Work on the program will start by mid-2009 and the program is expected to be completed by 2017. Indian Air Force will get 200 twin-seated and 50 single seated FGFAs. Sukhoi/HAL FGFA when fully developed is intended to replace the MiG-29 Fulcrum and Mikoyan MiG-27 in the Indian inventory.

HAL has also started design work on an Advanced Medium Combat Aircraft (AMCA), which is a twin-engined 5th generation stealth multirole fighter. It will complement the HAL Tejas, the Sukhoi/HAL FGFA, the Sukhoi Su-30MKI and the as yet undecided MRCA in the Indian Air Force. The main purpose of this aircraft is to replace the aging SEPECAT Jaguar & Dassault Mirage 2000 fighters.

Airborne Early Warning aircraft

In 2004, Defence Research and Development Organisation revived the Airavat Project, which was India's first attempt in developing an indigenous AEW aircraft. A $210 million deal signed with Brazil's Embraer in 2008 for the supply of three Embraer EMB-145 regional jets.

India has sent a request for proposal to six vendors for the supply of Active Array Antenna Unit (AAAU) and various other sub-systems. These vendors include Israel's Elta, the European consortium EADS, France's Thales, Sweden's SAAB Erikson and the United State's Raytheon and Northrop Grumman. The IAF has a requirement for 24 DRDO AEW&CS.

Transport aircraft

HAL entered a joint-venture with the United Aircraft Corporation (UAC) of Russia to develop the UAC/HAL Il-214 Multirole Transport Aircraft (MTA) which is a medium-lift military transport aircraft. Both companies will invest US$300 million each in joint venture. The aircraft will be able to perform regular transport duties and also deploy paratroopers. The jet is expected to fly by 2014 and inducted by 2015/16. The Indian Air Force plans to acquire 45 MTAs. The aircraft will have a maximum payload of 18.5 tons, with a range of 2500 km and a speed of 870 km/h. The Indian Air Force plans to acquire 45 MTAs. The IAF has also placed an order for 15 NAL Saras light transport aircraft designed by the National Aerospace Laboratory (NAL) which is still under development. The manufacturer has stated that the Indian Air Force intends to place an order for up to 45 aircraft.

Training aircraft

HAL has developed the HAL HJT-36 Sitara intermediate jet trainer aircraft for the IAF which carried out its maiden test flight in 2003. These aircraft are scheduled to replace the aging HJT-16 Kiran mk.I. The Indian Air Force has placed placed an order for 73 aircraft, of which the first 12 are in production. The order by the Indian Air Force could eventually grow to 250 aircraft. Two prototype aircraft have been built. These aircraft have undergone 280 test flights. The HJT-36 is scheduled to enter service with the Indian Air Force in June, 2010.

HAL will also develop the HAL HTT-40 which will replace HAL HPT-32 Deepak as basic trainer. HAL has decided to rope in an international partner for the design and development of the much needed ab initio turbo trainer for the Indian Air Force (IAF) and the Navy.

Helicopters

HAL is developing the Light Combat Helicopter (LCH) for the IAF based on the successful HAL Dhruv platform. It is being designed to fit into an anti-infantry and anti-armour role and will be capable to operate from altitudes of 6,500 metres. The first prototype of the LCH has successfully completed its first flight run on 29 March 2010. The Hindustan Aeronautics

Limited of India is now developing the HAL Light Observation Helicopter (LOH) to replace the fleet of Cheetah and Chetak helicopters. The project is in preliminary stages and is in the design phase. The project is expected to be completed within next 5–6 years.

Unmanned Aerial Vehicles

The DRDO of India is developing a Medium Altitude Long Endurance Unmanned Aerial Vehicle (UAV) called the Rustom (English: Warrior) for all three branches of the Indian Armed Forces. The Rustom will replace/supplement the Heron UAVs in service with the Indian armed forces. DRDO is also developing the AURA (Autonomous Unmanned Research Aircraft) which is an Unmanned Combat Aerial Vehicle for the Indian Air Force. The design work on the UCAV is carried out by Aeronautical Development Agency (ADE). The AURA UCAV will be a tactical stealth aircraft built largely with composites, and capable of delivering laser-guided strike weapons. It would be a stealthy flying-wing concept aircraft with internal weapons and a turbofan engine.

Surface to Air Missile Systems

India and Israel have agreed to expand their missile development cooperation with a longer-range version of their extended-range Barak ship defense system for the Indian Air Force. DRDO is in talks with MBDA to develop Maitri LLQRM (Low Level Quick Reaction Missile) for all three branches of the armed forces. Sources said that DRDL is preparing feasibility report and is awaiting formal clearance from defence ministry.

FUTURE PLANNING OF INDIAN AIR FORCE

Planning for the future has always been a daunting task, especially when it concerns the military of a nation. As the military is a vital component and in fact the ultimate instrument of national security, improper assessment or gross miscalculation of its pattern of development can have catastrophic ramifications. The task of forward planning is rendered particularly difficult in a scenario where long term plans need to be evolved in a coordinated fashion amongst the three wings of the Armed Forces – the Army, Navy and the

Air Force. Also, for any long term planning to be meaningful, two inputs are prerequisites for military planners – a clear long term strategic vision for the nation, and assured availability of resources commensurate with national security imperatives, in that order.

In the Indian context, the lofty and fiery rhetoric on both these aspects emanating from the highest levels of governance have rarely crystallized into reality. Over the last six decades since Independence, in the Indian Air Force (IAF) there has been piecemeal acquisition of hardware as cleared by the civilian bureaucracy to be sanctioned by the political leadership on the basis of stand alone case-by-case justification and not in conformity with any long term national plan. Possibly there has been none. The process of acquisition of new equipment has generally followed a pattern of one to one replacement with equipment procured from a source that is either the cheapest, politically expedient or both. Acquisition of hardware has often been contingent not on the availability of resources but on allocation of funds.

OBSOLESCENCE IN THE IAF

For decades the IAF had largely been tethered to one non-western source. Much of the inventory acquired through this route has now been overtaken by obsolescence. As a result, in recent years, there has been an alarming erosion in combat power and other capabilities. Even after prolonged and reportedly vigorous effort, the indigenous Research & Development Organisations and the Aerospace Industry have not been able to provide a respectable degree of self reliance to the IAF. The near total dependence on foreign sources for cutting edge technology and frontline equipment is potentially perhaps the most debilitating factor that often threatens to seriously undermine the capability of the IAF. Despite the limitations, the IAF has managed to attain and project an image of a potent force capable to preserving the sovereignty of the Indian skies and in more recent times, to project power albeit limited in quantum and reach. And even in the future there appears to be no option but to procure advanced technology and hardware from abroad. There is however an attempt to indigenize products through co-development, co-production and the difficult, but innovative, concept of "Offsets". Though not the best, this route is the most expedient under the circumstances to accord military hardware a semblance of Indian character.

Life of a modern weapon system is in the region of thirty years which is normally extendable by another 10 to 15 years after a mid-life upgrade. New equipment procured for the IAF over the next decade will remain operational up to 2050 at the very least, possibly up to 2060. As the nature of warfare itself is undergoing transformation, it is necessary to make a comprehensive reassessment of the contours of the operational scenario that the IAF will have to contend with and reconfigure its inventory accordingly. To do this at this point in time, the IAF needs to take note of India's regional power status in the emerging world order and assess its possible role and responsibility in the new geopolitical and geostrategic environment.

The Pakistan Factor

In view of the asymmetry, Pakistan is unlikely to take the initiative for large scale conventional military operations against India. While it will continue to retain the capability to put up stout defence against any assault, as indications are, it is more likely to engage in clandestine warfare against India in a variety of ways, some of which were amply demonstrated by way of attack on the Parliament in 2001 or the raid on Mumbai in November 2008. Such operations should no longer be seen as purely internal security problems. Our land and sea borders are extensive and quite impossible to seal through measures on the ground – such as erection of physical barriers or through the deployment of paramilitary forces/civil police that are riddled with porosity on account of corruption. In the present scenario, it is relatively easy for the well trained enemy agents or commandos collectively described by India as "terrorists", to penetrate unsecured borders and inflict disproportionately high levels of damage and human casualties. It should not come as a surprise if the various religious, political and social divides that afflict the nation actively facilitate such operations by the enemy.

Despite the perceived success in the recently held elections in the State of Jammu and Kashmir, the end to the turmoil is not in sight.

There is no doubt that Pakistan will continue its campaign in the state, in all likelihood, with renewed vigour and intensity to turn the tide against India. The techniques of warfare and tactics adopted by Pakistan in J&K will be similar to those employed by other regions in India and possibly with an enhanced level of support from the local populace.

The induction of nuclear weapons in South Asia has added a new dimension to the Indo-Pak military confrontation. Pakistan is believed to have unknown quantities of Chinese supplied nuclear weapons and has the capability to deliver these using surface-to-surface missiles with adequate range to cover most important cities and targets of strategic value. India too has nuclear weapons and has one advantage over Pakistan wherein the latter lacks strategic depth.

In order to neutralize the Pakistani nuclear threat and raise their threshold substantially, India needs to enlarge her own nuclear arsenal and diversify her delivery capability with bias towards surface-to-surface missiles complemented by combat aircraft in the ratio 75:25.

The nuclear warfare capability needs to be developed to the extent necessary to obliterate most cities in Pakistan in a single strike and this capability must be clearly made known to them by direct or indirect means. With such a capability in being, there would be a high probability that Pakistan would be deterred from first use of nuclear weapons. Although the President of Pakistan, Asif Ali Zardari has proclaimed a "no first use" policy, it would not be prudent to take this assurance at face value and neglect or delay the build up of own capability. We need to bear in mind the principle that nuclear weapons are not meant to win but to prevent wars.

Against the traditional enemy with whom India has fought three major conventional wars since Independence and who now is engaged in aggressive subversion in different parts of the country, it should be clear that in the future, the traditional military posture will progressively become less relevant as the clandestine warfare of the future will have no clearly defined fronts. This would necessitate redefined doctrines and restructured inventory.

First and foremost, there has to be a profound qualitative change in the capability of surveillance and communication intelligence through extensive employment of aerial platforms. Surveillance platforms parked at medium to high altitudes must be capable of providing resolution of a few centimeters with all-weather capability through cameras in the optical and infrared frequency range, Synthetic Aperture Radar or other new generation sensors to be introduced in the future.

These advanced sensors need to be mounted on new generation Unmanned Aerial Vehicles (UAV) with continental range and high endurance capable of being controlled and operated thousands of miles away from parent base through satellite based data link. Such a system can provide round-the-clock cover of any part of land and sea frontiers as also inland areas of the nation.

This will obviate the need to reposition the bulky control infrastructure in different parts of the country. The airborne platforms must also carry powerful and agile sensors to record, identify and pin-point the source of all radio transmissions on a wide range of frequency bands.

Intelligence gathering through UAVs on continuous patrol would have to be supported by high speed, possibly automated intelligence data processing and analysis systems, which should include capability of integration with intelligence inputs from other agencies. Threat thus analyzed must be available in the shortest possible time to security agencies required to respond. For swift response, an effective method is vertical envelopment through a heli-borne force with the helicopter fleet dedicated to this task, data linked with the UAV to get a real time view of the objective.

The ever increasing cost of fixed wing combat aircraft and their weapons, as also substantially enhanced lethality of enemy air defence weapon systems, would render employment of such aircraft both in the deep strike role and in the tactical battle areas, less and less cost effective in the future. It would be necessary therefore to place greater reliance on surface-to-surface missiles for deep strike against heavily defended targets in depth such as airfields. In the tactical battle area the fixed wing combat aircraft would have to be replaced by Unmanned Aerial Combat Vehicles (UCAV) and rotary wing platforms with stand-off weapons, both integrated with the ground forces. Fixed wing aircraft when employed would have to be effectively protected through versatile electronic warfare capability. Strategic Air Defence capability of the IAF would have to be augmented through the enlargement of the fleet of AWACS and AEW aircraft. These systems would effectively close the prevalent gaps in the low level surveillance capability of the IAF. Simultaneously, it would be necessary to induct new air defence missile systems for area and point defence and revamp electronic warfare capability across the board.

China, an Emerging Superpower

Riding the wave of stupendous economic growth, China has emerged as a major regional power and has clear aspirations to be a global power in' the not too distant future. Despite prolonged dialogue, there has been no progress in the settlement of Sino-Indian border dispute and none is likely in the foreseeable future. China is a nuclear power and is currently embarked on a major upgrade of its somewhat outdated military machine. She has enlarged her sphere of influence in Asia and has effectively thrown a cordon around India through political, economic and military support to all the immediate neighbours. India's growing proximity with and subservience to the US consequent to the Indo-US nuclear deal, has clearly pushed India on to the opposite side of the international political divide. With this development, the possibility of rapprochement with the emerging superpower has practically receded into oblivion. In the long term perspective, China is potentially a greater military threat to India than Pakistan is.

Thus it would be unwise for India to depend solely on diplomacy or support of the US to secure the nation against the awakening giant in the north. The limitations of diplomacy without the backing of military power have so clearly been exposed in the confrontation with Pakistan in the wake of 26/11. If India's diplomatic demarche has not succeeded against Pakistan which is relatively a weak state, it would be naive to assume that it will be effective against China. The character and level of threat from China is qualitatively different and the nation's armed forces must be geared to meet the long term threat beginning to loom over the horizon. Finally it would be the armed forces that would have to face the consequences of diplomatic failure and bear the brunt of a Chinese offensive in any form.

First and foremost, the IAF must have the capability to counter China's nuclear capability through a missile based credible nuclear deterrence. Simultaneously, the Sino-Indian borders need to be kept under surveillance through satellites and unmanned platforms. The IAF must also acquire the capability to launch precision attack in mountainous areas from high altitude using advanced precision guided munitions. In addition, it must have the capability to neutralize targets with mobile units of surface-to-surface missiles with conventional warheads in coordination with target data obtained from UAVs.

Space

A completely new dimension in future wars would be the employment of space-based assets for reconnaissance, surveillance and communication. There has been some progress in this area but much more needs to be done. However, the new problem that is emerging is the security of the space-based assets. There appears to be no clear solution at this point in time except for multiple redundancy which may be expensive and impractical. In addition to space-based assets, the IAF needs to acquire the capability to neutralize space-based capability of the enemy through hard or soft kill techniques with weapon systems located on the ground or mounted on airborne platforms.

POWER PROJECTION CAPABILITY

A major responsibility of the IAF in the future would be in the area of strategic airlift. Internal security compulsions will place growing demand for the movement of quick reaction as also regular security forces within the country on short notice. Given its emerging regional power status and the newly forged strategic partnership with the US if not abrogated by the incoming administration, India may be called upon to project power in the region which may involve airlift of large military forces to areas of interest of either of the partners in the region outside our borders and to provide sustained logistic support. Strategic airlift capability of the IAF would therefore need to be built up practically from scratch as the existing fleet is fast approaching the end of its total technical life. At the tactical level, the IAF should be equipped with a fleet of medium tactical transport aircraft and helicopters capable of speedy response with special forces over shorter ranges.

The IAF has taken some baby steps towards acquiring the capability of projecting combat power in the region. At this point in time, the capability is limited to a token force and cannot be described as significant. However, while steps are in hand to augment the existing fleet of long range combat aircraft as also to acquire a new fleet, the capability of power projection would in the ultimate analysis be limited by the size of the fleet of in-flight refuelling aircraft. This fleet would have to be suitably enlarged for any meaningful power projection that is capable of making an impact.

Summary

To summarise, the IAF needs to enhance some of the force multipliers already on the inventory as also to develop a range of new capabilities both in the strategic and tactical regimes. At the strategic level, the IAF must be able to provide the nation with credible nuclear deterrence against Pakistan and China.

Also, it should be capable of power projection in its perceived area of national security interests and those of our ally in the region beyond the national borders with combat aircraft, in-flight refuelling and strategic airlift capability. These forces should be geared to provide swift response to a crisis situation and be able to provide logistic support to sustain forces for significant length of time. For strategic strike deep into enemy territory, the IAF needs to have a combination of missile based and airborne platforms, the latter with powerful electronic warfare equipment to suppress and defeat enemy air defence systems. Tactical roles may be transferred to UCAVs and helicopters.

To provide effective air defence of the homeland, the IAF needs to acquire a fleet of AWACS and AEW aircraft over and above the few already on order to enhance surveillance capability at low level. New generation area and point defence missile systems need to be inducted to replace the ageing and obsolete systems currently deployed. For strategic and tactical intelligence, the IAF must have its own satellite systems and a fleet of UAVs with a range of advanced sensors to provide all weather day and night capability. The fleet of UAVs should be adequately supported by appropriate ground infrastructure for automated and speedy processing of intelligence information, and fleet of tactical transport aircraft and helicopters for quick response with special forces.

It goes without saying that in future wars, the IAF must be geared to operate in a network-centric environment. But perhaps most important of all, there is the imperative need for the IAF to shed the defensive mindset.

INDIAN AIR FORCE PLANS MODERNIZATION PROGRAMME

The Indian Air Force (IAF) in a bid to enhance every aspect of its capability, plans on a systematic modernization plan, which majorly includes launching a satellite in 2010 and an integrated air command and control system by the end of this year. The IAF would have complex grade radar facilities in the next few years. The Chief of Air Staff, Air Chief Marshall, Fali Homi Major while delivering the Air Chief Marshall L M Katre Memorial Lecture in Bangalore said that the IAF has already redesigned its training patterns and most of its inventory will be upgraded or changed including a robust network of robust network of sensors.

On a query related to the steps the IAF had taken in the wake of heightened tension between India and Pakistan, he straightforwardly said, "We are ready to meet any situation," When asked about the possibility of a war-like situation on the Indo-Pak border, he made his position clear as a simple prosecutor who carries out orders of the authorities.

On modernisation plans, he said induction of Jaguars, MIG-27s, MIG-29s and Sukhois with upgraded avionics have been accelerated. He further mentioned that the Inter-Governmental agreements for design and development of fifth generation fighter aircraft has been concluded and the light Combat Aircraft (LCA) Programme has gained momentum. The initial operations are expected to start by 2010-2011.

The first flight of the Light Combat Helicopter is likely by May-June, while technical evaluation of the medium Multi Role Combat Aircraft (MMCA) had been completed. The MMCA would go for test trials by April-May. IAF would soon commence work on upgrading AN-32 aircraft with better avionics, Major said. He, further informed that India is expecting 70-80 tonne aircraft very soon as it is in talks with Russia for supply of aircraft.

Approval for four more Embraer jets has been secured and efforts were on to get more to strengthen air defense, he said. Major said that IAF is trying the most for the attack helicopters which are supposed to be the best in the world, 38 ALH (Advanced light helicopters) and also 12 VVIP helicopters. Contracts to upgrade 30 airfields also have to be signed soon. He stressed the need of public-private partnership to boost production, which would result in lesser dependence on foreign equipment. Major said that the IAF authorities have decided that all the projects entered into will be turnkey projects. It would take up 30 airfields for infrastructure upgrade in the first phase, each of which would have an 11,000 feet runway. Major payed tribute to Katre by recalling his able leadership under which prestigious products like LCA and ALH have originated.(ANI)

INDIAN MRCA COMPETITION

The Indian Air Force Medium Multi-Role Combat Aircraft (MMRCA) Competition, commonly known as the MRCA Tender, is an ongoing competition to supply the Indian Air Force with 126 Multi-Role Combat Aircraft. The Defence Ministry has allocated Rs. 42000 crore for the purchase of these aircraft (Approx. 10.5 billion USD). There are six aircraft competing for this multi-billion dollar contract, which has been touted as India's single largest defence deal ever. These represent some of the latest combat aircraft being developed or fielded today.

INDIAN AIR FORCE

The Indian Air Force is the air-arm of the Armed Forces of India and has the primary responsibility of conducting aerial warfare, defending the Indian airspace, conducting strategic strikes inside enemy territory and providing aerial cover to ground troops. It was established on October 8, 1932 and is the fourth largest air force in the world, with a strength of 1,322 aircraft, including 625 combat aircraft and 305 helicopters. and presently operates a total of 42 squadrons.

Most of the IAF's 625 fighter jets are of Soviet/Russian origin. These include the MiG-21 Fishbed, MiG-27 Flogger-D, MiG-29 Fulcrum as well as the Sukhoi Su-30MKI Flanker-H. Added to these are the British SEPECAT Jaguar and French Mirage 2000 aircraft, produced under license. The MiG-21 forms the backbone of the IAF, which currently operates more than 230 of the type. These aircraft were acquired in the late 1960s and early '70s, and performed well in the 1971 Indo-Pakistan War. However, they have been aging, and have mostly become obsolete. Added to that is a poor safety record, which has made their replacement paramount for the Indian Air Force.

BACKGROUND

Sanctioned strength

The Indian Air Force plays a crucial role in securing Indian airspace and also in India's power projection in South Asia and Indian Ocean. Therefore, modernizing and expanding the Indian Air Force is a top priority for the Indian government. The minimum sanctioned strength of the IAF is 39.5 squadrons of combat aircraft, with a healthy level of 45 squadrons. [*A combat squadron in the IAF usually consists of 18 aircraft in service with another 3-4 in maintenance*] However, this level was achieved only in the mid-80s, with the acquisition of the Mirage 2000s, MiG-29s and Jaguars. In addition, at the time, most IAF aircraft were comparatively new, being less than 10 years old. Most of the older aircraft would have become obsolete by the mid-90s, with the rest needing replacement by 2010.

However, these aircraft were not replaced, for reasons mentioned below, which led to frequent crashes and attrition losses. The Force levels fell to 33 combat squadrons: a big worry for the IAF. Further phasing out of aircraft has meant that the IAF now operates only 31 fighter squadrons, which represents a serious depletion of force levels. This has led to a threat to India's traditional air-superiority over Pakistan, and further erosion of its position as compared to China, another Asian power. The ratios of aircraft has fallen from 2.79:1 to around 1.30:1 and could potentially fall further to 1.15:1 in the coming years. For the first time, the PAF would be inducting BVR missiles with its purchase of 500 AIM-120C5 AMRAAM missiles. Pakistan's acquisition of 36 F-16C/D Block 52+ aircraft from the U.S., and future JF-17 Thunder production, along with China's much bigger and modernizing air force, has led to further concern from the IAF.

Experts estimate that for India to exert influence over South Asia and the Indian Ocean region, it would require at least 60 squadrons of aircraft performing multi-role combat, deep penetration strike, air superiority, air defence, reconnaissance and electronic warfare tasks. However, the IAF presently operates only 42 aircraft squadrons, making the acquisition of new aircraft all the more vital.Fact | date=June 2007

"Flying coffins"

Due to budgetary constraints — specifically, the economic problems in the early 90s — the refurbishment of old planes and purchase of new ones was halted. Added to this was the Disintegration of the Soviet Union, which led to severe shortage of aircraft spares, which rendered many of them unserviceable. By this time, most of the MiG-21s were reaching the end of their service life and needed to be phased out or upgraded.

This led to frequent crashes of aircraft, cannibalization of aircraft and low serviceability, all of which contributed to the rapid decline of the Force levels. The safety record of the IAF's MiG-21s and other older aircraft has raised concern in the Indian Parliament and media, leading to the aircraft sometimes being referred to in the media as "flying coffins". The age of the MiG-21s, and their safety record, led the Public Accounts Committee of Parliament to call for their immediate phase out in a March 2002 report. However, the Chief of Air Staff, Air

Chief Marshal S. Krishnaswamy and Air Chief Marshal A.Y. Tipnis had stated that the aircraft were "fit to fly". Besides the raw age of the aircraft, their maintenance and upkeep had been called into question.

One source estimates that in the nine years from 1993 to 2002, the IAF lost over 100 pilots in 283 accidents. Around 50 pilots have been lost in MiG-21s alone. During its service life, the IAF has lost at least 116 aircraft to crashes (not including those lost in combat), with 81 of those occurring since 1990. This, predictably, led to much anguish and criticism among the Indian public and media, who, in the aftermath of the Kargil War, were much more concerned with the state of the Armed Forces and the emotive issue of loss of pilots.

The attrition was stemmed to some extent by extensive upgrade programs on the MiG-21 ("bis" upgrade), MiG-27, Jaguar ("DARIN I" upgrade) and other aircraft in the mid-90s. However, by the early 2000s, this crash rate had risen again, partly because of low-quality spares used, insufficient pilot training, inefficient aircraft health appraisals, all which led to many unsafe aircraft being allowed to fly with old airframes and engines.

An aggressive program of upgrades was initiated. The MiG-21bis aircraft have been upgraded to MiG-21 Bison levels (128 aircraft will be upgraded to that standard), Jaguars to "DARIN II" standards, and Mirage 2000s and MiG-27s were also upgraded. Along with that, a rigorous process of maintenance and quality control was initiated to ensure airworthiness. Older obsolete aircraft were also phased out. These steps led to the a drastic drop in accident rates, comparable to most other air forces. However, by this time, the Force levels had fallen drastically, which engendered the need to acquire new, modern aircraft.

Pilot training

Other sources blame the accident rate on failures in the pilot training system, due to lack of Advanced Jet Trainers (AJTs). This had led to trainee pilots jumping directly from subsonic HAL Kiran aircraft to the unforgiving and challenging Mach-2-capable MiGs. This was exacerbated by severe delays in the acquisition of BAe Hawk 132 AJTs. This deal for 66 AJTs has been one of the most protracted negotiations in aviation history. Although the IAF projected the requirement in 1984, the deal was signed only in March 2004. This led to widespread criticism of the Ministry of Defence by the public and the Defence staff alike. The IAF will receive 24 aircraft directly from BAE Systems starting in 2007 and another 42 will be assembled by Hindustan Aeronautics Limited (HAL) during 2008-10.

Added to this was the loss of valuable MiG-21UM trainer jets, which denied pilots enough training on the MiG-21. The loss of these aircraft in crashes also claimed the lives of highly-skilled instructors as well.

LCA Delayed

The IAF had initially planned to replace the MiG-21 fleet with the indigenously-built HAL Tejas (LCA) aircraft by 2006. The project was crippled in the early 90s (1991-1993) due to the weak Indian economy which led to a fund crunch. The liberalization policies of Dr. Manmohan Singh meant that funds were needed elsewhere. This delayed the program further.

Once full funding was restarted in June 1993, the schedule was revised to induction by 2003. However, the target could not be met due to developmental delays and U.S. sanctions following the Pokhran II nuclear tests, which blocked the development of the FBW Flight Control System and the delivery of GE F404 engines — both crucial components of the aircraft. This meant that the IAF would have to take other steps to stem the decline in numbers. The Tejas finally flew on January 4, 2001. Induction is expected to commence only in 2010.

Requirements

The IAF projected a requirement for about 126 aircraft in 2001, when the strength was at 39.5 squadrons (down from 45). There is an option for an additional 74 aircraft. [*Chief of Air Staff Air Chief Marshal F.H. Major said there was no proposal at the moment to increase the order to 200 aircraft, but "a review after induction, based on cost-benefit analysis, is of course possible in future."*] Initial requirements appeared to be for a 20-ton class fighter aircraft with the Mirage 2000 as the strongest contender. However, the 20-ton MTOW limit requirement has reportedly been removed. Also, considering the delays in the bidding, it is very likely that the LCA would be ready for induction by then. The IAF then would require replacements for its frontline strike aircraft like the MiG-27 and Jaguar, which would be retiring by 2015. India's indigenous Medium Combat Aircraft and the Indo-Russian joint 5th-generation aircraft projects are unlikely to be ready before 2020, thus providing the need for a replacement. Thus, the MRCA tender is more likely to be a medium-weight aircraft (MTOW of ~24 tons). This has led to a renaming of the competition as the Medium Multi-Role Combat Aircraft (MMRCA) tender.

The Indian government has officially stated that it would require 100% Transfer of Technology (ToT), as well as license manufacturing permission for the aircraft. It has stated that the first squadron of aircraft will be bought directly from the manufacturer, while later versions will be built in India, by HAL, initially from kits, and later, on its own.

The IAF was keen on buying the Mirage 2000-5, after it was impressed by the Mirage 2000's capabilities during the Kargil War. However, due to the upcoming manufacture of the Dassault Rafale and lack of orders, the Mirage production lines were to be closed down. French officials stated that they could be kept open if India had made a firm commitment. However, the Indian Government decided to go in for a multi-vendor tendering process. Requests for Information (RFI) were issued in 2004. The RFIs were initially sent to four vendors: Dassault Mirage 2000-5 Mk.2, Lockheed Martin F-16C/D, Saab JAS 39 Gripen and Mikoyan MiG-29OVT.

Due to the tendering process and delay in issuing the RFIs, Dassault decided to remove the Mirage 2000-5 from the bidding process and enter the Rafale in its place. The MiG-35 was entered in place of the prototype MiG-29OVT. Eurofighter Typhoon also expressed interest in entering the bidding, and have entered their aircraft into the competition. With the signing of the July 2005 Indo-U.S. nuclear deal, the F/A-18E/F Super Hornet also joined the tendering. The U.S. offered its latest AN/APG-79 AESA radar as well.

Bidders

Six aircraft are competing for the order-the Saab Gripen, Eurofighter Typhoon, Dassault Rafale, Mikoyan MiG-35 and the American F-16IN and F/A-18IN (a version of the Super Hornet).

Up to now, Mikoyan and Dassault have been regular suppliers of aircraft for the Indian Air Force and in terms of transfers of technology, licensed production in India, personnel training, supply of spare parts, maintenance and upgrading. IAF pilots and technicians are familiar with earlier aircraft from those two aircraft manufacturers, and would need minimal retraining. Infrastructural and logistical support for maintenance and spares would also be easier for these aircraft compared to the unfamiliar Gripen, Typhoon, F-16 and F/A-18.

Dassault Rafale

The Dassault Rafale is a French twin-engined delta-wing agile multi-role fighter aircraft designed and built by Dassault Aviation. The Rafale was brought in as the replacement for the Mirage 2000-5 that was originally a competitor for the tender, after the production lines for the Mirage closed down, as well as the entry of much more advanced aircraft into the competition. The Rafale has the advantage of being logistically and operationally similar to the Mirage 2000, which the IAF already operates, and has used with great success during the Kargil War.

This would require fewer changes in the existing infrastructure of the IAF, which in turn will reduce cost. Moreover, the Rafale type, at 30,000 EUR per hour, is cheaper to fly than any of its competitors.

Dassault has also offered to fit the Kaveri engine into the Rafale, which, if chosen, which would greatly improve commonality with the Tejas aircraft that will enter service into the IAF by 2010. Concerns have been raised about cost issues, the level of ToT that France would be willing to provide, as well as potential sales to Pakistan, which has also expressed interest in the Rafale. However, no such jets have been sold to Pakistan, and India and France have recently agreed to "go beyond a buyer-seller relationship".

EUROFIGHTER TYPHOON

The Eurofighter Typhoon is a twin-engine multi-role canard-delta strike fighter aircraft, designed and built by a consortium of European aerospace manufacturers through Eurofighter GmbH. For the Indian tender, EADS has been leading the contract negotiations, although there have been reports that India has requested that BAE Systems take over contract negotiations.

Eurofighter is offering the Tranche-3 Typhoon for the Indian requirement, equipped with the E-Captor (CAESAR) AESA radar. EADS has invited India to become a "partner" of the Eurofighter Typhoon programme if the Typhoon wins the contract, and will be given technological and development participation in future tranches of the Typhoon.

Lockheed Martin F-16IN

India initially sent the RFI for a F-16C/D Block 52+ configuration aircraft. On January 17, 2008, Lockheed Martin offered a customized version of the F-16, the F-16IN for the Indian MMRCA contract. The F-16IN, which is similar to the F-16 Block 60, will be a 4.5 generation aircraft. Lockheed Martin has stated that it will be the most advanced F-16 variant developed. It will be more advanced than the F-16 Block 52s that the Pakistan Air Force has acquired. Another factor that will play in its favour is its low price at $29 mn per plane.

Lockheed Martin has described the F-16IN as "the most advanced and capable F-16 ever." Based closely on the F-16E/F Block 60 as supplied to the UAE, the features on the F-16IN include:Lockheed Martin.

* Conformal Fuel Tanks (CFTs)-This will give the F-16IN a combat range of 1700 km with 1500 kg weapons load.
* A Northrop Grumman AN/APG-80 AESA (active electronically scanned array) radar. This is the same radar in service on the F-16 Block 60s in service in UAE.
* General Electric F110-132A engine with 143 kN full reheat thrust with FADEC Controls.

* Electronic warfare suites and infra-red searching.
* Advanced all-color glass cockpit.
* Helmet-mounted cueing system.

Lockheed Martin has offered to sell India the F-35 Lightning II aircraft in the future, as replacements, if the F-16 is chosen. However, some reports indicate that the Indian Air Force is not too keen on buying the F-16, since the Pakistan Air Force already operates the same type, and, having had exercises along with F-16s of the USAF, RSAF and other air forces. The capabilities of the F-16 appear to be similar to the Mirage 2000s that the IAF currently operates. The F-16 is also more prone to pilot errors than the Mirage 2000H, which would also work against the F-16., "Collected news about IAF and MRCA tender from Various news sources during March-April 2005".]

BOEING F/A-18E/F SUPER HORNET

The U.S. Navy operates over 340 F/A-18E/F Super Hornets (with 411 on order), and is presently the only user of the aircraft. Australia is buying 24 F/A-18Fs, and Boeing is trying to gain other contracts as well.Boeing,, Boeing, 24 April 2008. Accessed 26 April 2008] The MMRCA contract represents a prime opportunity for U.S. defence companies to gain a foothold in the Indian defence market, which is estimated to be about $100 billion USD in the next 10 years. Initially, the Request for Information (RFI) was not issued to Boeing, which decided to field the Super Hornet. The U.S. Government allowed Boeing to participate in the RFI, and later gave permission for RFP as well. However, any sale of aircraft will need to be approved by the U.S. Congress.

Initial reactions within the IAF were enthusiastic, although there were apprehensions of support issues in case of future sanctions. There were concern over the availability of the Super Hornet's APG-79 AESA radar, but export of the radar has been approved by the U.S. government. Although it is expected that there would be some restrictions. In particular, Boeing has refused to provide Transfer of Technology (ToT) for these radars.fact Boeing has proposed joint manufacture of the jets with Indian partners. It also plans to offset the cost by setting up a US$100 million maintenance and training hub in Nagpur.

This is the first time the Super Hornet has been offered for production in a foreign country. On 14 February 2008, Boeing and Tata Industries agreed to form a joint-venture company. The new entity, which will be formed in June 2008, will supply components for Boeing military aircraft, including the Super Hornet.

On 24 April 2008, Boeing (through the U.S. Embassy in New Delhi) submitted their 7000-page proposal to the Ministry of Defence, before the April 28 deadline for the submission for proposals. The Super Hornet variant being offered to India, the F/A-18IN, is based on the F/A-18E/F model flown by the U.S. Navy and currently being built for the Royal Australian Air Force (RAAF). Raytheon's APG-79 AESA radar is being offered on the aircraft. Delivery of the first F/A-18IN Super Hornets can begin approximately 36 months after contract award. In order to satisfy its offset requirements, Boeing has signed long-term partnership agreements with Hindustan Aeronautics Limited (HAL), Tata Industries, and Larson and Toubro, who will play a significant role in production and assembly of the aircraft.

Saab Gripen

The Saab JAS 39 Gripen ("Griffin" or "Gryphon") is a fighter aircraft manufactured by the Swedish aerospace company Saab. The aircraft is in service with the Swedish, Czech, Hungarian and the South African air forces, and has been ordered by the Royal Thai Air Force. The Gripen was one of the aircraft that the IAF sent the Request for Information. The Gripen participated at Aero India 2007, where JAS 39C (single seater) and JAS 39D (two-seater) variants were brought. Gripen International is offering the Gripen IN, a version of the Gripen NG (Next Generation) for India's competition., *Gripen International, 28 April 2008.*] The Gripen NG has increased fuel capacity, more powerful powerplant, higher payload, upgraded avionics and other improvements.

Mikoyan MiG-35

The Mikoyan MiG-35 (NATO reporting name Fulcrum-F) is the production version of the latest MiG-29 and incorporates mature development of the MiG-29M/M2 and MiG-29K/KUB technology, such as glass cockpit and fly-by-wire technology. The IAF already operates 65 MiG-29s, and the Navy has ordered 16 MiG-29Ks for its aircraft carrier "INS Vikramaditya" (formerly "Admiral Gorshkov").

Russia unveiled the MiG-35 at Aero India 2007 in Bangalore, amid Moscow's keen interest to sell these planes to India. This was the first time that the final version of the MiG-35 was publicly displayed at an international air show, and thus, generated a great deal of interest. Since the IAF already has maintenance and upgrade facilities for the MiG-29, this would mean that the plane could be brought into service with a minimum of expenditure on infrastructure. Added to that is Russia's willingness to give full ToT, as well as customization for the IAF,Fact|date=May 2008 as seen with the Su-30MKI; in addition to the continued support for equipment in the event of a international embargo. However, Russian product support, esp. for the MiG-29 fleet, has been inadequate.

Additionally, buying the MiG-35 would mean an almost total dependence on a single supplier for India's entire fighter fleet. Recent Russian demands for renegotiation of earlier contracts, the sale of RD-93 engines (a variant of the Klimov RD-33 that powers the Indian MiG-29s) to Pakistan for its JF-17 Thunder aircraft and concurrently supplying combat aircraft to China has also caused concern in New Delhi.

COMPARISON OF THE COMPETING AIRCRAFT

The Order is for 126 aircraft with the option to buy another 64 more. David Donald and Chris Pocock,, AINonline, 21 February 2008. Accessed 27 April 2008] While there were reports of the direct order being increased to 200, or split between two vendors, Former Chief of Air Staff of the IAF, Air Marshal S.P. Tyagi stated during Aero India 2007 that the number would remain the same, and would be sourced from a single vendor. The first squadron would be directly supplied by the vendor, while the rest would be manufactured under license in India by HAL. He stated however, that as the bidding progressed, this could change.

The Government of India has sanctioned approximately US$10 billion (Rs. 42,000 crore),, "Domain-b report from May-

2007"] with reports that another US$2 billion might be added to this. This is indicative of the high importance of the order to the respective vendors.

Offset clause

In 2005, in response to allegations of corruption in defence procurements, the Defence Ministry formulated the Defence Procurement Policy (DPP) 2005. According to the DPP, at least 30% of any order over Rs. 300 crores (~US$70 million) is to be sourced from Indian companies. This would enable Indian companies to gain expertise in defence-related technologies, as well as cycle back a large amount of any order back into the country.

This tender will be the first time that an Offset clause has been included in an Indian defence deal, which led to many changes in the RFP as the Offset policy and life-cycle costs needed to be improved and finalized. This led to delays in issuing the RFPs. The economic offset for the MMRCA tender was increased to 50% under the DPP 2006. The bidders must confirm the offset details in a separate proposal, to be submitted by 9 June 2008. This brings the value of offsets in the MMRCA deal to almost Rs. 25000 Crores (US$6 Bn).

Status

The issuing of RFPs was expected in June 2007. During Aero India 2007, Defence Minister Pranab Mukherjee had stated that the RFP would be issued by 31 March 2007. However, Air Marshal A.S. Tyagi, in his last press conference before he retired, had stated that there were delays in issuing the RFP. His successor, Air Marshal F.H. Major had said that the RFP would be issued by June. The delays were said to be due to new factors added into the RFP such as Total Life-cycle Costs as well as fine-tuning the Offset policy, under the new DPP 2005. The Total Life-cycle Cost has been introduced for the first time in Indian defence procurements, and has reportedly been a major source of the delay.

On 29 June, the Defence Acquisition Council (DAC), headed by the Defence Minister, cleared the process for the procurement of 126 aircraft. The 211-page RFP was approved for release to the respective bidders. On August 28, the RFP was released to the 6 bidding companies. The bidders had to give their Formal Proposals within six months from the release of the RFP, latest by March 3 2008.

However, some of the bidders asked for an extension of the deadline, citing complexity of the RFP. The deadline for submission of the proposals was then extended by a month. The Formal Proposals will have to be submitted by April 28 2008. The Proposals will then be technically evaluated to check for compliance with IAF's requirements and other RFP conditions. After that, field trials will be carried out to evaluate the performance. Finally, the Commercial Proposal of the vendors, short-listed after technical and field evaluations, will be examined and compared, and a winner announced.

After the winner is chosen, there will be further rounds of negotiation to decide the final price, as well as sensor suite and aircraft configuration, along with other factors, like offsets and maintenance. The first 18 aircraft (1 squadron) will come in a 'fly away' condition, while the remaining 108 will be manufactured in India under ToT. There have been fears that this process would take a few years at least, and getting the aircraft after that would take longer. It is reasonable to expect that the aircraft can be delivered by 2011 at the earliest. This might take longer for the Super Hornet, Rafale and Typhoon, considering their numbers on order.

THE SAGA OF INDIAN AIR FORCE : GLIMPSES INTO THE PAST

Indian Air Force (IAF) has air warriors in its ranks to fulfil the aspirations and the objectives reposed by the nation. History of IAF is replete with innumerable instances of unflinching commitment and dedication to the security and prosperity of our great country, written with the sweat and blood of the devoted air warriors.

Every citizen of our great nation is indebted to this great force in some form or the other, be it confronting the enemy or standing up to render timely help to its brethren in need, be it the earthquakes, floods or tsunamis. This article salutes the untiring and unflinching dedication to duty rendered by air warriors at all times. While conveying our sincere gratitude, we the IAF Medical Services, the medicos hope that we have been there to provide the healing touch that goes a long way in helping an air warrior become physically fitter and mentally stronger to face future adversities to protect our skies for all times to come.

BIRTH OF A FORCE TO RECKON WITH

The saga of the men in blue started from its inception as the Royal Indian Air Force (RIAF) on 8 October 1932. The RIAF had a strength of six RAF trained Indian officers and 19 *Havai Sepoys*, literally air soldiers. The young Air Force had an inventory comprising of four Westland Wapiti IIA Army Cooperation biplanes at Drigh Road as the "A" Flight nucleus of the planned No.1 (Army Co-operation) Squadron. From such humble beginnings to the IAF (the prefix Royal was dropped after India became a Republic) becoming the fourth largest Air Force in the world, in its platinum jubilee year, makes every Indian proud of the sentinels of the Indian skies.

The Founding Visionary

On 1 April 1954, Air Marshal Subroto Mukherjee OBE took over from Air Marshal Gerald Gibbs as the Chief of Air Staff of the Indian Air Force. At that time he was just about 43 years old. The immediate task of re-equipping and restructuring the Air Force with newer aircraft and equipment fell upon Mukherjee. With the first Indian Chief of Air Staff at its helm the IAF was destined for undiminished glory and unmatched greatness in the coming years. During his tenure, the Air Force inducted a variety of state of the art aircraft viz. Dassault Mystere, Hawker Hunter, BAe Canberra and Folland Gnat. Mukherjee took care to see that even the human resources planning and development received much attention to benefit the IAF personnel. His task was commendable for he had to deal with the post-independence nonviolence driven defence policy but it was his vision and foresight which has placed IAF where it is today.

The Saga of Valour and Courage

The air warriors have lived through a wonderful and exciting journey that has been etched by the valor and selfless sacrifice of many. It is the told and the untold stories of the heroes of the IAF, that makes this path so exciting and humbling for those who follow in their footsteps. Here is a glimpse into a few notable ones; the ones to miss out will only be because of paucity of space and not for the dearth of bravery and valour.

The Burma Campaign & Sqn Ldr Arjan Singh

The RIAF with its Lysanders, Wapitis and Audaxes flew umpteen number of low level dangerous missions to the Japanese bases in Thailand. For almost a month they provided the vital air cover for Rangoon harbour against the marauding Japanese.

In 1944, Sqn Ldr Arjan Singh led his Squadron against the Japanese during the Arakan Campaign. Flying close support missions during the crucial Imphal Campaign and later assisting the advance of the Allied Forces to Rangoon, Burma. For his role in successfully leading the squadron in combat, Sqn Ldr Arjan Singh received the Distinguished Flying Cross (DFC) in 1944.

He later commanded the first IAF Display Flight, flying Hawker Hurricanes, after the war and his flight toured all over the country for aerobatic displays. On 16 August 1947, he had the unique honour of leading the fly-past of over a hundred IAF aircraft over the Red fort. At the age of 44 years he was entrusted to lead the Air Force as its first Air Chief Marshal. Under his leadership the IAF saw its first modern combat, the war against Pakistan in 1965. In recognition of his services he was awarded the Padma Vibhushan after the war. In 2002 he was conferred with the rank of the Marshal of the Air, the only five star general of the IAF.

Independence & Partition: Baptism with Fire & Mehar Baba

The RIAF lost several of its permanent bases and other establishments as a result of the division of the country. The young divided nation did not have the breathing space to recover from the division of assets before the IAF was called to service. On 27 October 1947, No.12 Sqn was to accomplish the remarkable feat of air-lifting the 1st Sikh Regiment from Palam,

Delhi to the rough and dusty Srinagar airstrip without planning or reconnaissance as an initial response to the sizeable insurgent forces that were pouring across the border into Jammu and Kashmir. On 30 October 1947, the first Spitfires from the Advanced Flying School at Ambala reached Srinagar and were soon engaged in strafing the raiders beyond Pattan. Within a week, the Tempests of No. 7 Squadron were playing a decisive role in the battle of Shelatang which halted the forward momentum of the insurgents.

The indefatigable and indomitable spirit of IAF was exemplified by the we inspiring Air Cmde Mehar Singh MVC DSO, fondly called as 'Mehar Baba'. During those years he was in charge of the operations of the IAF, leading the 1st Operational Group.

His sorties to Poonch and Ladakh, when both these areas were in imminent danger of being run over by the insurgents are stuff of legends in the IAF. He was relentless in his Dakota and was the first to land at Leh, the highest air base in the world, accompanied by none other than commander of land forces in the Srinagar Valley sector, Major General KS Thimmayya, DSO, and his troops. The daring act of flying by Mehar Baba on previously uncharted route helped the Indian troops stop the invaders from isolating Ladakh. The fighting in Jammu and Kashmir continued for 15 months with intense IAF involvement throughout. The ceasefire eventually came into force on 01 January 1949. Despite active operations during this period, the reorganization and modernization of the Service continued unabated.

Congo Campaign 1960-62: IAF in aid of the United Nations

The IAF was committed to support United Nations (UN) operations in Congo (now Zaire) in 1961-62. Following an appeal by the U.N. for both troops and combat aircraft to restore law and order and maintain peace, six Canberra B(1) 58s of No.5 Squadron were flown from Agra to Central Africa. Operating from Leopoldville and Kamina, the Canberras destroyed the rebel air force, raided Katangan targets and provided the UN ground forces the vital long-range air support force.

Liberation of Goa 1961

Goa was under Portuguese occupation till 1961. The Portuguese refused to give up this colony inspite of repeated requests by the Indian Government, on behalf of the Goan people. India decided to deploy its forces in late 1961 after failure of prolonged negotiations to evict the Portuguese out. The IAF provided the support elements to a massive effort by the ground forces.

Air Vice Marshal Erlic Pinto, Air Officer Commanding in Chief (AOC-in-C) of the Western Air Command, IAF was the theater commander during the campaign to liberate Goa. The main staging airbases were Poona and Sambre. Poona hosted two Canberra Squadrons No.16 and No. 35 along with Hunter from No.17 and No.37 Squadrons.

The air power was first used on 18 December 1961. No.35 Squadron sent in a massive wave of 12 Canberra led by Wg Cdr NB Menon to attack Dabolim. The bombers dropped 63,000 lbs of bombs within a span of few minutes on Dabolim runway. The pilots took care not to bomb the terminals and the ATC. A second raid by eight Canberra of No.16 Squadron led by Wg Cdr Surinder Singh dropped more bombs on the runway area. In another strike, six Hunter of No.17 Sqn led by Sqn Ldr Jayawant Singh took off from Sambre and attacked the Wireless station at Bambolim. Attacking with a mixture of rockets and gun cannon ammunition, the station was soon left a smoldering wreck. The Army requested close support now and then which was supported by the Vampire of No. 45 Sqn. Shortly before the Portuguese surrender on the 19th, the Liberator of No. 6 Sqn flew over Marmagao dropping leaflets heralding the surrender. Daman sector saw about 14 sorties by Mystere of No. 1 Squadron flying from Santa Cruz, Bombay. Flying in pairs of two, the Mystere harassed Portuguese gun positions continuously throughout the day. Part of air efforts during the Goa Operations were directed at Diu, another small Portuguese enclave.

The Chinese Aggression 1962

The real test of IAF airlift capability came in October 1962, when open warfare erupted on the Sinolndian border in the

North-East. Between 20 October 1962 to 20 November 1962 there was extreme pressure on IAF's transport and helicopter units. The need was to airlift the troops and supplies to support the border posts virtually round the clock and at extreme altitudes. The helicopters constantly ran the gauntlet of Chinese small arms and anti-aircraft fire while landing at make-shift helipads in the mountains. Many notable feats were performed by the IAF during this conflict, including the operation of C-119Gs from airstrips 17,000 ft (5180m) above sea level in the Karakoram Himalayas, and air-lifting by An-12Bs of two troops of AMX-13 light tanks to Chushul, Ladakh, at a small airstrip located at 15,000 ft (4570m) above sea level.

Indo-Pak Conflict 1965

India was attacked on 1 September 1965 in the Chhamb sector by Pakistani forces, after years of mounting border tensions since independence. Pakistan had seized the initiative, having chosen the time and the place, besides enjoying the numerical superiority of both the armour and troops. This posed a grave threat to the Indian forces on the ground. IAF, responding to urgent requests from Army for air strikes against advancing Pakistani armour in the Chhamb-Jaurian sector, launched its Vampire FB Mk52 of No. 45 Sqn from a forward base at 1745 hours on the very first day of the conflict.

This was followed by strikes by the Mystere of Nos.3 and 31 Sqn from Pathankot. This effort halted the Pakistani armoured thrust. The IAF Gnat proved its mettle in shooting down several PAF Sabres in this sector, with the first aerial victories being notched by Nos. 23 and 9 Sqn. IAF Canberras raided major PAF bases at Sargodha and Chaklala at night, flying 200 counter air and interdiction missions during the war also to Akwal, Peshawar, Kohat, Chakjhumra and Risalwala. The virtuosity of the Hunter was amply demonstrated with Nos. 7, 20 and 27 Squadrons employed in counter-air as well as interdiction and close air support missions in the West, while No. 14 Squadron battled with PAF Sabres at Kalaikunda in the East.

The Mystere were extremely effective in the ground attack role, where their swaths of 55 mm rockets proved highly effective against armoured vehicles. The most outstanding operational success was enjoyed by the Gnat. The three Gnat squadrons provided the air defence mainstay by flying CAPs over most operational IAF bases as well as flying escort missions. Indeed, such was its success, particularly against the F-86, that it earned the appellation of "*Sabre Slayer*".

East Pakistan - Creation of Bangladesh 1971

The professional standards, capability and flexibility of the much expanded IAF was put to test in 1971. With the deteriorating political situation in East Pakistan, the IAF was alerted to the possibility of another armed conflict in early 1971. By November 1971, both Indian and Pakistan governments protested violations of their national airspace along the Western border, before the aerial conflict broke out on 22nd November, preceding full-scale war between India and Pakistan by 12 days.

At 1449 hours, four Pakistani Sabres strafed Indian and Mukti Bahini positions in the Chowgacha Mor area, and 10 minutes later, while engaged on a third strafing run, the Sabre were intercepted by four Gnats from No. 22 Sqn, a detachment of which was operating from Dum Dum Airport, Calcutta. During the ensuing melee, three of the Sabre were shot down and all the Gnats returned to base unscathed. Other aerial encounters followed over the next 10 days.

The IAF carried out some 4,000 sorties in the West from bases in Northern India, while in the East, another 1,978 sorties were flown. Throughout the conflict, the strategy was to maintain defensive postures on the Western and Northern fronts whilst undertaking lightning campaign in the East, the IAF established a highly credible serviceability rate exceeding 80 per cent. Mission emphasis throughout was on interdiction. IAF's primary tasks on the Western front were disruption of enemy communications, destruction of fuel and ammunition reserves, and prevention of concentration of ground forces so that no major offensive could be mounted against India while Indian forces were primarily engaged in the East.

The versatility of the MiG-21's was amply demonstrated in this war, with highly effective short range, precision attacks with 500 kg bombs on the PAF's air bases at Tezgaon and Kurmitola, while pin point 57 mm rocket attacks were carried out against key command centres in Dhaka.

The MiG-21 finally met its original adversary, the F-104 Starfighter, in air combat during the conflict and in all the four recorded cases of classic dog fights, the MiG-21 outclassed and out-fought the F-104. The first aerial victory was on 12 December 1971, when MiG-21FL of No. 47 Squadron shot down a PAF F-104 over the Gulf of Kutch.

This was followed by three more victories in quick succession on 17 December, when MiG-21FL of No. 29 Squadron escorting HF-24 Marut, shot down intercepting F-104s near Uttarlai in the Rajsthan desert in gun-missile encounters, while a third F-104, on an intruding mission, was shot down by another MiG 21FL of No.29 Squadron.

Param Vir Chakra-Fg Off Nirmal Jit Singh Sekhon

The Param Vir Chakra (PVC) is the highest gallantry award given to the Indian Armed Forces. Thus far only 21 PVC have been awarded with as many as 14 of these being posthumous. The IAF received its first Param Vir Chakra during the 1971 conflict.

This was awarded posthumously to Fg Off Nirmal Jit Singh Sekhon. Fg Offr Nirmal Jit Singh Sekhon was commissioned on 4 June 1967. During the 1971 Operations, Fg Off Sekhon was with No.18 *"Flying Bullets"* Squadron flying the Folland-Gnat fighter at Srinagar. In accordance with the international agreement dating back to 1948, no air defence aircraft could be based at Srinagar, until the outbreak of hostilities with Pakistan. Flying Officer Sekhon was, therefore, unfamiliar with the terrain and was not acclimatised to the altitude of Srinagar, especially with the bitter cold and biting winds of the Kashmir winter. Nevertheless, from the onset of the war, he and his colleagues fought successive waves of intruding Pakistani aircraft with valour and determination, maintaining the high reputation of the Gnat aircraft.

On the morning of 14 December 1971, Srinagar airfield was attacked by a wave of six enemy Sabre aircraft. Flying Officer Sekhon was on readiness duty at the time. However, he could not take off at once because of the clouds of dust raised by another aircraft which had just taken off. By the time the runway was fit for take-off, no fewer than six enemy aircraft were overhead, and strafing of the airfield was in progress. Nevertheless, inspite of the mortal danger of attempting to take off during an attack, and with all the odds against him, Flying Officer Sekhon took off and immediately engaged a pair of the attacking Sabre.

He succeeded in damaging two of the enemy aircraft. In the fight that followed, at tree top height, he all but held his own, but was eventually overcome by sheer weight of numbers. His aircraft crashed and he was killed.

Thus sacrificing himself for the defence of Srinagar, Flying Officer Sekhon achieved the objective of deterring the enemy from attack. The remaining enemy aircraft fled from the scene of battle without pressing home their attack against the town and the airfield. The sublime heroism, supreme gallantry, flying skill and determination, above and beyond the call of duty, displayed by Flying Officer Sekhon in the face of certain death, set new heights of bravery in the true Air Force traditions.

Operation Safed Sagar –The Kargil Heroics

Early in May 1999, the Indian Army discovered large scale infiltration by Pakistani soldiers across the LOC in the Indian territory in the desolate Kargil sector.

The operation to evict the mountain tops of the Pakistani army has now etched itself in living memory as 'Operation Vijay' and 'Operation Safed Sagar' (the IAF Campaign). IAF was called upon by the army to bamboozle the insurgents. Mi-17 helicopters, MiG-21,-27,-29 and Mirage 2000 were deployed. They provided battlefield close support, logistical supply and casualty evacuation along with the Army Aviation Units.

The mild winter in Jammu and Kashmir during 1998 enabled Pakistani Army regulars and mercenaries to infiltrate, and set up camps on the Indian Side of the Line of Control (LOC). The build-up of forces, unknown to Indian authorities at the time was to have a major impact on the IAF the following year as it fought to dislodge the enemy.

The battle in Kargil took place over some of the highest terrain in the world, where aircraft and weapons were limited in their effectiveness. Conventional targets like airfields, command and control centre and convoys did not exist.

Instead, the IAF were to be confronted with tents and fortified bunkers. The advance along the LOC was eventually to penetrate up to 10 Km in some areas along a line 200 Km long. All the ridges in the area were off-shoots of Mount K2 (8611 metres), the world's second tallest mountain or Nanga Parbat (8126 metres), both located on the Pakistan side. Because of the climatic conditions and wind directions, a large number of features are sheer cliffs on the Indian side with gradual gradients on the other.

Heights varied along the line, with a low of 2700 metres at Kargil, going up to 3400 metres in Dras and Tiger Hill being at 5000 metres. The area had no habitation and was covered in snow for most of the year. Strategically, the area could not be used as a launch pad for a major offensive, its sole importance being the heights and the threat to the strategic National Highway 1A.

IAF was limited in what could be used at such demanding altitudes. Mi-17 helicopters and MiGs were initially deployed for low level strike missions. The use of shoulder fired surface-to-air (SAM) missiles such as the Stingers by the enemy restricted the effective use of both helicopter and fighter due to hostile flying environment.

During the early part of operations IAF sacrificed two fighter and a Mi-17. This was the turning point in IAF's mission planning. It was decided that high altitude bombing by fighter aircraft, particularly precision bombing by Mirage 2000, was the best option. Mirage 2000 could operate at high altitude but did not have high altitude attack capability.

The aircraft which had already moved to forward ops location in its air defence role, thus had to be made ready for an offensive role. It has always been regarded as an air defence fighter with limited ground attack capability. Consequently it lacked certain resources such as bombs, hard-point pylons, tools, testers and ground crew experience in such matters. But the IAF personnel stood up to the challenge and ironed out most of the requirements for the redefined role of Mirage 2000, making twelve aircraft available at any given time for bombing missions. Each aircraft was configured with 12 bombs, 1 ventral fuel tank and 2 'Magic-2' Matra air-to-air missiles. The mission would meet up with fighter escorts to fly into the Indian side of Jammu and Kashmir, with MiG 29s providing top cover. The early attacks took place on Point 5140 near Tololing in the Dras Sector facilitating the Indian Army to recapture this position after fighting in tandem with continuous IAF Strikes.

Notable amongst approximately 200 plus attack missions flown by Mirage 2000 were air strikes on Muntho Dhalo, Tiger Hill and Point 4388 in the Drass Sector. During Kargil ops, three Officers and two airmen made the ultimate sacrifice for the nation. The IAF was awarded two Vir Chakras and 23 Vayusena Medals for the valour and courage shown by air warriors.

6

Types of Aircraft in Indian Air Force

The Indian Air Force, often abbreviated as the IAF with over 1,300 aircraft is the world's fourth largest air force after the United States Air Force, Russian Air Force and China's People's Liberation Army Air Force. The Indian Air Force has aircraft of British, French and Russian (erstwhile Soviet) origins. However, Russian aircraft dominate its inventory. HAL produces some of the Russian and British aircraft in India under license. The exact number of aircraft in service with the Indian Air Force cannot be determined with precision from open sources. Various reliable sources provide notably divergent estimates for a variety of high-visibility aircraft. The IAF currently operates approximately 363 fighter aircraft, over 224 ground-attack/bomber aircraft, 740 non-combat aircraft as well as approximately 135 UAVs. The following is a list of aircraft that have served in or are in service with the IAF, for aircraft programmes still under development refer to Future of the Indian Air Force.

MIKOYAN-GUREVICH MIG-21

The Mikoyan-Gurevich MiG-21 is a supersonic jet fighter aircraft, designed by the Mikoyan-Gurevich Design Bureau in the Soviet Union. It was popularly nicknamed "balalaika", from the aircraft's planform-view resemblance to the Russian stringed musical instrument or *o³ówek* by Polish pilots due to the shape of its fuselage. Early versions are considered second-generation jet fighters, while later versions are considered to be third-generation jet fighters. Some 50 countries over four continents have flown the MiG-21, and it still serves many nations a half-century after its maiden flight. The fighter made aviation records. At least by name, it is the most-produced supersonic jet aircraft in aviation history and the most-produced combat aircraft since the Korean War, and it had the longest production run of a combat aircraft (1959 to 1985 over all variants).

Development

Development of what would become the MiG-21 began in the early 1950s, when Mikoyan OKB finished a preliminary design study for a prototype designated Ye-1 in 1954. This project was very quickly reworked when it was determined that the planned engine was underpowered; the redesign led to the second prototype, the Ye-2. Both these and other early prototypes featured swept wings—the first prototype with delta wings as found on production variants was the Ye-4. The Ye-4 made its maiden flight on 16 June 1955 and made its first public appearance during the Soviet Aviation Day display at Moscow's Tushino Airport in July 1956. The MiG-21 was the first successful Soviet aircraft combining fighter and interceptor characteristics in a single aircraft. It was a lightweight fighter, achieving Mach 2 with a relatively low-powered afterburning turbojet, and is thus comparable to the American F-104 Starfighter and F-5 Freedom Fighter and the French Dassault Mirage III. Its basic layout was used for numerous other Soviet designs; delta-winged aircraft included Su-9 interceptor and the fast E-150 prototype from MiG bureau while the mass-produced successful front fighter Su-7 and Mikoyan's I-75 experimental interceptor combined a similar fuselage shape with swept-back wings. However, the characteristic layout with the shock cone and front air intake did not see widespread use outside the USSR and finally proved to have limited development potential, mainly because of the very small space available for the radar.

Like many aircraft designed as interceptors, the MiG-21 had a short range. This was not helped by a design defect where the center of gravity shifted rearwards once two-thirds of the fuel had been used. This had the effect of making the plane uncontrollable, resulting in an endurance of only 45 minutes in clean condition. The issue of the short endurance and low fuel capacity of the MiG-21F, PF, PFM, S/SM and M/MF variants—though each had a somewhat greater fuel capacity than its predecessor—led to the development of the MT and SMT variants. These had a range increase of 250 km (155 mi) compared to the MiG-21SM, but at the cost of worsening all other performance figures (such as a lower service ceiling and slower time to altitude).

The delta wing, while excellent for a fast-climbing interceptor, meant any form of turning combat led to a rapid loss of speed. However, the light loading of the aircraft could mean that a climb rate of 235 m/s (46,250 ft/min) was possible with a combat-loaded MiG-21bis, not far short of the performance of the later F-16A. Given a skilled pilot and capable missiles, it could give a good account of itself against contemporary fighters. It was replaced by the newer variable-geometry MiG-23 and MiG-27 for ground support duties. However, not until the MiG-29 would the Soviet Union ultimately replace the MiG-21 as a maneuvering dogfighter to counter new American air superiority types.

The MiG-21 was exported widely and continues to be used. The aircraft's simple controls, engine, weapons, and avionics were typical of Soviet-era military designs. The use of a tail with the delta wing aids stability and control at the extremes of the flight envelope, enhancing safety for lower-skilled pilots; this in turn enhanced its marketability in exports to developing countries with limited training programs and restricted pilot pools. While technologically inferior to the more advanced fighters it often faced, low production and maintenance costs made it a favorite of nations buying Eastern Bloc military hardware. Several Russian, Israeli and Romanian firms have begun to offer upgrade packages to MiG-21 operators, designed to bring the aircraft up to a modern standard, with greatly upgraded avionics and armaments.

Due to the lack of available information, early details of the MiG-21 were often confused with those of the similar Sukhoi fighters also under development. *Jane's All the World's Aircraft 1960–1961* describes the "Fishbed" as a Sukhoi design, and uses an illustration of the Su-9 'Fishpot'.

Operational history

India

In 1961, the Indian Air Force (IAF) opted to purchase the MiG-21 over several other Western competitors because the Soviet Union offered India full transfer of technology and rights for local assembly. In 1964, the MiG-21 became the first supersonic fighter jet to enter service with the IAF. Due to limited induction numbers and lack of pilot training, the IAF MiG-21 played a limited role in the Indo-Pakistani War of 1965. However, the IAF gained valuable experience while operating the MiG-21 for defensive sorties during the war. The positive feedback from IAF pilots during the 1965 war prompted India to place more orders for the fighter jet and also invest heavily in building the MiG-21's maintenance infrastructure and pilot training programs. By 1969, India had acquired more than 120 MiG-21s from the Soviet Union.

Safety record

The safety record of the IAF's MiG-21s has raised concern in the Indian Parliament and media, leading to the aircraft sometimes being referred to in the IAF as a "flying coffin". One source estimates that in the nine years from 1993 to 2002, the IAF lost over 100 pilots in 283 accidents. During its service life, the IAF has lost at least 116 aircraft to crashes (not including those lost in combat), with 81 of those occurring since 1990.

Indo-Pakistani War of 1971

The expansion of IAF MiG-21 fleet marked a growing India-Soviet Union military partnership which enabled India to field a formidable air force to counter Chinese and Pakistani threats. The capabilities of the MiG-21 and the skills of its Indian pilots were soon put to the test during the Indo-Pakistani War of 1971. During the war, the MiG-21s played a crucial role in giving the IAF complete air superiority over vital points and areas in the western theater of the conflict.

The 1971 war witnessed the first supersonic air combat in the subcontinent when an Indian MiG-21FLs shot down a PAF F-104 Starfighter with its GSh-23 twin-barrelled 23 mm cannon. By the time the hostilities came to an end, the IAF MiG-21s had shot down four PAF F-104s, two PAF F.6, one PAF F-86 and one PAF C-130 Hercules. According to Western military analysts, the MiG-21s had clearly "won" the much anticipated air combat between the MiG-21 and the F-104 Starfighter. Because of the formidable performance of the MiG-21s, several nations, including Iraq, approached India for MiG-21 pilot training. By the early 1970s, more than 120 Iraqi pilots were being trained by the Indian Air Force.

Kargil War and Atlantique Incident

It was also used as late as 1999 in the Kargil War, in which one Indian Air Force MiG-21 was shot down by a Pakistani hand-held "Stinger" surface-to-air missile. The MiG-21's last known kill took place in 1999 during the Atlantique Incident, when two MiG-21 aircraft of the Indian Air Force intercepted and shot down an Breguet Atlantique reconnaissance aircraft of the Pakistani Navy with the R-60MK (AA-8 Aphid) air-to-air missile.

MIKOYAN MIG-29

The Mikoyan MiG-29 is a 4th-generation jet fighter aircraft designed in the Soviet Union for an air superiority role. Developed in the 1970s by the Mikoyan design bureau, it entered service with the Soviet Air Force in 1983, and remains in use by the Russian Air Force as well as in many other nations. The NATO name "Fulcrum" was unofficially used by Soviet pilots in service. The MiG-29, along with the Sukhoi Su-27, were developed to counter new American fighters such as the McDonnell Douglas F-15 Eagle, and the General Dynamics F-16 Fighting Falcon.

Development

In 1969 the existence of the United States Air Force's "F-X" program, which would result in the McDonnell Douglas F-15 Eagle, became public knowledge. At the height of the Cold War, a Soviet response was necessary to avoid the possibility of a new American fighter becoming a serious technological advantage over existing Soviet fighters, thus the development of a new air superiority fighter became a priority. The Soviet General Staff issued a requirement for a *Perspektivnyy*

Frontovoy Istrebitel (*PFI*, translating directly as "Perspective Frontline Fighter", roughly "Advanced Frontline Fighter"). Specifications were extremely ambitious, calling for long range, good short-field performance (including the ability to use austere runways), excellent agility, Mach 2+ speed, and heavy armament. The aerodynamic design for the new aircraft was largely carried out by the Russian aerodynamics institute TsAGI in collaboration with the Sukhoi design bureau.

However, in 1971 Soviet studies determined the need for different types of fighters. The PFI program was supplemented with the *LPFI* (*Perspektivnyy Lyogkiy Frontovoy Istrebitel*, or "Advanced Lightweight Tactical Fighter") program; the Soviet fighter force was planned to be approximately 33% PFI and 67% LPFI. PFI and LPFI paralleled the USAF's decision that created the "Lightweight Fighter" program and the General Dynamics F-16 Fighting Falcon and Northrop YF-17. The PFI fighter was assigned to Sukhoi, resulting in the Sukhoi Su-27, while the lightweight fighter went to Mikoyan. Detailed design work on the resultant Mikoyan *Product 9*, designated MiG-29A, began in 1974, with the first flight taking place on 6 October 1977. The pre-production aircraft was first spotted by United States reconnaissance satellites in November of that year; it was dubbed *Ram-L* because it was observed at the Zhukovsky flight test center near the town of Ramenskoye. Early Western speculations suggested that the Ram-L was very similar in appearance to the YF-17 and powered by afterburning Tumansky R-25 turbojets.

Despite program delays caused by the loss of two prototypes in engine-related accidents (third prototype on 15 June 1978 and the fifth prototype on 31 October 1980), the MiG-29B production version entered service in August 1983 at the Kubinka air base. State acceptance trials were completed in 1984, and deliveries began the same year to the Soviet Frontal Aviation.

The workload split between TPFI and LPFI became more apparent as the MiG-29 filtered into front line service with the Soviet Air Forces (Russian: *Voenno-Vozdushnye Sily* [VVS]) in the mid-1980s. While the heavy, long range Su-27 was tasked with the more exotic and dangerous role of deep air-to-air sweeps of NATO high-value assets, the smaller MiG-29 directly replaced the MiG-23 in the frontal aviation role. The MiG-29 was positioned relatively close to the front lines, tasked with providing local air superiority to advancing Soviet motorized army units. Rugged landing gear and protective intake grates meant the MiG-29 could operate from the damaged or under-prepared airstrips Soviet war planners expected to encounter during a rapid armored advance. The MiG-29 was also tasked with escort duties for local strike and interdiction air packages, protecting vulnerable ground attack aircraft from NATO fighters such as the F-15 and F-16. Frontal aviation MiG-29s would ensure Soviet ground forces could operate under a safe air umbrella, moving forward with the troops as they advanced.

In the West, the new fighter was given the NATO reporting name "Fulcrum-A" because the pre-production MiG-29A, which should have logically received this designation, remained unknown in the West at that time. The MiG-29B was widely exported in downgraded versions known as MiG-29B 9-12A and MiG-29B 9-12B (for Warsaw Pact and non-Warsaw Pact nations, respectively), with less capable avionics and no capability for delivering nuclear weapons. Total production was about 840 aircraft.

Improved versions

In the 1980s, Mikoyan developed the improved MiG-29S to use longer range R-27E and R-77 air-to-air missiles. It added a dorsal 'hump' to the upper fuselage to house a jamming system and some additional fuel capacity. The weapons load was increased to 4,000 kg (8,800 lb) with airframe strengthening. These features were included in new-built fighters and upgrades to older MiG-29s. Refined versions of the MiG-29 with improved avionics were fielded by the Soviet Union, but Mikoyan's multi-role variants, including a carrier-based version designated MiG-29K, were never produced in large numbers. In the post-Soviet era, MiG-29 development was influenced by the Mikoyan bureau's apparent lesser political clout than rival Sukhoi. Some more advanced versions are still being pursued for export, and updates of existing Russian aircraft are likely. New fighter versions called MiG-29M/M2 and MiG-29SMT have been developed. Furthermore, development of the MiG-29K carrier version has been resumed for the Indian Navy's INS *Vikramaditya* aircraft carrier.

The Soviet Union did not assign official names to most of its aircraft, although nicknames were common. Unusually, some Soviet pilots found the MiG-29's NATO reporting name, 'Fulcrum', to be a flattering description of the aircraft's intended purpose, and it is sometimes unofficially used in Russian service.

India

India was the first international customer of the MiG-29. The Indian Air Force (IAF) placed an order for more than 50 MiG-29s in 1980 while the aircraft was still in its initial development phase. Since its induction into the IAF in 1985, the aircraft has undergone a series of modifications with the addition of new avionics, sub-systems, turbofan engines and radars. The upgraded Indian version is known as *Baaz* (Hindi for *Hawk*) and forms a crucial component of the second-line offensive aircraft-fleet of the IAF after the Sukhoi Su-30MKI.

Indian MiG-29s were used extensively during the 1999 Kargil War in Kashmir by the Indian Air Force to provide fighter escort for Mirage 2000s, which were attacking targets with laser-guided bombs. According to Indian sources, MiG-29s from the IAF's No. 47 squadron (Black Archers) gained missile lock on two F-16s of the Pakistan Air Force (PAF) which were patrolling close to the border to prevent any incursions by Indian aircraft, but did not engage them because no official declaration of war had been issued. The Indian MiG-29s were armed with beyond-visual-range air-to-air missiles whereas the Pakistani F-16s were not.

The MiG-29's good operational record prompted India to sign a deal with Russia in 2005—2006 to upgrade all of its MiG-29s for US$888 million. Under the deal, the Indian MiGs were modified to be capable of deploying the R-77RVV-AE (AA-12 'Adder') air-to-air missile, also known as the *Amraamski*. The missiles had been successfully tested in October 1998 and were integrated into IAF's MiG-29s. IAF has also awarded the MiG Corporation another US$900 million contract to upgrade all of its 69 operational MiG-29s. These upgrades will include a new avionics fit, with the N-109 radar being replaced by a Phazatron

Zhuk-M radar. The aircraft is also being equipped to enhance beyond-visual-range combat ability and for air-to-air refuelling to increase endurance. In 2007, Russia also gave India's Hindustan Aeronautics Limited (HAL) a licence to manufacture 120 RD-33 series 3 turbojet engines for the upgrade. The upgrade will also include a new weapon control system, cockpit ergonomics, air-to-air missiles, high-accuracy air-to-ground missiles and "smart" aerial bombs. The first six MiG-29s will be upgraded in Russia while the remaining 63 MiGs will be upgraded at the HAL facility in India. India also awarded a multi-million dollar contract to Israel Aircraft Industries to provide avionics and subsystems for the upgrade.

In January 2004, the Indian Navy signed a contract for the delivery of 12 MiG-29K and 4 MiG-29KUB fighters which will be operated from INS *Vikramaditya*. The first MiG-29KUB manufactured for the Navy took to the skies in May 2008. The first four aircraft were delivered to India in February 2009.

In March 2009, the Indian Air Force expressed concern after 90 MiG-29s were grounded in Russia. After carrying out an extensive inspection, the IAF cleared all MiG-29s in its fleet in March 2009. In a disclosure in Parliament, Defence Minister A. K. Antony said the MiG-29 is structurally flawed in that it has a tendency to develop cracks due to corrosion in the tail fin. Russia has shared this finding with India, which emerged after the crash of a Russian Air Force MiG-29 in December 2008. "A repair scheme and preventive measures are in place and IAF has not encountered major problems concerning the issue," Antony said. Despite concerns of Russia's grounding, India sent the first six of its 78 MiG-29s to Russia for upgrades in 2008. The upgrade program will fit the MiGs with a phased array radar (PESA) and in-flight re-fuelling capability. In January 2010, India and Russia signed a US$1.2 billion deal under which the Indian Navy would acquire 29 additional MiG-29Ks, bringing the total number of MiG-29Ks on order to 45. The MiG-29K entered service with the Indian Navy on 19 February 2010. The upgrade of all IAF MiG-29 "Baaz" to latest MiG-29SMT standard is in process, which will include latest avionics, Zhuk-ME Radar, engine, weapon control systems etc., enhancing multi-role capabilities by many-fold.

SUKHOI SU-30MKI

The Sukhoi Su-30MKI (NATO reporting name: Flanker-H) is a variant of the Sukhoi Su-30 jointly-developed by Russia's Sukhoi Corporation and India's Hindustan Aeronautics Limited (HAL) for the Indian Air Force (IAF). It is a heavy class, long-range air superiority fighter which can also act as a multirole, strike fighter aircraft. The development of the variant started after India signed a deal with Russia in 2000 to manufacture 140 Su-30 fighter jets. The first Russian-made Su-30MKI variant was accepted into the IAF in 2002, while the first indigenously assembled Su-30MKI entered service with the IAF in 2004. In 2007, the IAF ordered 40 additional MKIs. As of July 2010, the IAF has 124 MKIs under active service with plans to have an operational fleet of 280 MKIs by 2015. The Su-30MKI is expected to form the backbone of the Indian Air Force's fighter fleet to 2020 and beyond.

The aircraft is tailor-made for Indian specifications and integrates Indian systems and avionics as well as French and Israeli subsystems. It has abilities similar to the Sukhoi Su-35 with which it shares many features and components.

Development

The Su-30MKI was jointly designed by Russia's Sukhoi Corporation and India's Hindustan Aeronautics Limited (HAL). The MKI's airframe evolved from that of the Sukhoi Su-27 while most of the avionics were developed by India.

The Su-30MKI is more advanced than the basic Su-30MK, the Chinese Su-30MKK, and the Malaysian Su-30MKM. The aircraft features state of the art avionics developed by Russia, India and Israel which includes display, navigation, targeting and electronic warfare systems. Other key avionics used in the aircraft were sourced from France and South Africa. It is also speculated that the passive phased array Radar Irbis-E could be added to the fighter jet by 2010. In 2004 India inked a deal with Russia to domestically produce the Novator K-100 missile for its Su-30MKI fighters. The Novator K-100 missile is designed to shoot down AWACS and other C4ISTAR aircraft whilst keeping the launch platform out of range of any fighters that might be protecting the target.

The United Aircraft Corporation (UAC) and HAL plan to integrate several features developed from the Fifth Generation Fighter Aircraft program into the Su-30MKI. These features include internal weapons carriage and radar absorbent material, Active Phased Array Radar, and enhancement of situational awareness by incorporating active electronically scanned transmit/receive arrays on the aircraft's wings and pumping up the defensive-aids suite by installing a combined radar/laser warning system and a missile approach warning system.

Although not initially designed to carry nuclear or strategic weapons, the Indian Air Force will receive 40 upgraded SU-30MKIs capable of carrying the BrahMos cruise missile possibly by 2012. In addition, there are also plans to integrate the nuclear-capable Nirbhay missile with the aircraft as well. In May 2010, India Today reported that Russia had won a large contract to upgrade 40 Su-30MKI fighters with new radars, onboard computers, electronic warfare systems and the ability to carry the BrahMos missile. The first two prototypes with the 'Super-30' upgrade will be delivered to the Indian Air Force in 2012, after which the same upgrades will be performed on the last batch consisting of 40 production aircraft. The exact value of the contract has yet to be disclosed however.

Procurement

In 1996, after 2 years of evaluation and negotiations, India decided to purchase Su-30MKI aircraft. India signed a US$1.462 billion deal with the Sukhoi Corporation on 30 November 1996 for the delivery of 50 Su-30 aircraft. These aircraft were to be delivered in five batches. The first batch were 8 Su-30MKs, the basic version of Su-30. The second batch were to be 10 Su-30Ks with French and Israeli avionics. The third batch were to be 10 Su-30MKIs featuring canard foreplanes. The fourth batch of 12 Su 30MKIs and final batch of 10 Su-30MKIs aircraft all were to have the AL-31FP turbofans.

In October 2000, a MoU (Memorandum of Understanding) was signed confirming the license production of 140+ Su-30MKIs and in December 2000, the deal was sealed at Russia's Irkutsk aircraft plant, with full technology transfer. The first Su-30MKIs from Nasik are to be delivered from 2004, with the original plan of carrying production up to 2017-18. However in November 2002, it was decided that the delivery schedule would be completed within ten years-by 2014-by increasing the annual rate of production from 10 to 14 aircraft annually.

An estimated 920 AL-31FP turbofans are to be manufactured at HAL's Koraput Division, while the mainframe and other accessories are to be manufactured at HAL's Divisions in Lucknow and Hyderabad. Final integration of the aircraft and its test flight are to be carried out at HAL's Nasik Division. The MKI production was planned to be done in four phases: Phase I, II, III and IV respectively.

In 2007 another order of 40 Su-30MKIs have been made. In 2009, India planned to acquire 230 Su-30-MKIs. HAL has been directed to end the production of 140 of the original 230 jets under transfer of technology by 2015, instead of the originally scheduled 2017-2018.

In 2008, Samtel HAL Display Systems (SHDS), a joint venture between Samtel Display Systems and HAL won a contract to develop and manufacture multi-function avionics displays for the MKI.. A Helmet Mounted Sight & Display system-Topsight-I, based on technology from Thales and developed by SHDS will be integrated on the Su-30MKI in the next upgrade.

As of March 2010, sources in the Indian Defense Ministry announced that a contract for 42 more Su-30MKI was in the final phases. In June 2010, it was reported that the Cabinet Committee on Security had cleared the 15,000 crore (US$3.26 billion) deal and that the 42 aircraft would be in service by 2018. By August 2010 the number of aircraft had shrunk to 40 and the cost increased to $4.3 billion or $102 million each, comparable in cost to the Lockheed Martin F-35 Lightning II, but lacking in features such as AESA radar or stealth.

HAL also expects that total indigenisation of the SU-30MKI program will be in 2010. V. Balakrishnan, general manager of the Aircraft Manufacturing Division stated that "HAL will achieve 100 per cent indigenisation of the Sukhoi aircraft — from the production of raw materials to the final plane assembly,".

Design

Airframe

The Su-30MKI is a highly integrated twin-finned aircraft. The airframe is constructed of titanium and high-strength aluminium alloys. The engine nacelles are fitted with trouser fairings to provide a continuous streamlined profile between the nacelles and the tail beams. The fins and horizontal tail consoles are attached to tail beams. The central beam section between the engine nacelles consists of the equipment compartment, fuel tank and the brake parachute container. The fuselage head is of semi-monocoque construction and includes the cockpit, radar compartments and the avionics bay.

Cockpit and ergonomics

The displays include a highly customised version of the Elbit Su 967 head-up display consisting of bicubic phase conjugated holographic displays and seven liquid crystal multifunction displays, six 127 mm x 127 mm and one 152 mm x 152 mm. Variants of the same HUD have also been chosen for the IAF's MiG-27 and SEPECAT Jaguar upgrades, on grounds of standardisation. Flight information is displayed on four LCD displays which include one for piloting and navigation, a tactical situation indicator, and two for display systems information including operating modes and overall operation status. The rear cockpit is fitted with a larger monochromatic screen display for the air-to-surface missile guidance.

Flight control

The aircraft has a fly by wire (FBW) with quadruple redundancy. Depending on the flight conditions, signals from the control stick position transmitter or the FCS will be coupled to the remote control amplifiers. These signals are combined with feedback signals fed by acceleration sensors and rate gyros. The resultant control signals are coupled to the high-speed electro-hydraulic actuators of the elevators, rudders and the canard. The output signals are compared and, if the difference is significant, the faulty channel is disconnected. FBW is based on a stall warning and barrier mechanism which prevents development of aircraft stalls through a dramatic increase in the control stick pressure. This allows a pilot to effectively control the aircraft without running the risk of reaching the limit values of angle of attack and acceleration. Although the maximum angle of attack is limited by the canards the FBW acts as an additional safety mechanism.

General features

The displays include a highly customized version of the Israeli Elbit Su 967 head-up display consisting of bi-cubic phase conjugated holographic displays and seven liquid crystal multifunction displays, six 127 mm x 127 mm and one 152 mm x 152 mm. The HUD was widely misreported to be the VEH 3000 from Thales.

Variants of the same HUD have also been chosen for the IAF's MiG-27 and SEPECAT Jaguar upgrades, on grounds of standardization. Flight information is displayed on four LCD displays which include one for piloting and navigation, a tactical situation indicator, and two for display systems information including operating modes and overall operation status.

The rear cockpit is fitted with a larger monochromatic screen display for the air-to-surface missile guidance. The Su-30MKI on-board health and usage monitoring system (HUMS) monitors almost every aircraft system and sub-system including the avionics sub-systems. It can also act as an engineering data recorder

Navigation

The aircraft is fitted with a satellite navigation system (A-737 GPS compatible), which permits it to make flights in all weather, day and night. The navigation complex includes the high accuracy SAGEM Sigma-95 integrated global positioning system and ring laser gyroscope inertial navigation system.

Pilot ejection

The crew are provided with zero-zero KD-36DM ejection seats. The rear seat is raised for better visibility. The cockpit is provided with containers to store food and water reserves, a waste disposal system and extra oxygen bottles. The KD-36DM ejection seat is inclined at 30°, to help the pilot resist aircraft accelerations in air combat.

Aerodynamics

Su-30MKI aerodynamic configuration is an unstable longitudinal triplane. The canard increases the aircraft lifting ability and deflects automatically to allow high angle-of-attack (AoA) flights allowing it to perform Pugachev's Cobra. The integral aerodynamic configuration combined with thrust vectoring results in extremely capable maneuverability, taking off and landing characteristics. This high agility allows rapid deployment of weapons in any direction as desired by the crew. The canard notably assists in controlling the aircraft at large angles-of-attack and bringing it to a level flight condition. The wing will have high-lift devices featured as deflecting leading edges, and flaperons acting as flaps and ailerons.

Radar

The forward facing NIIP N011M Bars (Panther) is a powerful integrated passive electronically scanned array radar. The N011M is a digital multi-mode dual frequency band radar. The N011M can function in air-to-air and air-to-land/sea mode simultaneously while being tied into a high-precision laser-inertial or GPS navigation system. It is equipped with a modern digital weapons control system as well as anti-jamming features. N011M has a 350 km search range and a maximum 200 km tracking range, and 60 km in the rear hemisphere. The radar can track 15 air targets and engage 4 simultaneously. These targets can even include cruise missiles and motionless helicopters. The Su-30MKI can function as a *mini-AWACS* as a director or command post for other aircraft. The target co-ordinates can be transferred automatically to at least four other aircraft. The radar can detect ground targets such as tanks at 40–50 km.

Avionics

Laser-optical locator system

OLS-30 laser-optical locator system to include a day and night FLIR capability and is used in conjunction with the helmet mounted sighting system. The OLS-30 is a combined IRST/LR device using a cooled, broader waveband, sensor. Detection range is up to 90 km, whilst the laser ranger is effective to 3.5 km. Targets are displayed on the same LCD display as the radar.

LITENING targeting pod

Israeli LITENING targeting pod is used to target the laser guided munitions. Litening incorporates in a single pod all the targeting features required by a modern strike fighter. The original Litening pod includes a long range FLIR, a TV camera, a flash-lamp powered laser designator, laser spot tracker for tracking target designated by other aircraft or from the ground, and an electro-optical point and inertial tracker, which enabled continuous engagement of the target even when the target is partly obscured by clouds or countermeasures. The pod integrates the necessary laser rangefinder and designator, required for the delivery of Laser Guided Bombs, cluster and general purpose bomb.

Electronic countermeasures

Sukhoi Su-30MKI has electronic counter-measure systems. The RWR system is of Indian design, developed by India's DRDO, called *Tarang*, (*Wave* in Sanskrit). It has direction finding capability and is known to have a programmable threat library. The RWR is derived from work done on an earlier system for India's MiG-23BNs known as the Tranquil, which is now superseded by the more advanced Tarang series. Elta EL/M-8222 a self-protection jammer developed by Israel Aircraft Industries is the MKI's standard EW pod, which the Israeli Air Force uses on its F-15s. The ELTA El/M-8222 Self Protection Pod is a power-managed jammer, air-cooled system with an ESM receiver integrated into the pod. The pod contains an antenna on the forward and aft ends, which receive the hostile RF signal and after processing deliver the appropriate response.

Propulsion

The Su-30MKI is powered by the two Al-31FP turbofans, each rated at 12,500 kgf (27,550 lbf) of full afterburning thrust. These by-pass, thrust-vectoring engines push the aircraft up to mach two in horizontal flight (about 2450 kmh at ground-level) and give a rate of climb of 230 m/s. The mean time between overhaul for the AL-31FP is given at 1,000 hours with a full-life span of 3,000 hours. The titanium nozzle has a mean time between overhaul of 500 hours. Al-31FP builds on the Al-37FU with the capability to vector in two planes. The Thrust Vectoring nozzles of the MKI are mounted 32 degrees outward to longitudinal engine axis (i.e. in the horizontal plane) and can be deflected ±15 degrees in the vertical plane. This produces a cork-screw effect, thus enhancing the turn capability of the aircraft. There is no strain-gauge engine control stick to change the engine thrust in the cockpit, rather just a conventional engine throttle control lever. The pilot controls the aircraft with help of a standard control stick. On the pilot's right there is a switch which is turned on for performing difficult manoeuvres. After the switch-over, the computer determines the level of use of aerodynamic surfaces and swiveling nozzles and their required deflection angles.

Fuel system

The Su-30MKI has a range of 5,000 km with internal fuel which ensures a 4.5 hour combat mission. Also, it has an in-flight refueling (IFR) probe that retracts beside the cockpit during normal operation. The air refueling system increases the flight duration up to 10 hours with a range of 8,000 km at a cruise height of 11 to 13 km. Su-30 MKIs can also use the Cobham 754 buddy refueling pods.

Operational history

The Sukhoi Su-30MKI is the most potent fighter jet in service with the Indian Air Force in the late 2000s. The MKIs are often fielded by the IAF in bilateral and multilateral air exercises. India exercised its Su-30MKIs against the Royal Air Force's Tornado ADVs in October 2006. This was the first large-scale bilateral aerial exercise with any foreign air force during which the IAF used its Su-30MKIs extensively. This exercise was also the first in 43 years with the RAF. During the exercise, RAF's Air Chief Marshall, Glenn Torpy, was given permission by the IAF to fly the MKI. RAF's Air-Vice Marshall, Christopher Harper, praised the MKI's dogfight ability, calling it "absolutely masterful and unbeatable".

In July 2007, the Indian Air Force fielded the MKI during the *Indra-Dhanush* exercise with Royal Air Force's Eurofighter

Typhoon. This was the first time that the two jets had taken part in such a exercise. The IAF did not allow their pilots to use the radar of the MKIs during the exercise so as to protect the highly-classified N011M Bars. During the exercise, the RAF pilots candidly admitted that the Su-30MKI displayed maneuvering superior to that of the Typhoon.

An earlier variant of the Su-30MKI, the MK, took part in war games with the United States Air Force (USAF) during *Cope-India 04*. The results have been widely publicized, with the Indians winning "90% of the mock combat missions" against the American force's F-15C. When questioned on the capabilities of IAF pilots, Col Greg Newbech, USAF Team Leader made the following remarks:-"What we've seen in the last two weeks is, the IAF can stand toe-to-toe with best AF in the world. Indian hospitality from everyone has been truly overwhelming. The greatest compliment we heard from an IAF pilot, 'You American pilots are just like us, simply down to earth people.' We depart India with great respect for the Indian Air Force. Your pilots, maint and support crew are exceptional professionals.".

In July 2008, the IAF sent 6 Su-30MKIs and 2 aerial-refueling tankers, the Il-78MKI, to participate in the Red Flag exercise.. The IAF again did not allow their pilots to use the radar of the MKIs during the exercise so as to protect the highly-classified N011M Bars. In October 2008, a video surfaced on the internet which featured a USAF colonel, Corkey Fornoff, criticizing Su-30MKI's high friendly kill rate and serviceability issues during the Red Flag exercise. Several of his claims were later rebutted by the Indian side.

Notable accidents

A Su-30MKI aircraft crashed on 30 April 2009 in the Pokhran region of Rajasthan after it took off from Pune during its routine sortie, killing one of its two pilots. Defence minister A. K. Antony, stated that the likely cause of the April 30 crash was "failure of the fly-by-wire system". The Sukhoi fleet had then been grounded for around three weeks. However it was found that this crash at Rajmathai village, around 170 km from Jaisalmer, in April was because of the position of the various critical switches of the aircraft. The switches were behind the pilots and they would have to turn them on and off without looking back. At one point, a wrong switch was turned on, leading to the crash on April 30. Wing Commander PS Nara was killed in the mishap, while Wing Commander SV Munje was injured. After investigators identified the problem, a couple of difficult switches were sealed off.

Another Su-30MKI aircraft crashed on 30 November 2009 in Jathegaon, about 40 km from Jaisalmer. The pilots ejected after they saw fire alarm buttons glowing red. Both the pilots are unharmed. This is second such crash of this fighter. The Sukhoi mishaps have come as a setback to the 12 year safety record IAF had achieved with the aircraft which was inducted into the force in 1996. As a result the entire fleet of Su-30MKIs was grounded while the cause of the problem was investigated. It was attributed to accidental ingestion of a foreign material in the engine intake.

HAL TEJAS

The HAL Tejas is a 4th generation lightweight multirole jet fighter being developed by India. It is a tailless, compound delta wing design powered by a single engine. Originally known as the Light Combat Aircraft (LCA)—a designation which continues in popular usage—the aircraft was officially named "*Tejas*" by then Prime Minister Atal Bihari Vajpayee. The IAF is reported to have a requirement for 200 single-seat and 20 two-seat conversion trainers, while the Indian Navy may order up to 40 single-seaters to replace its Sea Harrier FRS.51 and Harrier T.60. During its sea level flight trials off Goa, Tejas notched a speed of over 1,350 km per hour, thus becoming the second supersonic fighter manufactured indigenously by Hindustan Aeronautics Limited after the HAL Marut.

Development

LCA programme

In 1969, the Indian government accepted the recommendation by its Aeronautics Committee that HAL should design and develop an advanced technology fighter aircraft around a proven engine. Based on a 'Tactical Air Support Aircraft' ASR markedly similar to that for the *Marut*, HAL completed design studies in 1975, but the project fell through due to inability to procure the selected "proven engine" from a foreign manufacturer and the IAF's requirement for an air superiority fighter with secondary air support and interdiction capability remained unfulfilled.

The LCA programme was launched in 1983 for two primary purposes. The principal and most obvious goal was the development of a replacement aircraft for India's ageing MiG-21 fighters. The MiG-21 has been the mainstay of the Indian Air Force since the 1970s. The "Long Term Re-Equipment Plan 1981" noted that the MiG-21s would be approaching the end of their service lives by the mid-1990s, and that by 1995 the IAF would lack 40% of the aircraft needed to fill its projected force structure requirements.

The LCA programme's other main objective was to serve as the vehicle for an across-the-board advancement of India's domestic aerospace industry. The value of the aerospace "self-reliance" initiative is not simply the production of an aircraft, but also the building of a local industry capable of creating state-of-the-art products with commercial spin-offs for a global market. The LCA program was intended in part to further expand and advance India's indigenous aerospace capabilities.

To better accomplish these goals, the government chose to take a different management approach, and in 1984 established the Aeronautical Development Agency (ADA) to manage the LCA programme. Although the *Tejas* is most often described as a product of Hindustan Aeronautics Limited (HAL), responsibility for the development of the *Tejas* actually belongs to ADA, a national consortium of over 100 defence laboratories, industrial organisations, and academic institutions with HAL being the principal contractor.

The Indian government's "self-reliance" goals for the LCA include indigenous development of the three most sophisticated — and hence most challenging — systems: the fly-by-wire (FBW) flight control system (FCS), multi-mode pulse-doppler radar, and afterburning turbofan engine. Although India has had a policy of strictly limiting foreign participation in the LCA programme, these are the only major LCA systems on which the ADA has had to invite significant foreign technological assistance and consultancy. Moreover, the engine and radar are also the only major systems for which the ADA has seriously considered substituting foreign equipment.

The ambitiousness of the LCA programme in terms of pursuing self-reliance in aviation technologies is illustrated by the fact that out of a total of 35 major avionics components and line-replaceable units (LRUs), only three involve foreign systems. These are the multi-function displays (MFDs) by Sextant (France) and Elbit (Israel), the helmet-mounted display and sight (HMDS) cueing system by Elbit, and the laser pod supplied by Rafael (Israel). However, even among these three, when the LCA reaches the production stage, the MFDs are expected to be supplied by Indian companies. A few other important items of equipment (such as the Martin-Baker ejection seat) have been imported. As a consequence of the embargo imposed on India after its nuclear weapons tests in May 1998, many items originally planned to be imported were instead developed indigenously.

Of the five critical technologies the ADA identified at the beginning of the LCA programme as needing to be mastered for India to be able to design and build a "completely indigenous" fighter, two have been entirely successful: the development and manufacture of advanced carbon-fibre composite (CFC) structures and skins and a modern "glass cockpit." In fact, ADA has had a profitable commercial spin-off in its Autolay integrated automated software system for the design and development of 3-D laminated composite elements (which has been licensed to both Airbus and Infosys). These successes have gone mostly unnoticed in the shadow of the problems encountered with the other three key technology initiatives. Nonetheless, as a result of the accomplishments of India's domestic industries, presently about 70% of the components in LCA are manufactured in India and the dependence on imported components used would be progressively reduced in the coming years.

HAL serves as the prime contractor and has leading responsibility for LCA design, systems integration, airframe manufacturing, aircraft final assembly, flight testing, and service support. The ADA itself has primary responsibility for the design and development of the LCA's avionics suite and its integration with the flight controls, environmental controls, aircraft utilities systems management, stores management system, etc.

Of particular importance are the initiatives to develop an indigenous flight control system, radar, and engine for the LCA. The National Aeronautics Laboratory (NAL)—now called the National Aerospace Laboratories—was selected to lead the development of the flight control laws, supported by the Aeronautical Development Establishment (ADE). HAL and the Electronics and Radar Development Establishment (LRDE) are jointly developing the *Tejas'* Multi-Mode Radar (MMR). The GTRE is responsible for the design and parallel development of the GTX-35VS *Kaveri* afterburning turbofan engine for the *Tejas*.

The IAF's Air Staff Requirement for the LCA were not finalised until October 1985. This delay rendered moot the original schedule which called for first flight in April 1990 and service entry in 1995; however, it also proved a boon as it it gave the ADA time to better marshal national R&D and industrial resources, recruit personnel, create infrastructure, and to gain a clearer perspective of which advanced technologies could be developed indigenously and which would need to be imported.

Project definition commenced in October 1987 and was completed in September 1988. Dassault Aviation of France was hired as a consultant to review the PD and provide advice based on its extensive aviation expertise. The PD phase is a critical early element in the aircraft design and development process because from this flow key elements of the detailed design, manufacturing approach, and maintenance requirements.

Development history

The LCA design was finalised in 1990 as a small delta-winged machine with relaxed static stability(RSS) to enhance maneuverability performance. The sophisticated avionics and advanced composite structure specified caused some concern almost immediately, and the IAF expressed doubt that India possessed sufficient technological infrastructure to support such an ambitious project. A governmental review committee was formed in May 1989 which reported out a general view that Indian infrastructure, facilities and technology had advanced sufficiently in most areas to undertake the project. As a measure of prudence, though, it was decided that the full-scale engineering development (FSED) stage of the programme would proceed in two stages.

Phase 1 would focus on "proof of concept" and would comprise the design, development and testing (DDT) of two technology demonstrator aircraft (TD-1 and TD-2) and fabrication of a structural test specimen (STS) airframe; only after successful testing of the TD aircraft would the Indian government give its full support to the LCA design. This would be followed by the production of two prototype vehicles (PV-1 and PV-2), and creation of the necessary basic infrastructure and test facilities for the aircraft would begin.

Phase 2 would consist of the manufacturing of three more prototype vehicles (PV-3 as the production variant, PV-4 as the naval variant, and PV-5 as the trainer variant) and a fatigue test specimen, and the construction of further development and test facilities at various work centres.

Phase 1 commenced in 1990 and HAL started work on the technology demonstrators in mid-1991; however, a financial crunch resulted in full-scale funding not being authorized until April 1993, with significant work on FSED Phase 1 commencing in June. The first technology demonstrator, TD-1, was rolled out on 17 November 1995 and was followed by TD-2 in 1998, but they were kept grounded for several years due to structural concerns and trouble with the development of the flight control system.

One of the most ambitious requirements for the LCA was the specification that it would have "relaxed static stability" (RSS). Although Dassault had offered an analogue FCS system in 1988, the ADA recognised that digital flight control technology would soon supplant it. RSS technology was introduced in 1974 on the General Dynamics (now Lockheed Martin) YF-16, which was the world's first production aircraft to be slightly aerodynamically unstable by design. Most aircraft are designed with "positive" static stability, which means they have a natural tendency to return to level and controlled flight in the absence of control inputs; however, this quality tends to oppose the pilot's efforts to manoeuvre. An aircraft with "negative" static stability (i.e., RSS), on the other hand, will quickly depart from level and controlled flight unless the pilot constantly works to keep it in trim; while this enhances manoeuvrability, it is very wearing on a pilot relying on a mechanical flight control system.

Development of a FBW flight control system requires extensive knowledge of flight control laws and the expensive writing of a considerable amount of software code for the flight control computers, as well as its integration with the avionics and other electronic systems. When the LCA programme was launched, FBW was a state-of-the-art technology and such a sensitive one that India could find no nation willing to export it. Therefore, in 1992 the LCA National Control Law (CLAW) team was set up by the National Aeronautics Laboratory to develop India's own version. The CLAW team's scientists and mathematicians were successful in developing their control laws, but could not test them since India did not possess advanced real-time ground simulators at that time. Accordingly, British Aerospace (BAe) and Lockheed Martin were brought in to help in 1993, but the effort required for the Aeronautical Development Establishment to code the control laws into the FCS software proved a much larger job than originally anticipated.

Specific control law problems were tested on BAE's simulators (and on HAL's, once theirs became available). As it was being developed, progressive elements of the coding were checked out on the "Minibird" and "Ironbird" test rigs at the ADE and HAL, respectively. A second series of inflight simulation tests of the integrated flight control software were conducted on the F-16 VISTA (Variable In-flight Stability Test Aircraft) simulator in the U.S. in July 1996, with 33 test flights being carried out. However, Lockheed Martin's involvement was terminated in 1998 as part of an embargo enacted by the U.S. in response to India's second nuclear tests in May of that year.

The NAL's CLAW team eventually managed to successfully complete integration of the flight control laws indigenously, with the FCS software performing flawlessly for over 50 hours of pilot testing on TD-1, resulting in the aircraft being cleared for flight in early 2001. The LCA's maiden flight was made by TD-1 from National Flight Test Centre (NFTC), near Bangalore, on 4 January 2001, and its first successful supersonic flight followed on 1 August 2003. TD-2 made its first flight on 6 June 2002. The automatic flight control system (AFCS)of the Tejas has been highly praised by all of its test pilots, one of whom said that he found it easier to take off with the LCA than in a Mirage 2000.

Another critical technology area tackled for indigenous development by the ADA team is the Multi-Mode Radar (MMR). It was initially planned for the LCA to use the Ericsson Microwave Systems PS-05/A I/J-band multi-function radar, which was developed by Ericsson and Ferranti Defence Systems Integration for the Saab JAS-39 *Gripen*. However, after examining other radars in the early 1990s, the DRDO became confident that indigenous development was possible. HAL's Hyderabad division and the LRDE were selected to jointly lead the MMR program and the radar development effort began in 1997.

The DRDO's Centre for Airborne Studies (CABS) is responsible for running the test programme for the MMR. Between 1996 and 1997, CABS converted the surviving HAL/ HS-748M Airborne Surveillance Post (ASP) testbed into a testbed for the avionics and radar of the LCA. Known as the 'Hack', the only major structural modification besides the removal of the rotodome assembly was the addition of the LCA's nose cone in order to accommodate the MMR.

By mid-2002, development of the MMR was reported to be experiencing major delays and cost escalations. By early 2005 only the air-to-air look-up and look-down modes — two very basic modes — were confirmed to have been successfully tested. In May 2006 it was revealed that the performance of several modes being tested still "fell short of expectations." As a result, the ADA was reduced to running weaponisation tests with a weapon delivery pod, which is not a primary sensor, leaving critical tests on hold. According to test reports, the crux of the problem is a serious compatibility issue between the radar and the advanced signal processor module (SPM) built by the LRDE. Acquisition of an "off-the-shelf" foreign radar is an interim option being seriously considered. The LSP-3 which flew on April 23, 2010 was flying with a hybrid version of Elta's EL/M-2032 pulse-doppler radar.

Engine and propulsion

Kaveri engine

Initially, it was decided to equip the prototype aircraft with the General Electric F404-GE-F2J3 afterburning turbofan engine. Simulataneously, in 1986, a parallel programme to develop an indigenous powerplant was also launched. Led by the Gas Turbine Research Establishment, the GTRE GTX-35VS, named "*Kaveri*", was expected to replace the F404 on all production aircraft. However, progress in the *Kaveri* development programme was slowed by technical difficulties. In mid-2004, the *Kaveri* failed its high-altitude tests in Russia, ending the last hopes of introducing it with the first production *Tejas* aircraft.

Continued development snags with the *Kaveri* resulted in the 2003 decision to procure the uprated F404-GE-IN20 engine for the eight pre-production LSP aircraft and two naval prototypes. The ADA awarded General Electric a US$105 million contract in 2004 for development engineering and production of 17-IN20 engines, delivery of which began in 2006.

An RFP inviting companies for further development of *Kaveri* was issued. In February 2006, the ADA awarded a contract to the French aircraft engine company Snecma for technical assistance in working out the *Kaveri's* problems. The Kaveri engine based on Snecma's new core, an uprated derivative of the M88-2 engine that powers the French Rafale fighter, providing 83-85 Kilonewtons (KN) of maximum thrust is being considered a third option by DRDO leading the IAF to object that since Snecma has already developed the core of the engine it is offering the DRDO will not participate in any "joint development" but merely provide Snecma with an indigenous stamp.

In 2007, HAL ordered an additional 24 F404-IN20 afterburning engines to power the first operational squadron of Tejas fighter aircraft for the Indian Air Force. Before the subsequent order, F404-GE-IN20 was trial-installed in the Tejas as part of final evaluations toward flight-testing, scheduled for mid-2007. The F404-GE-IN20 engine generated more than 19,000 pounds (85 kN) uninstalled thrust and completed 330 hours of Accelerated Mission testing, equivalent of 1,000 hours of flight operation.

In 2008, it was announced that the Kaveri would not be ready in time for the Tejas, and that an in-production powerplant would have to be selected in the 95 to 100 kilonewton (kN) (21,000–23,000 lbf) range. The contenders are likely to be the Eurojet EJ200 and the General Electric F414.The single crystal turbine blade technology, originally denied to Indian scientists, has also been offered to India by Eurojet via the EJ200 engine.

The current F404 engine does not produce enough thrust to enable the aircraft to carry out combat manoeuvres with optimal weapons load. Eurojet Turbo and General Electric will be competing to supply 100 engines for the LCA. The Eurojet EJ200 and the GE F414 engines meet the IAF's requirement as they generate a thrust of 95–100 kilonewtons. It has also been said by IAF sources that the airframe will have to be redesigned in order to accommodate the heavier engine which is expected to take up to three-four years. The initial batch of Tejas aircraft will be powered by the F404 engine.

It was reported that Eurojet was offering two variants of the EJ200, which through a software change would also be able to meet the requirements of the Naval variant of the LCA. Eurojet also offered to help India in the development of the Kaveri engine

Status

In March 2005, the IAF placed a 2,000 crore (US$434 million) order for 20 aircraft, with a similar purchase of another 20 aircraft to follow. All 40 will be equipped with the F404-GE-IN20 engine. The Tejas is presently undergoing flight testing. It will be inducted into the IAF when it has received Initial Operating Clearance (IOC) which is expected to be in December 2010. Consequently, the IAF has created a 14 member "LCA Induction Team" stationed in Bangalore that is composed of

IAF pilots and officers and headed by an Air Vice Marshal. The team's objectives are to reportedly oversee the induction of the LCA, help solve any challenges that may arise, assist HAL in customizing the Tejas for operational use, and to create doctrines, training and maintenance programs and finally to assist the IAF in ensuring a smooth introduction of 'Tejas' into operational service.

The first production variant of the 'Tejas' (LSP-1) flew on June 2008. Tejas completed 1000 Test Flights by January, 2009 with more than 530 hours of in-flight testing. By February 2009 officials of the Aeronautical Development Agency stated that the *Tejas* had started flying with weapons and integration of radars would be completed by March 2009.

In addition, they stated that nearly all system development activity would be completed by that time. On April 2010, the third production aircraft (LSP-3) flew with a hybrid version of the Elta EL/M-2032 multi-mode radar and by June 2010, the fourth production aircraft took flight in the configuration it would be delivered to the Indian Air Force in.

By June 2010, Tejas had also completed the second phase of hot weather trials. The objective of the hot weather trials was to prove that the aircraft was in an IOC configuration with the weapon system and sensors integrated. The sea trials of the aircraft is being carried out.

The trainer variant prototype took to the skies in November 2009. In December 2009, the Indian government sanctioned 8,000 crore (US$1.74 billion) to begin production of the fighter jet for the Indian Air Force and Indian Navy. The Indian Navy has a requirement of 50 Tejas and the first protoype, NP-1 was rolled out in July 2010. IAF had ordered 20 additional Tejas fighter jets and the defence acquisition council had cleared the plan.

HAL HPT-32 DEEPAK

The HAL HPT-32 Deepak is an Indian prop-driven primary trainer manufactured by Hindustan Aeronautics Limited. The student and the instructor sit side-by-side. The aircraft can accommodate one passenger.

Operational history

The Deepak is used for primary training, observation, liaison and target towing.

Grounding

The entire fleet of HPT 32 Deepak aircraft in service with the IAF was grounded "owing to a series of crashes and engine failures" during August 2009 after two senior flight instructors were killed in a crash near Hyderabad.

Retro-fitting safety systems

It has been long known that the aircraft has two major design flaws : 1. When it flies upside-down the flow of fuel gets blocked, shutting the engine. 2. Deepak cannot glide without engine power for even a short distance, a serious crash in inevitable

It has been reported the IAF and HAL are looking into radical safety systems such as attaching 'enormous parachute' to the aircraft to enable it to glide in the event of an engine failure. On May 16 2010 the IAF gave clearance for a parachute recovery system to be fitted on the trainer. During an emergency the pilot can deploy the parachute by using a lever. With no other basic trainer available, the IAF envisions that the parachute system will make the training process safer in the future.

Accidents

An aircraft crashed in the outskirts of the city of Medak, Andhra Pradesh on July 31, 2009, killing both the pilots. The causes of the crash are being investigated. In 17 Deepak crashes so far, 19 pilots have died. The Comptroller and Auditor General (CAG) of India has been reported as saying the aircraft is "technologically outdated and beset by flight safety hazards" when discussing the grounding of the fleet in 2009

HAL KIRAN

The HAL HJT-16 Kiran (*Ray of Light*) is an Indian two-seat basic jet trainer built by Hindustan Aeronautics. Used by the Indian Air Force for intermediate training for pilots trained on the HPT-32 Deepak. It is used by the Indian Air Force aerobatic team Surya Kiran and Indian naval acrobatic team Sagar Pawans.

Development

The Kiran was designed to meet an Indian air force requirement for a basic jet trainer. The first aircraft powered by the Rolls Royce Viper Mk 11 was flown for the first time on the 4 September 1964. The production aircraft was designated the Kiran I, and first deliveries from a pre-production batch were delivered to the Indian Air Force in March 1968. Later production aircraft were fitted with hardpoints under each wing for weapon training (as the Kiran IA. A total of 190 Mk I and 1A aircraft were built. An improved version powered by a 4,200 lbf (19,000 N) thrust Bristol-Siddeley Orpheus engine and improved weapon-carrying capability was designated the Kiran II, first flying on 30 July 1976, and was delivered from 1985, 61 being delivered by the time production ended in 1989.

Replacement

Kiran will be replaced with the new HAL HJT-36 trainer undergoing flight trials. The Indian Air Force has already placed orders for 12 such aircraft to replace the Kiran jets used by the Surya Kiran team.

Notable accidents

A Kiran Mk II of the Sagar Pawan Aerobatic Team of the Indian Navy crashed at Hyderabad during the Indian Aviation 2010 air show on 3 March 2010, killing both crewmembers.

Variant

Kiran Mk.I: Two-seat basic jet trainer powered by a Rolls-Royce Viper turbo-jet engine. 118 built.

Kiran Mk.IA: Improved version with four hardpoints and integral twin 7.62 mm machine guns in nose and a Rolls-Royce Orpheus engine.

Dornier Do 228: The Dornier 228 is a twin-turboprop STOL utility aircraft, manufactured by Dornier GmbH (later DASA Dornier, Fairchild-Dornier) from 1981 until 1998. In 1983, Hindustan Aeronautics (HAL) bought a production licence and manufactures the 228 for the Asian market sphere.

Approximately 270 Do 228 were built at Oberpfaffenhofen, Germany and Kanpur, India. In August 2006, 127 Dornier Do 228 aircraft (all variants) remain in airline service. RUAG will commence building a Dornier 228 New Generation in Germany using structural parts supplied by HAL. It will be basically the same aircraft with improved technologies and performances, such as a new five blade propeller, glass cockpit and longer range.

Design and development

In the late 1970s, Dornier GmbH developed a new kind of wing, the TNT ("*Tragflügel neuer Technologie*"), subsidized by the German Government. Dornier tested it on a modified Do 28D-2*Skyservant* and with Pratt & Whitney Canada PT6A-110 turboprop engines.

Finally, Dornier changed the engine and tested the new aircraft, which was named Do 128 with two Garrett AiResearch TPE-331-5 engines. The company developed a new fuselage for the TNT and TPE 331–5 in two variants (15-and 19-passenger) and named both project-aircraft E-1 (later Do 228-100) and E-2 (later Do 228-200). At ILA '80, Dornier presented the new aircraft in public. Both the prototypes were flown on 28 March 1981 and 9 May 1981 for the first time.

After German certification was granted on 18 December 1981, the first Do 228 entered service in the fleet of Norving Flyservice in July 1982. British and United States certification followed on 17 April and 11 May 1984 respectively. Over the years Dornier offered the 228 in upgraded variants and with special equipment for special missions. In 1998 the production line was stopped for better development of the successor Fairchild-Dornier 328.

Do 228 NG

The Dornier 228 NG was certified by EASA on 18 August 2010. First delivery, to a Japanese customer, is scheduled to take place in 3rd quarter 2010. The main changes from the previous Dornier 228-212 model are a new 5-blade propeller made of composite material, more powerful engines, and an advanced glass cockpit featuring electronic instrument displays.

HAL DHRUV

The HAL Dhruv is a multi-role helicopter developed and manufactured by India's Hindustan Aeronautics Limited (HAL). It is being supplied to the Indian Armed Forces, and a civilian variant is also available. The helicopter was first exported to Nepal and Israel, and is on order by several other countries for both military and commercial uses. Military versions in production are for transport, utility, reconnaissance and MedEvac roles. The HAL Light Combat Helicopter (LCH) is a helicopter gunship based on the Dhruv platform. A naval version for anti-submarine operations was proposed, but has been dropped.

Development

Hindustan's Advanced Light Helicopter (ALH) program was first announced in November 1984, the ALH was designed with assistance from MBB in Germany and shows strong resemblance to MBB's smaller BK-117 helicopter. The twin 1000 shp Turbomeca TM333-2B turboshafts are mounted above the cabin and drive a four-blade composite main rotor. The ALH makes use of an advanced integrated dynamic system which combines several rotor control features into an integrated module. The civil prototype ALH (Z-3182) first flew on 23 August 1992, at Bangalore, followed by a second civil aircraft (Z-3183), an Army version (Z-3268) and a navalised prototype (N.901) with Allied Signal CTS800 engines and a retractable tricycle undercarriage.Even after the first prototype flew in August 1992, problems arose due to the changing demands of the Indian military, funding, and contractual issues with Messerschmitt-Bölkow-Blohm, which was the consultant for design. Further delay was caused by U.S. sanctions after Indian nuclear tests in 1998, which embargoed the engine originally intended to power the helicopter. Then the helicopter used Turbomeca TM 333-2B2 turboshaft producing 746 kW (1000 shp) each and an agreement was signed with Turbomeca to develop a more powerful engine.

HAL is also developing the Light Combat Helicopter (LCH) based on the Dhruv platform for the Indian Armed Forces. It will have stub wings fitted to carry up to eight anti-armour missiles, four air-to-air missiles or four rocket pods for 70mm and 68mm rockets. The LCH will also have FLIR (Forward Looking Infrared), CCD (Charge Coupled Device) camera and a target acquisition system with thermal sight and laser rangefinder. Recent versions of the Dhruv entering production use the more powerful Shakti engine developed jointly by HAL and Turbomeca. The first test flight of the Dhruv with the new engine and the weaponised version took place on 16 August 2007.

Design

HAL Dhruv is of conventional design and about two-thirds by weight of composite construction. The high tail boom allows easy access to the rear clamshell loading doors.The four-bladed hingeless main rotor can be manually folded. The blades are mounted between cruciform-shaped carbon-fibre-reinforced plastic plates on a fibre elastomer constructed rotor head. The helicopter is equipped with an active vibration control system developed by Lord Corporation of North Carolina that uses sensors to monitor on-board conditions and outputs signals to actuators to cancel fuselage floor vibrations.

Cockpit

The cockpit section of the fuselage is of Kevlar and carbon-fibre construction and is fitted with crashworthy seats.The aircraft is equipped with a SFIM Inc. four-axis automatic flight control system. The navigation suite includes a global positioning system, a Doppler navigation system, distance measuring equipment, a true air speed indicator, automatic direction finder, a heading reference system, radio altimeter, VHF omnidirectional ranger and instrument landing system (VOR/ ILS) and marker beacons. The communications suite includes HF, UHF, and VHF radio communications.

Operational history

Military service

Deliveries of the Dhruv commenced in 2002, a full ten years after the prototype's first flight, and nearly twenty years after the program was initiated. The Indian Coast Guard became the first service to bring Dhruv helicopters into service. This was followed by the Indian Army, Indian Navy, Indian Air Force and the Border Security Force. Dhruvs were delivered to the Indian armed forces by 2007 and the plan is to produce 40 helicopters yearly. One of only three helicopter display teams in the world, the Sarang aerobatic display team of the Indian Air Force performs with 4 Dhruv helicopters.

The Dhruv is capable of flying at high altitudes, a crucial requirement for the Army, which requires helicopters for operations in Siachen Glacier and Kashmir. In September 2007, the Dhruv was cleared for high-altitude flying in the Siachen Sector after six-month long trials. In October 2007, a Dhruv flew to an altitude of 27,500 feet (8,400 m) ASL in Siachen. This was the highest that the Dhruv had flown, and was higher than the 25,000 feet (7,600 m) record set by an IAF *Cheetah* helicopter in 2005.

A further order for 166 helicopters were placed with HAL since the helicopter is working well in higher altitude areas with the Indian Army. The Armed Forces may order 12 ambulances versions for use by the Armed Forces Medical Services for MEDEVAC operations. HAL Dhruv ambulances will have all the emergency medical equipment for the treatment of injured soldiers.

In June 2008, the *Hindustan Times* reported that the Indian Navy had decided against placing further orders for the Dhruv Naval variant, stating it has failed to meet basic operational requirements. However these rumours were put to rest by the recent comments of the defence minister who stated in the parliament that the navy had not rejected the Dhruv as eight Dhruv helicopters are already operating in the Utility role. The Anti-submarine version will not be inducted since it did not suit the requirements of the Indian Navy in anti-submarine role.

Civilian service

HAL also produces a civilian variant of the Dhruv for VIP transport, rescue, policing, offshore operations and air-ambulance role, among others. In April 2008, HAL chairman Mr Baweja confirmed that the Home Ministry had "placed an order for six ALHs"

The National Disaster Management Authority (NDMA) has placed an order for 12 Advanced Light Helicopters (ALH) with Hindustan Aeronautics Limited (HAL). Chief Test Pilot Wing Commander Upadhyay said the helicopters will have a full set of medical equipment, including ventilators and two stretchers. Other buyers include the Geological Survey of India (GSI) (1 Helicopter), ONGC for its offshore operations, as well as state governments for VIP transport and policing.

Foreign sales

The Dhruv has become the first major Indian weapons system to have secured large foreign sales. HAL hopes to sell 120 Dhruvs over the next eight years, and has been displaying the Dhruv at airshows, including Farnborough and Paris in order to market the Dhruv. With a unit price at least 15% less than its rivals, Dhruv has elicited interest in many countries, mostly from Latin America, Africa, West Asia, South East Asia and the Pacific Rim nations. Air forces from around 35 countries have sent in their inquiries, along with requests for demonstrations.

The first foreign orders for the Dhruv were placed by Nepal in early 2004, for 2 Dhruvs. Another Dhruv, a civilian version, was leased to the Israeli Defense Ministry in 2004. In June 2008, the government of Peru ordered two air ambulance Dhruvs for use by the Peruvian health services. Peru has also shown interest in the military version Dhruv.

HAL also secured an order from the Ecuadorian Air Force for 7 Dhruvs. HAL has gained this order amidst strong competition from Elbit, Eurocopter and Kazan. HAL's offer of $ 50.7 million for seven helicopters was about 32% lower than the second lowest bid from Elbit. 5 helicopters were delivered in February 2009, during the Aero India 2009. The remaining 2 helicopters will be delivered within six months Ecuadorian Army and Ecuadorian Navy have also expressed unofficial interest in purchasing the helicopter.

Dhruv also participated in a Chilean tender for eight to ten 5.5 tonne, twin engined new generation helicopter, but lost to the Bell Helicopters Bell 412 amid allegations of arm-twisting by the US Government. The evaluation included flights at high altitudes, hot and desert conditions, ship deck landing, search and rescue at 12,500 feet (3,800 m) MSL at a temperature of 2°C as well as long distance ferry flights, clocking 107 flying hours. On August 10, 2008 HAL chairman confirmed it had finalized a deal with Turkey to supply 3 Dhruvs for $20 million. Turkey is planning to buy as many as 17 helicopters in medical assistance role.

India is also reportedly planning to transfer several Dhruvs to Burma. This led to protests from Amnesty International, who pointed to the use of components sourced from European suppliers as a possible violation of the EU Arms Embargo of Burma. In a letter to the President of the EU Council of Ministers, Amnesty stated that it had evidence that India planned to transfer two Dhruvs (with European components) to Burma.

These reports have been denied by the Indian Government. HAL is negotiating with Bolivia for delivery of five Dhruvs and with Venezuela for seven of the choppers in transport roles, and in Europe. The Dhruv is also being offered to Malaysia. Indonesia is also evaluating Dhruv helicopters for the Indonesian Army.

Flight certification for Europe and North America is also being planned, in order to tap the large civilian market there. On 18 April 2010. the Indian navy supplied a Dhruv to Maldives to use in Maldivian defense force in search and rescue operations.

DRDO LAKSHYA

The Lakshya is an Indian remotely piloted high speed target drone system developed by the Aeronautical Development Establishment (ADE) of DRDO. The drone, remote piloted by a ground control station provides realistic towed aerial sub-targets for live fire training. The drone is ground or ship launched from a zero length launcher and recovery is by a two stage parachute system developed by ADE (DRDO), for land or sea based recovery. The drone has a crushable nose cone, which absorbs the impact of landing, minimizing damage. The flight path may be controlled or pre-programmed, based upon the type of mission.

Development

The requirement for a pilotless target aircraft (PTA) arose in 1976. Feasibility studies were carried out by ADE to provide for a target system that met the requirements of all 3 services of the armed forces. An Inter Services Qualitative Requirement (ISQR), common to the three Services, was formulated by a Working Group constituted by the Ministry of Defence in January 1977 and 35 ISQR points were identified. Subsequently, based on a feasibility study carried out by ADE, the project for the design and development of Inter-Services PTA by ADE, satisfying the ISQR was sanctioned by Government in September 1980 at a cost of₹. 170 million including a foreign exchange element of. 80 million. The development activity was planned for completion within five years. In parallel, a development project for indigenous development of PTA Engine (PTAE-7) was also sanctioned at an estimated cost of.45 million (. One crore = 10 million) to Hindustan Aeronautics Limited(HAL) in September 1980, based on a feasibility study and project proposal submitted by HAL. The engine was to be developed by HAL by September 1985, concurrently with the PTA. HAL announced the successful trial of the indigenously-designed and developed remote-controlled PTAE-7 jet engine on 24 January 2001.

Between December 1985 and July 1986, four Lakṣhya PTA prototypes powered by Microturbo TRI-60-5 engines were launched for trials. While the first two launches were successful for planned flight times of 20 and 38 minutes respectively, the next two launches failed. By June 1994, 18 Lakshya PTA prototypes were fabricated by ADE itself and 43 trials were conducted, 24 of which were between December 1985 and February 1992. Due to rigorous evaluation and stringent quality control, a total of 10 prototypes were lost during the testing phase between 1985 and 1990. The project was formally closed on June 1994 and a final closure report was issued in April 1995 after incurring a total expenditure of 218.2 million. The first 6 Lakshya drones were given to the Indian Air Force in 1998. Laskhya units are manufactured and overhauled at HAL's Aircraft division, Bangalore. The Lakshya was formally inducted into the services by CAS AY Tipnis, on 9 November 2000 at

Interim test range (ITR) Chandipur. On May 9, 2002, an upgraded version of the Laskhya featuring the new engine from HAL was flown from ITR Chandipur, bringing user trials to a close. On 6 November 2002, HAL announced that they had received an initial order for 25 Lakshya drones and that limited series production to satisfy the order for all three services had already begun. By 16 January 2003, the drone had completed over 100 flights.

A modified reconnaissance version of the Lakshya is under development. This version was fitted with oblique cameras and a digital on board computer with a faster data-link enabling the drone to carry out completely autonomous operations. The development of this version was formally announced by Dr VK Aatre, then Scientific Adviser to the Defence Minister, during his lecture on "Evolving Battlefields and Role of Technology" organized by Bangalore Science Forum on 5 July 2003.

Operational history

Indian Air Force had received the aircraft, ground systems and expendables in September 1999 and Indian Navy was scheduled to receive its first deliveries in November 2000. 23 Pilotless Target Aircraft Lakshya have been inducted into the defence services. The production cost of one aircraft is. 293.75 lakh. Some countries, like Singapore, Malaysia and Israel have expressed interest for "paid demonstration" of the Lakshya aircraft as a target. A similar "paid demonstration" was conducted for Israel's Air Force during the year 2002. This information was given by the Defense Minister Shri AK Antony on 5 September 2007.

7

Indian Air Force : Down the Memory Lane

The Indian Air Force (IAF) has come a long way from its modest beginning to become one of the finest air forces in the world, renowned for its professionalism and competence. The IAF came into being on October 8, 1932. At that time, there were only six officers-five pilots and one equipment officer apart from 19 Havai Sepoys (air soldiers) and its aircraft inventory comprised four Westland *Wapiti* biplanes at Drigh Road (now in Pakistan).

The outbreak of second world war resulted in the expansion of IAF. By the end of 1941, the IAF had three squadrons and five coastal defence flights. The Japanese attack on Pearl Harbour brought the war to India's doorstep and in December 1942, the IAF was inducted into Burma for the first Burma Campaign. In recognition of its achievements, the service was bestowed with the prefix "Royal" in March 1945 and was then known as the Royal Indian Air Force (RIAF).

The principal components of RIAF at the time of partition in 1947 were Nos 3,4,7,8 and 10 Squadrons with *Tempest II,* No 2 Squadron with *Spitfires,* and No 12 Squadron with C-47s and No 1 Air Observation Flight. The RIAF lost many permanent bases and other establishments as a result of the division of the country. It had virtually no breathing space to recover from the surgery that had accompanied the partition. Tribal raiders-clothed, fed and armed by Pakistani military commanders-raided Kashmir in October 1947. On October 26, the same year, the Maharaja of Kashmir signed the Instrument of Accession as per the requirements of the partition process and asked for military help. The next day, RIAF flew to Srinagar carrying the first contingent of the Indian Army in three DC-3 *Dakotas* of 12 Squadron. A couple of days later, the *Spitfires* from Ambala reached Srinagar and were soon engaged in strafing the raiders beyond Pattan. Within a week, the *Tempests* of No 7 Squadron were playing a decisive role in the battle of Shelatang and had halted the movement of the insurgents. The fighting continued for 15 months and the RIAF was involved throughout the operations.

In January 1950, India became a Republic within the British Commonwealth and the Indian Air Force dropped its "Royal" prefix. At this time, it possessed six fighter squadrons of *Spitfires*, *Vampires* and *Tempests* operating from Kanpur, Poona, Ambala and Palam, one B-24 bomber squadron, one C-47 *Dakota* transport squadron, one AOP flight, a communication squadron at Palam and a growing training organisation.

The real test of IAF's airlift capability came in October 1962 when an open warfare erupted on the Sino-Indian border. During the period, October 20–November 20, pressure on the transport and helicopter units was intense, troops and supplies having to be flown to the support of the border posts virtually round-the-clock and at high altitudes. The helicopters had to constantly run the gauntlet of Chinese small arms and anti-aircraft fire, while operating on tricky helipads in the mountains. Many notable feats were performed by the IAF during this conflict, including the operation of C-119 Gs from airstrips 17,000 ft AMSL in the Karakoram Himalayas and the airlifting by AN-12Bs of two troops of AMX-13 light tanks to Chushul, in Ladakh, where the small airstrip was 15,000 ft AMSL.

An unusual task given to the IAF was to support United Nations in Congo (now Zaire) in 1961-62 for dealing with the Katanga rebellion. Following an appeal by the UN troops to restore law and order in Congo six Canberra B(1) 58s of No 5 Squadron were flown from Agra to Central Africa. Operating from Leopoldville and Kamina, the *Canberras* soon destroyed the rebel Air Force, raided Katangan targets and provided the UN ground forces with its only long-range air support force.

On September 1, 1965 Pakistan launched a massive attack in the Chhamb sector. In response to the urgent requests for air strikes against Pakistani armour advancing in the Chhamb-Jaurian sector, IAF fighters went into action. *Vampires* of No 45 Squadron undergoing operational training at a forward base, mounted their first sorties at 1745 hrs on the first day of the conflict and on their heels came the *Mystere* of Nos 3 and 31 Squadrons operating from Pathankot. IAF Gnats proved their mettle in shooting down several PAF F-6 *Sabres* in this sector, the first aerial victories being notched up by Nos 23 and 9 Squadrons. Full-scale war broke out on September 6 all along the international border between West Pakistan and India. Pakistan attempted a pre-emptive strike on the same day, attacking IAF bases at Adampur, Halwara, Pathankot, Srinagar, Jamnagar and Kalaikunda. On the following day, IAF retaliated with air raids and shot down a PAF star fighter in air combat in Sargodha. The IAF provided close air support to the Indian Army in the famous battle of 'Assal Uttar' in Khemkaran sector. In this battle, the thrust of Pakistani Armoured Division was beaten back. The IAF also interdicted Pakistan's railway network, successfully hitting at the Pakistani forces as well as their stores of necessary war-material and also their lines of communication and supply by blowing up trains carrying these goods. With the assistance of IAF, India's ground forces advanced to the outskirts of Lahore. A cease-fire was shortly declared.

As the political situation in the sub-continent deteriorated, the load of 10 million Bangladeshi refugees in India was too much for a weak Indian economy. The IAF was alerted to the possibility of another armed conflict.

On November 22, the same year, four Pakistani *Sabres* strafed Indian and Mukti Bahini position in the Chowgacha Mor area. After 10 minutes, while engaged on a third strafing run, the *Sabres* were intercepted by four *Gnats* from No 22 Squadron, a detachment of which was operating from Dum Dum airport, Kolkata. During the ensuing *melee,* three of the *Sabres* were shot down and all Gnats returned to the base unscathed. On December 3, 1971, pre-emptive strikes were launched by the Pakistani Air Force against IAF bases at Srinagar, Amritsar and Pathankot followed by attacks on

Ambala, Agra, Jodhpur, Uttarlai, Awantipur, Faridkot, Halwara and Sirsa. In response to these strikes, the IAF carried out some 4000 sorties in the west from major and forward bases in Jammu, Kashmir, Punjab and Rajasthan while, in the east, a further 1978 sorties were flown. It was in the western theatre that the *MiG-21* was employed in Pathankot in the north to Jamnagar in the southwestern area. The *MiG-21* mounted combat air patrol missions over vital points and vital areas, flew escort missions for bombers and strike-fighters and was continuously scrambled to intercept hostile intruders. The first aerial victory was on December 12, 1971, when MiG-21s of No 47 Squadron shot down a PAF F-104 over the Gulf of Kutch. This was followed by three more victories in quick succession on December 17 when *MiG-21s* of No 29 Squadron escorting *Maruts,* shot down intercepting F-104s near Uttarlai in Rajasthan desert in gun-missile encounters while a third F-104, on an intruding mission, was shot down by another *MiG-21* of No 29 Squadron. This singular contribution by IAF resulted in a decisive victory for India that resulted in the birth of an independent state of Bangladesh with the unconditional surrender of 90,000 soldiers of Pakistan's armed forces.

The IAF has been strenuously involved in many other major operations that have extended the capacity of its transport and helicopter fleet. With the support of the Indian Army and para-military forces in Northern Ladakh, IAF launched operation *Meghadoot* to control the heights predominating the Siachen glacier. The *IL-76, AN-32, Mi-17 IV* and *Chetak/ Cheetah* helicopters of the IAF still continue with their untiring zeal ferrying men and material to the dizzy heights under the most inhospitable conditions.

To support the mission of the Indian Peace Keeping Force (IPKF) in northern and eastern Sri Lanka, IAF launched operation *Pawan* which lasted almost some thirty months. Some 70,000 sorties were flown by the IAF's transport and helicopter fleet to and within Sri Lanka without a single aircraft lost or mission aborted. In November 1988, in response to the Maldives government's appeal for military help against a mercenary invasion, IAF launched operation *Cactus* to airlift a parachute battalion group from Agra to Maldives. IL-76 aircraft of No 44 Squadron landed at Hulule with in short time. The Indian paratroopers secured the airfield and restored the government's rule at Male within hours. IAF *Mirage-2000* and *AN-32* aircraft also supported the operation.

The IAF took part in the UN peace-keeping duties in Somalia in 1993-94 and once again in Sierra Leone in 2000-2001 sending its helicopters including Mi-8, Mi-17 and Mi-25s.

Operation *Safed Sagar,* as the air operation in the Kargil area was called, was indeed a milestone in the history of military aviation. This was the first time that air power was employed in such an environment.

Fighters as well as armed helicopters carried out many hundreds of sorties against the armed intruders who had infiltrated into the Indian territory. The use of air power in this theatre was instrumental in accelerating the end of the conflict to India's advantage. IAF's air strikes against enemy supply camps and other targets yielded rich dividends. A noteworthy fact is that there was not a single operation on ground that was not preceded by air strikes, each and every action was a result of coordinated planning between 15 Corps and AOC, J&K. The enemy was kept off the back of the Indian Army. In the area of interdiction of enemy supplies, the successful and incessant attacks on the enemy's logistic machines, over the weeks, culminated in a serious degradation of the enemy's ability to sustain them.

Over the years, the IAF has time and again come to the aid of millions of Indians during natural calamities and disasters. Whether battling floods or rescuing marooned crew from floundering ships on the high seas, the IAF has lived up to its reputation and aspiration of the nation.

INDIAN AIR FORCE

The Indian Air Force was officially established on 8 October 1932. Its first ac flight came into being on 01 Apr 1933. It possessed a strength of six RAF-trained officers and 19 *Havai Sepoys* (literally, air soldiers). The aircraft inventory comprised of four Westland Wapiti IIA army co-operation biplanes at Drigh Road as the "A" Flight nucleus of the planned No.1 (Army Co-operation) Squadron.

Cutting its teeth

Four-and-a-half years later, "A" Flight was in action for the first time from Miranshah, in North Waziristan, to support Indian Army operations against insurgent Bhittani tribesmen. Meanwhile, in April 1936, a "B" Flight had also been formed on the vintage

Wapiti. But, it was not until June 1938 that a "C" Flight was raised to bring No. 1 Squadron ostensibly to full strength, and this remained the sole IAF formation when World War II began, although personnel strength had by now risen to 16 officers and 662 men.

Problems concerning the defence of India were reassessed in 1939 by the Chatfield Committee. It proposed the re-equipment of RAF (Royal Air Force) squadrons based in India but did not make any suggestions for the accelerating the then painfully slow growth of IAF except for a scheme to raise five flights on a voluntary basis to assist in the defence of the principal ports. An IAF Volunteer Reserve was thus authorised, although equipping of the proposed Coastal Defence Flights (CDFs) was somewhat inhibited by aircraft availability. Nevertheless, five such flights were established with No. 1 at Madras, No. 2 at Bombay, No. 3 at Calcutta, No. 4 at Karachi and No. 5 at Cochin. No. 6 was later formed at At the end of March 1941, Nos. 1 and 3 CDFs gave up their Wapitis which were requisitioned to equip No. 2 Squadron raised at Peshawar in the following month, and were instead issued with Armstrong Whitworth Atalanta transports, used to patrol the Sunderbans delta area south of Calcutta. No. 2 CDF had meanwhile received requisitioned D.H. 89 Dragon Rapides for convoy and coastal patrol, while No. 5 CDF took on strength a single D.H. 86 which it used to patrol the west of Cape Camorin and the Malabar Coast.

Meanwhile the creation of a training structure in India became imperative and RAF flying instructors were assigned to flying clubs to instruct IAF Volunteer Reserve cadets on Tiger Moths.364 pupils were to receive elementary flying training at seven clubs in British India and two in various princely States by the end of 1941. Some comparative modernity was infused in August 1941, when No. 1 Squadron began conversion to the Westland Lysander at Drigh Road, the Unit being presented with a full establishment of 12 Lysanders at Peshawar by the Bombay War Gifts Fund in the following November. No. 2 Squadron had converted from the Wapiti to the Audax in September 1941 and, on 1 October No. 3 Squadron, similarly Audax-equipped, was raised at Peshawar.

The IAF VR was now inducted into the regular IAF, the individual flights initially retaining their coastal defence status, but with Japan's entry into the war in December, No. 4 Flight, with four Wapitis and two Audaxes, was despatched to Burma to operate from Moulmein. Unfortunately, four of the flight's six aircraft were promptly lost to Japanese bombing and, late in January 1942, No. 4 Flight gave place in Moulmein to No. 3 Flight which had meanwhile re-equipped with four ex-RAF Blenheim Is. For a month, these Blenheims were to provide almost the sole air cover for ships arriving at Rangoon harbour.

WAR IN BURMA

On 1 February, No.1 Squadron arrived in Burma with its Lysanders, flying tactical recce missions from Toungoo before transferring to Mingaladon with a flight deployed at Lashio. IAF personnel were soon hanging pairs of 250-lb. bombs on each of their Lysanders and with these, flew low-level unescorted missions against the principal Japanese air bases at Mae-Haungsaun, Cheingmai and Chiangrai in Thailand. However, the Japanese advance was relentless and with the final evacuation of Burma, No.1 Squadron personnel were flown to India, where at Risalpur in June 1942, the unit began conversion to the Hurricane IIB fighter. No.2 Squadron had also equipped with Lysanders by the end of 1941, being confined to anti-invasion exercises until, in September 1942, it emulated the IAF's premier unit by converting to Hurricanes. The third IAF unit to operate the Lysander was No.4 Squadron, formed with four aircraft on 16 February 1942. This squadron was to continue to operate the Westland aircraft until it, too was re-equipped with the Hurricane in June 1943. Six months earlier, No.6 Squadron was raised with personnel from Nos 1 and 2 flights, being Hurricane-equipped from the outset. Between March and December 1942, 10 aircrew schools were opened in India, and the first Harvard Is and IIs were delivered to No. 1 Flying

Training School at Ambala, this school having been established to provide basic and advanced training for IAF pilots over a four-and-half month course. By the end of that year, however,or a decade after the IAF's creation and three years into World War II, the Service could muster just five squadrons. The coastal defence flights had now been disbanded and most personnel of Nos.3 and 6 Flights were combined with regular IAF personnel to form No. 7 Squadron which was equipped with the U:S.-built Vengeance 1 dive bomber in mid-February 1943. No. 8 Squadron was raised meanwhile, on 1 December 1942, absorbing the remaining coastal defence flight personnel, and also issued with the Vengeance, to achieve operational status on 25June 1943.

The Vengeance suffered numerous defects and teething troubles, necessitating temporary withdrawal from the two IAF squadrons, but the problems were eventually mitigated if not eradicated, and No. 8 Sqn flew its first operational Vengeance sorties against Japanese targets from Double Moorings, Chittagong, on 15 December 1943, No. 7 Squadron, which had flown its Vengeances on some missions against dissident tribesmen in North Waziristan, started operations in the Arakan from an airstrip at Uderbund, near Kumbigram, where it arrived on 12 March 1944, the two squadrons converting to Vengeance IIIs during the course of operations and both flying with considerable distinction.No. 7 Squadron discarded its dive bombers in favour of Hurricane IIs for the tactical-reconnaissance role in November 1944, No. 8 Squadron becoming the first to convert onto the Spitfire VIII during the previous month and commencing operations on 3 January 1945 in the Kangaw area.

Both Nos 9 and 10 Squadrons were raised on Hurricanes in the early months of 1944, and thus, by the end of the year, the operational element of the IAF had risen to nine squadrons, with Nos. 1,2,3,4,6,7,9 and 10 on Hurricanes and No.8 on Spitfires. Five of the

Hurricane-equipped squadrons played a major role in the Arakan offensive which began in December 1944, disrupting the enemy's lines of communication and constantly harrying the Japanese forces until victory was achieved with the re-occupation of Rangoon on 3 May 1945. In that month, No. 4 Squadron became the second IAF Spitfire unit when it re-equipped with the Mk VIII version of this fighter, and No. 9 followed suit to complete conversion byJuly, by which time No. 10 had begun conversion, and the Hurricane, backbone of the IAF combat element for much of the war, was rapidly phased out.

During the war years, the steady expansion of the IAF had placed all emphasis on army co-operation and tactical reconnaissance; it had continued to fly ageing equipment such as the Hurricane when such aircraft as the Thunderbolt and Mosquito were being inducted in large numbers by other Allied forces in the theatre and it had, in consequence, suffered a sense of equipment inferiority.

Nevertheless, assigned the least glamorous of tasks and flying obsolescent equipment, the Service established traditions of courage and efficiency second to none; its personnel had been awarded 22 Distinguished Flying Crosses and a host of other decorations, and in recognition of its achievements, the Service had been honoured by bestowal of the prefix "Royal" on its title in March 1945.

INDEPENDENCE AND PARTITION

The stimulus provided by the Second World War had raised RIAF personnel strength to 28,500 including some 1,600 officers, by the time hostilities terminated. In August 1945, No. 4 Squadron was designated a component unit of the British

Commonwealth Occupation Forces in Japan, exchanging its Spitfire VIIIs for Mk XIVs in October and arriving in Japan aboard HMS vengence on 23 April 1946. Meanwhile, from late 1945, the remaining Hurricane-equipped RIAF fighter squadrons converted to the Spitfire at Kohat, Samungli and Risalpur and by mid-1946 the entire RIAF fighter force was Spitfire-equipped. The year 1946 also saw the establishment of the first RIAF transport unit, No.12 Squadron which had first been raised on Spitfires at Kohat in December 1945 and received C-47 Dakotas in Panagarh in late 1946. A decision had also been taken to re-equip the fighter squadrons with the Tempest II, and implementation of this decision began during the autumn of 1946, No. 3 Squadron at Kolar becoming the first to re-equip, followed by No.10 Squadron later in 1946.

Personnel strength had meanwhile been virtually halved to some 14,000 officers and men in the post-war rundown, but the British authorities had made their own assessment of India's post-war defence needs. As of October 1946, they envisaged expansion of the existing ten RIAF squadrons into a balanced force of twenty fighter, bomber and transport squadrons. Owing to the rapidly changing political situation, however, definitive decisions concerning Indian defence were, in the event, to be left to the emerging Government of Independent India. No. 4 Squadron converted to the Tempest 11 upon its return to India from Japan and Nos.7 and 8 Squadrons also relinquished their Spitfires for the more efficacious Tempest fighter during the summer of 1947. Nos. 1 and 9 Squadrons, too, received Tempest lls at this time, but on 15 August 1947, and with the division of both India and its armed forces, these units stood down and their equipment was transferred to the newly created Royal Pakistan Air Force. Thus, the principal components of the RIAF at partition were Nos. 3,4,7,8 and 10 Squadrons with Tempest us, No. 2 Squadron with Spitfires and No. 12 Squadron with C-47s, plus No. 1 Air Observation Flight, the establishment of which with AOP Auster 4s, 5s, and 6s, coincided with independence. No. 6 Squadron, which had been in process of converting from Spitfires to C-47s at Drigh Road, had been stood down and its transports transferred to Pakistan.

The RIAF had lost many permanent bases and other establishments as a result of the division of the country, but was to have virtually no breathing space in which to recover from the surgery that had accompanied partition before the Service was to find itself once more firing its guns in earnest. On 27 October 1947, No.12 Sqn was to initiate the remarkable feat of air-lifting the Ist Sikhs from Palam onto the rough and dusty Srinagar airstrip without planning or reconnaissance as the initial Indian response to the sizeable insurgent forces that were pouring across the border into Jammu and Kashmir. On 30 October, the first Spitfires from the Advanced Flying School at Ambala reached Srinagar and were soon engaged in strafing the raiders beyond Pattan. Within a week, the Tempests of No. 7 Squadron were playing a decisive role in the battle of Shelatang which halted the forward momentum of the insurgents.

The fighting was to continue for 15 months, with heavy RIAF involvement throughout, a ceasefire eventually coming into force on 1 January 1949, but despite being continuously on an operational footing throughout this period, the reorganisation and modernisation of the Service continued unabated. The Combined Services Headquarters had meanwhile been separated for command purposes and Air Headquarters established in New Delhi. This included the Operational and Training Commands, No. 1 Operational Group having been formed to supervise all RIAF units and their support elements engaged in the campaign in Jammu and Kashmir.

Heavy bombers and jet fighters

No. 2 Squadron had re-equipped with Spitfire XVllls in the interim, and No. 9 Squadron re-raised on this type; No. 101 Photo Reconnaissance Flight was formed in January 1948 on Spitfire PR Mk. XlXs, this unit being destined to achieve full squadron status in April 1950. To make up attrition suffered in the Kashmir operations, a further batch of Tempest IIs was procured from the UK in December 1948. The same year witnessed various equipment changes, one of which was to have a profound effect on the composition of the RIAF. The Service, wishing to establish a heavy bombing element, contracted with HAL to "re-construct" a force of B-24 Liberators from the mouldering remains of nearly 100 ex USAF bombers of this type at the immense Care and Maintenance Unit Depot at Kanpur.

Despite the scepticism on the part of the US and British advisers concerning the feasibility of the scheme, the first half-dozen HAL-reconditioned B-24s were ready by November 1948 and, on the 17th of that month, No. 5 Squadron was formed with these heavy bombers. Later, in early 1950, No. 6 Squadron was to re-form at Poona also with B-24s, while No.16 Squadron was to be established to provide back-up training on the type. To supplement the Tiger Moths, Prentice basic trainers were delivered to the RIAF during the course of 1948, eventually to see service at Jodhpur, Tambaram and Ambala, but truly epoch making in so far as the Service was concerned, was the arrival in India on 4 November 1948 of three Vampire F.Mk.3 jet fighters.

Republic status

In January 1950, India became a Republic within the British Commonwealth and the Indian Air Force dropped its "Royal" prefix. At this time, it possessed six fighter squadrons of Spitfires, Vampires and Tempests, operating from Kanpur, Poona, Ambala and Palam, one B-24 bomber squadron, one C-47 Dakota transport squadron, one AOP flight, a communications squadron at Palam and a growing training organisation. Training adhered closely to the pattern established by the RAF, most instructors having graduated from the CFS in the UK and in addition to No.1. Flying Training School at Hyderabad with Tiger Moths and Harvards and No. 2 FTS atJodhpur with Prentices and Harvards, there were IAF colleges at Begumpet, Coimbatore andJodhpur.

Licence manufacture of the de Havilland Vampire had been initiated by HAL which, after building a batch from imported major assemblies, went on to manufacture a further 250. In addition, 60 Vampire T Mk. 55s were to be built of which 10 were assembled from imported kits. Nos.2,3 and 8 Squadrons followed No.7 Squadron on the Vampire, but, extraordinarily, 1951 also saw the formation of the last piston-engined fighter combat unit when No. 14 Squadron was raised on the Spitfire Mk. XVIII. Vampire NF Mk. 54 two-seat night fighters were obtained in May 1953 to re-equip No. 10. Sqn at Palam, thus endowing night-intercept capability upon the IAF for the first time. At this time, relations between India and Pakistan were again steadily deteriorating and the IAF, its combat strength virtually unchanged since partition in 1947, was scarcely ready for any full-scale conflict. Plans were accordingly framed for major expansion during the period 1953-57, and the Government began to seek non-traditional and alternative sources of combat aircraft procurement.

Selection of the Dassault Ouragan fighter from France at this time reflected the decision to initiate diversification of supply sources. The first four of over 100 Ouragans, or *Toofanis* as they were to become known in the IAF, reached Palam from France on 24 October 1953, and this type re-equipped Nos.8, 3 and 4 Squadrons in that order. The *Toofanis* were eventually to be passed on to newly-raised units Nos. 29 and 47 Squadrons, with the re-equipment in 1957 of Nos. 3 and 8 Squadrons with the Mystere IVA from the same Gallic stable.

Re-equipment of the combat units necessarily assumed an overriding priority in view of the growth of what were seen as threats to India's integrity, but expansion of airlift capability was also vital. A second transport squadron, No. 11, had been formed on C-47 Dakotas in September 1951, and considerable enhancement of the Service's logistic support capacity was heralded by procurement of 26 Fairchild C-119G Packets from the United States which reached India by the end of 1954. Rapidly to assume the status of an airlift backbone, the C-119Gs were issued to No. 12 Squadron, which, for some years, operated them in concert with the C-47s, the older transports eventually passing to a newly-raised unit, No. 43 Squadron. A second batch of 29 C-119Gs was obtained in July 1960, and the transport fleet was further augmented by another 24 C-119Gs in May 1963 under US emergency military aid.

Both the establishment of a Maintenance Command and resurrection of the Auxiliary Air Force took place in 1955, two units of the latter being formed as Nos. 51 and 52 Squadrons at New Delhi and Bombay. A third AAF unit, No. 53 Sqn, was raised at Madras in the following year, and four more added over the next two years, Nos. 54 (Allahabad), 55 (Calcutta), 56 (Bhubaneshwar) and 57 (Chandigarh) Squadrons. The AAF squadrons were equipped with the HAL-designed HT-2 trainer-officially introduced into service on 10 January 1955-and the Harvard, although Vampire FB Mk. 52s were added in 1959.

Expansion and modernisation Particularly significant in IAF was the year 1957, which witnessed true beginnings of the major re-equipment programme that was to raise the Service fully to world standards. Deliveries began of 110 Dassault Mystere IVAs, carrying the service into the realms of transonic flight for the first time, and both Hawker Hunters and English Electric Canberras began to enter the IAF inventory. A new

No. 1 Squadron was raised on the Mystere, the existing Vampire-equipped No. 1 Squadron being redesignated as No. 27 Squadron; No. 5 Squadron re-equipped with the Canberra B(I) Mk. 58, and, at the year's end, No. 7 Squadron began conversion to the Hunter FMk.56. It was perhaps appropriate that the year which saw commencement of an immense infusion of modern hardware should also witness the end of the IAF's piston-engined fighter epoch: No. 14 Squadron, the last firstline piston-engined fighter unit, flew in its Spitfire Mk. XVIIIs to Halwara in preparation for re-equipment with the Vampire.

The IAF's energies were now taxed heavily with implementation of an expansion programme aimed at raising the Service from a 15-squadron force to no fewer than 33 squadrons over an extremely short span of years: a Herculean task when performed simultaneously with sweeping equipment changes. Several new squadrons, such as Nos. 15, 17, 20, 24, 27 and 45, were raised on Vampire FB.Mk. 52s as interim equipment; Canberra B(I) Mk. 58s had equipped two additional squadrons, Nos. 16 and 35 by 1959, No. 106 Squadron having equipped with Canberra PR Mk. 57s and by the end of the 1961, six squadrons (Nos.7, 14, 17, 20, 27 and 37) were equipped with the Hunter. Growth was not restricted to the combat elements for, in parallel, the IAF's transport force was enlarged to six squadrons, three with C-47s (Nos. 11, 43 and 49), two with C-119Gs (Nos. 12 and 19) and one with DHC-3 Otters (No.41).

The early sixties were accompanied by the IAF's induction of yet more new aircraft types, the most interesting of these arguably being the Folland Gnat lightweight fighter. With its startling agility, the Gnat proffered outstanding cost effectiveness and during the mid-fifties a licence agreement was concluded for its manufacture by HAL following delivery of 23 complete aircraft and 20 sets of components by the parent company. The first IAF unit, No. 23 Squadron, converted from the Vampire FB Mk. 52 to the Gnat in March 1960. No. 2 Squadron re-equipped with the Gnat at Ambala early in 1962, and No.9 Squadron soon followed suit.

Canberras in the Congo

An unusual commitment of the IAF was to support United Nations operations on the Congo (now Zaire) in 1961-62.

Following an appeal by the U.N. for both troops and combat aircraft to restore law and order and keep peace, six Canberra B(1) 58s of No.5 Squadron were flown from Agra to Central Africa. Operating from Leopoldville and Kamina, the Canberras soon destroyed the rebel air force, raided Katangan targets and generally provided the U.N. ground forces with its only long-range air support force.

Soviet transports and helicopters

Further procurement source diversification had been signified late in 1960 when, as a result of the increasing frequency of clashes with Chinese forces on the Sino-Indian Himalayan border and the need that these revealed for yet further increase in airlift capability, together with a requirement for medium helicopters suitable for high-altitude operation, orders were placed in the Soviet Union for eight Antonov An-12B and 24 IL-yushin 11-14 transport aircraft plus 10 Mi-4 helicopters. The first An-12B arrived in India on 1 March 1961, No. 44 Squadron being formed on this type, the 11-14s that followed equipping another newly-raised squadron, No. 42. A follow-on order for a further eight An-12Bs was placed early in 1962, the IAF finally beginning to build up a really credible heavy airlift capability which was to be immensely enhanced with the arrival of a further 25 An-12Bs under a loan agreement signed in July 1963, a second squadron, No.25, meanwhile being formed on this type.

The Mi-4 helicopter was to have as profound an effect on IAF capability as did the An-12B. Prior to the phase-in on this Soviet type, the Service had but a handful of ageing Sikorsky S-55s, plus a number of small Bell 47Gs, and with the delivery of Mi-4s, major expansion of the IAF rotorcraft inventory began. No.109 Helicopter Unit was formed with the first Mi-4s and following an order for further 16 Mi-4s in early 1962, other helicopter units were formed in North-East India, successive orders in 1963-64 and 1966 eventually bringing the total number of Mi-4s procured to 120.

Conflict with China

The real test of IAF airlift capability came in October 1962, when open warfare erupted on the Sino-Indian border. During the period 20 October to 20 November, pressure on the Service's transport and helicopter units were intense, troops and supplies having to be flown to the support of the border posts virtually around the clock and at extreme altitudes. The helicopters had to constantly run the gauntlet of Chinese small arms and anti-aircraft fire, while operating to.the tricky helipads in the mountains. Many notable feats were performed by the IAF during this conflict, including the operation of C-119Gs from airstrips 17,000 ft (5180m) above sea level in the Karakoram Himalayas, and the air-lifting by An-12Bs of two troops of AMX-13 light tanks to Chushul, in Ladakh, where the small airstrip was 15,000 ft (4570m) above sea level.

The state of emergency declared as a result of the Sino-Indian fighting resulted in disbandment of the Auxillary Air Force and absorption of its personnel and equipment by the regular IAF. An emergency training scheme was instituted in which the services of five flying clubs at Madras, Kanpur, New Delhi, Nagpur and Patiala were enlisted, more than 1,000 cadets receiving primary flying instruction with these clubs by the end of 1964. Furthermore, Vampire FBMk.52s "mothballed" since 1961, were restored to service as the equipment of newly-raised squadrons. The IAF was expanding rapidly, its personnel strength of 28,000 officers and men at the time of the Sino-ludian conflict increasing by some two-thirds by the end of 1964, but the manpower requirements of the 33-squadron force had still to be implemented fully when the scheme was overtaken by even more ambitious expansion to a 45-squadron force which was sanctioned by the Government in October 1962, this calling for the raising of IAF personnel strength to some 100,000 by the early seventies.

Together with the arrival of successive batches of An-12Bs from the Soviet Union and a third batch of C-119Gs from the USA, the IAF began to receive the Canadian DHC-4 Caribou, two being presented to the Service by the Canadian Government as assistance in wake of the Sino-Indian conflict and 16 more being ordered, with deliveries commencing in September 1963, resulting in the establishment of No.33 Squadron.

An epoch-making decision was taken in August 1962 which was to profoundly alter the complexion and strength of the

Indian Air Force into the decades ahead. The Government of India signed protocols with the Soviet Union for the very first supply of combat aircraft and missiles for the Indian Air Force. The purchase of 12 MiG-21 fighters from the Soviet Union-the IAF's first combat aircraft of non-western origin-and for Soviet technical assistance in setting up production facilities for the fighter in India was followed by the procurement of SA-2 *(Dvina)* surface-to-air missiles. Re-equipment and expansion of the IAF was now being pursued in parallel with major changes in the operational infrastructure. Prior to the Sino-Indian conflict, the IAF had been geared to provide defence against attack from the West only, but appreciation of the vulnerability of the entire Northern and Eastern border had called for profound rethinking of the operational infrastructure. It was now patently apparent that, for a country of the immensity of India, a system of purely functional Commands was impracticable and that, to cater for all potential-threats, operational command would in future, have to be exercised on a regional basis. Thus the Indian periphery was divided into three for purposes of operational control, the Western, Central and Eastern Air Commands eventually emerging. However, in order to maintain uniform standards in training and maintenance, the Training and Maintenance Commands were to remain functional.

WAR IN THE SUB CONTINENT

Tension between India and Pakistan had steadily escalated over the years, culminating on 1 September 1965 in a massive attack in the Chhamb sector by Pakistani forces. Possessing the initiative in having chosen the time and place to strike and enjoying overwhelming numerical superiority in the sector in both armour and troops, Pakistan posed a grave threat to Indian forces on the ground and so, in response to urgent requests for air strikes against Pakistani armour advancing in the Chhamb-Jaurian sector, Vampire FBMk.52s of No. 45 Squadron, at the time undergoing operational training at a forward base, mounted their first sorties at 1745 hours on the first day of the conflict, and on their heels came the Mysteres of Nos.3 and 31 Squadrons operating from Pathankot. The Pakistani armoured thrust was staggered. IAF Gnats proved their mettle in shooting down PAF Sabres in this sector, the first of aerial victories being notched by Nos. 23 and 9 Squadrons. Rapidly escalating, full scale warfare broke out on 6 September all along the international border between West Pakistan and India.

In the days that followed, IAF Canberras raided the major PAF bases at Sargodha and Chaklala at night, flying 200 counter air and interdiction missions against these and other Pakistani bases, including those at Akwal, Peshawar, Kohat, ChakJhumra and Risalwala. The virtuosity of the Hunters was fully demonstrated, Nos. 7, 20 and 27 Squadrons being employed in counter-air as well as interdiction and close air support missions in the West while Hunters of No. 14 Squadron battled with Sabres of the PAF No. 14 squadron raiding the IAF base at Kalaikunda in the East. The Mysteres were employed primarily in the ground attack role in which they proved extremely effective, with their swaths of 5 5 mm rockets most effective against armoured vehicles. Perhaps the most outstanding operational success was enjoyed by the Gnat, the three squadrons of which provided the air defence mainstay by flying CAPs over most operational IAF bases as well as fulfilling escort missions. Indeed, such was its success particularly against the F-86, that it was to earn the appellation of "Sabre Slayer". The September conflict was the first full-scale war in which the post-independence IAF was involved and the Service learned many lessons as a result. Post mortem examination revealed some requirements, the pace of expansion being slowed while lessons were digested. It was realised that too much emphasis had been placed on quantity at some cost in quality in order to cater for the dictates of the very high tempo IAF expansion embarked upon following the Sino-Indian War. This had necessitated cutting the duration of training courses to maximise personnel output and there was evidence that this could have some adverse effect on operational efficiency.. Emphasis was now reversed in that quality once more took precedence over quanitity and training underwent major reorganization in consequence.

Consolidation and modernisation

There could, of course, be no abatement in equipment modernisation. While the Indo-Pakistan conflict had underlined the vital importance of the state or readiness of the men flying and servicing the aircraft, their training and motivation, the efficacy of their equipment was of equal concern. When the September 1965 hostilities began, the MiG-21 had still to achieve operational status. No. 28 Squadron had been formed on the MiG-21 clear-weather day intercept model but was still very much a trials unit then flying localised CAPs. Early acquisition of MiG-21s of a later and more potent version was considered essential to accelerate re-equipment of squadrons still flying such patently obsolete types as the Vampire FBMk. Thus sufficient numbers of the improved MiG-21FL (Type 77 in IAF parlance) were imported in flyaway condition to initiate the programme, and these, together with others imported in CKD form for HAL assembly, were to be sufficient for the re-equipment of nine squadrons during the period 1966-69.

Owing to the success enjoyed by the Gnat during the conflict, plans for its early-1966 phase-out by HAL were halted and production was fully reinstated, to result in a further four Gnat squadrons (Nos 15, 21, 22 and 24) being formed during 1966-68. Delay in availability of the HAL-designed HF-24 Marut for the ground attack fighter mission led, in 1966, to the IAF evaluating and the Government purchasing the Sukhoi Su-7BM, deliveries of which from the Soviet Union were to commence in March 1968, with No.26 Squadron being the first of a half-dozen squadrons that were to operate the type. Within three years of the Indo-Pakistan conflict, the IAF, which had achieved equal status with the Army on 15 January 1966, possessed in excess of 70,000 personnel and was nearing its 45-squadron goal. Its composition in the autumn of 1968 included 23 fighter category squadrons, three tactical bomber squadrons, a maritime patrol squadron (with ex-Air India L. 1049G Super Constellations), 11 transport squadrons, four AOP squadrons, a number of helicopter units and a few SAM squadrons.

Numerically predominating in the fighter inventory was the Gnat, equipping eight squadrons; six squadrons were equipped with the Hunter, a further four on the MiG-21FL and two on the Mystere IVA. Two squadrons fulfilled the photo-recce fighter role with adapted Vampire T Mk. 55s and one squadron was operating the HF-24 Marut. The bombing element comprised three squadrons equipped with the Canberra; the maritime reconnaissance unit, No. 6 Sqn, had finally relinquished its Liberators late in 1967, and was operating adapted L-1049G Super Constellations. The airlift component consisted of two squadrons with An-12Bs, three with C-119Gs, three with C-47s, two with Otters and one each with 11-14s and Caribous while one squadron was in process of converting from the C-47 to the HS. 748. The AOP squadrons operated a mix of Auster AOP-9s and HAL-designed HAOP-27 Krishaks, and the Helicopter Units, which were not formed into separate squadrons, were equipped with the Mi-4 and the Alouette 111 (Chetak). As the sixties translated to the seventies, the IAF consolidated its expansion plans, attaining its 45-squadron goal. Obsolescent equipment was steadily withdrawn to be succeeded by increasing numbers of HF-24s, MiG-21FLs and SU-7BMs and in March 1971, planning began on the creation of an extensive Air Defence Ground Environment System (ADGES), the emphasis initially being placed on strengthening surveillance of the Sino-Indian border. Flying training was rationalised and expanded and, inJanuary 1971, the Air Force Academy at Dundigal (near Hyderabad) was inaugurated.

The War of December 1971

The professional standards, capability and flexibility of the much expanded Service were soon to be put to the acid test. From early 1971, as the political situation on the sub-continent deteriorated, the IAF was alerted to the possibility of another armed conflict. For some weeks in November, both Indian and Pakistan governments protested violations of national airspace along the western border, but aerial conflict between the respective air arms began in earnest on 22 November, preceding full-scale warfare between India and Pakistan by 12 days. At 1449 hours, four Pakistani Sabres strafed Indian and Mukti Bahini positions in the Chowgacha Mor area, and 10 minutes later, while engaged on a third strafing run, the Sabres were intercepted by four Gnats from No. 22 Sqn, a detachment of which was operating from Dum Dum Airport, Calcutta. During the ensuing melee, three of the Sabres were shot down, all Gnats returning to base unscathed. The first blood of a new Indo-Pakistan air war had been drawn. Other encounters were to follow over the next 10 days, within both Indian and Pakistani airspace, before full-scale war began on 3 December. Pre-emptive strikes were launched by the Pakistan Air Force against IAF bases at Srinagar, Amritsar and Pathankot, followed by attacks on Ambala, Agra, Jodhpur, Uttarlai, Avantipur, Faridkot, Halwara and Sirsa. Apart from IAF bases, the PAF attacked railway stations, Indian armour concentrations and other targets. In response and during the ensuing two weeks, the IAF carried out some 4,000 sorties in the West from major and forward bases in Jammu, Kashmir, Punjab and Rajasthan, while, in the East, a further 1,978 sorties were flown.

Throughout the conflict, in which Indian strategy was to maintain basically defensive postures on the western and northern fronts whilst placing emphasis on a lightning campaign in the east, the IAF established a highly credible serviceability rate which exceeded 80 per cent. Mission emphasis throughout was on interdiction. In the West the IAF's primary tasks were disruption of enemy communications, the destruction of fuel and ammunition reserves, and the prevention of any ground force concentrations so that no major offensive could be mounted against India while Indian forces were primarily engaged in the East. On the Eastern front, the Indian forces launched a sophisticated campaign which included rapid-moving infantry and armour advancing from three directions, airborne and heliborne assaults, missile bombardments from ships and an amphibious landing, the IAF's task being primarily direct support of the ground forces. In a classic air action in the Western desert, four Hunters of the OCU, detachment at Jaisalmer destroyed an entire armoured regiment at Longewala, literally stopping the enemy offensive in its tracks.

The IAF had good reason for satisfaction with its showing during the December 1971 conflict. Although Pakistan had initiated the war with pre-emptive air strikes against major forward air bases, the IAF rapidly gained the initiative and had thereafter dominated the skies over both fronts. Admittedly, there had to be war losses but the IAF flew many more sorties than its opponent with interdiction missions predominating, and the bulk of the Service's attrition was the result of intensive anti-aircraft fire; in aerial combat, the IAF proved its superiority in no uncertain manner. First round had gone to the Gnats, again, but its later compatriots, the MiG-21s, were to shortly demonstrate the superiority of this supersonic fighter, flown by professionals. Six squadrons of MiG-21FLs were part of the IAF's order-of battle, participating in operations both in the Eastern and Western Sectors. Three MiG-21 squadrons, operating from Gauhati and Tezpur,took part in counter-air, escort and close air support tasks during the blitzkrieg action in Bangladesh. That the MiG-21 was highly effective in short range, precision attacks was amply demonstrated during the attacks with 500 kg bombs on the PAF's air bases at Tezgaon and Kurmitola, while pin point 57 mm rocket attacks were carried out against key command centres in the capital Dacca itself.

It was in the Western theatre that the MiG-21 was employed in its primary task, that of air defence, escort and interception. Deployed at all the major air bases, from Pathankot in the north to Jamnagar in the South Western area, the MiG-21FLs mounted hundreds of combat air patrol sorties over Vital Points (VP) and Vital Areas (VA), flew escort missions for bombers and strike fighters and were continuously scrambled to intercept hostile intruders. The MiG-21 finally met its original adversary, the F-104 Starfighter, in air combat over the Subcontinent during the December 1971 conflict and in all four recorded cases of classic dog fights, the MiG-21s outclassed and out fought the F-104s. The first aerial victory was on 12 December 1971, when MiG-21FLs of No. 47 Squadron shot down a PAF F-104 over the Gulf of Kutch and this was followed by three more victories in quick succession on 17 December, when MiG-21FLs of No. 29 Squadron escorting HF-24 Maruts, shot down intercepting F-104s near Uttarlai in the Rajsthan desert in gun-missile encounters, while a third F-104, on an intruding mission, was shot down by another MiG 21FL of No.29 Squadron.

Mig 21 pair

The December 1971 war also meant the gaining of India's highest award for gallantry to the IAF. Flying Officer Nirmal Jit Singh Sekhon, flying Gnats with No. 18 Squadron from Srinagar, was posthumously awarded the Param Vir Chakra. Notwithstanding the successful campaign of December 1971 which created both history and geography, the Indian Air Force had lessons to draw from subsequent analyses of the conflict, although for the most part, these lessons dictated refinement rather than any fundamental change.

A MATURE AND MODERN FORCE

Aircraft Systems Testing Establishment (ASTE) the Tactics & Air Combat Development Establishment, (TACDE), the 'College of Air Combat' and other specialist establiments continued to mature. Work on the ADGES was resumed in 1974-75 and plans for the qualitative upgrading of the entire Air Force were continually refined. The IAF handed over its Super Constellations to the Navy in 1975. The early seventies saw force levels being consolidated, and training in new weapons-systems and evolution of new tactics being honed.

By the mid '70s, the IAF was clearly in need of urgent re-equipment decisions and various requirements, better known by their acronyms DPSA, TASA, METAC and HETAC, were pursued and decisions were forthcoming at last. The period, the IAF was to benefit from a crest in the eighties, the period 1978-88 witnessing a major modernisation programme which replaced most of the earlier generation and obsolete equipment with spanking new aircraft types and weapon systems. No less than twenty new aircraft types and sub-types entered the IAF's service over these years, including various strike fighters, third-generation supersonic interceptors, tri-sonic reconnaissance aircraft, strategic heavy lift transports, medium tactical transports, light transport aircraft, heavy lift and medium-assault helicopters, basic trainers, surface-to-air missiles and an array of sophisticated weaponry propelling the IAF, or *Bharatiya Vayu Sena,* into one of the world's better equipped air arms.

First off the mark was selection of the Jaguar strike fighter, to meet the IAF's urgent Deep Penetration Strike Aircraft (DPSA) requirement, to replace the Canberra and Hunter still soldiering on in this exacting role. After many years of evaluation and negotiation, the Anglo-French fighter was contracted for, an interim batch of ex-RAF Jaguars being accepted to re-equip No. 14 Squadron. IAF pilots and technicians received conversion training with the RAF and British Aerospace in Lossie mouth, Coltishall and Warton before ferrying the first Jaguars to India in July 1979. These were followed by a batch of U.K. built Jaguars to re-equip No. 5 Squadron even as simultaneously, HAL prepared for production of the aircraft, its powerplants, avionics and accessories in India. By the mid-80s, the Jaguar was in service with Nos. 5, 14, 16 and 27 Squadrons while a flight of No.6 Squadron was equipped with the Maritime Jaguar carrying the new generation Sea Eagle anti-ship sea-skimming missile. The Jaguar strike fighter was equipped also with Magic air-to-air missiles on unique overwing pylons, featured advanced nay-attack systems and able to carry formidable warload till the far ends of the sub-continent.

Meanwhile, in 1976, the "third generation" MiG-21bis, considered the definitive variant of the classic tailed-delta fighter design, was to follow-on the "M" sub-type, as a multi-role air superiority/ground attack version. The MiG-21bis assumed the prime air defence mantle and sufficient numbers were acquired in 1976-77 to equip three squadrons (Nos. 15, 21 and 23) formerly operating the Gnat light fighter. With some 580 MiG-21s delivered by HAL and nearly 250 MiG-21s (including the two-seat operational trainers) imported as "fly aways", the type remained an immense asset for the Indian Air Force for over a quarter century. The quantity vs. quality dilemma inevitably faced by most of the world's air forces as a consequence of spiralling costs was mitigated for the IAF by the large scale availability of the MiG-21, which type will surely go down as one of aviation history's all-time classics.

The next requirement to be met was for a Tactical Air Strike Aircraft (TASA). With the various development programmes to enhance the operational performance of the HF-24 Marut by HAL abandoned for one reason or the other, the Government of India concluded an agreement with the Soviet Union for the MiG-23 variable-sweep fighter. Four squadrons, then flying the HF-24 and Sukhoi Su-7 were re-equipped with the MiG-23BN and induction into IAF service of this swing-wing fighter. Nos. 10 and 220 Squadrons were shortly operational on the new type and Nos. 31 and 221 followed to add a considerable measure of potency to the offensive air support formations of the IAF. The dedicated strike derivative, selected for licence production by HAL, was the MiG-27M which shared the overall configuration of the BN but was optimised for low-level, high-speed performance. The last Sukhoi Su-7 Squadron (No.222) became the first MiG-27M unit and the Ajeet light fighter squadrons were gradually re-equipped with the MiG-27ML, No.9 being followed by Nos.18,22 and lately, No.2.

Induction of the new generation F-16 fighter by the PAF in 1981-82 was a "dejavu" type situation for India and in order to counter such a challenge, the Government contracted for the MiG-23MF air superiority version of the swing-wing fighter, equipped with beyond-visual range missiles, and two new squadrons (Nos. 223 and 224) were formed on the type in 1982. However, these were considered only an interim solution and, in the absence of suitable, known, Soviet equivalents, India turned to Western sources for an advanced technology interceptor. In 1982, a contract was finalised with France for the Mirage 2000 delta-wing, fly-by-wire fighter, with high agility and a formidable radar/missile combination. IAF pilots and technicians had converted to the Mirage 2000 at Mont de Marsan and ferried the fighters from France in the summer of 1985. Two squadrons (Nos. 1 and 7) were re-equipped with the new French fighter in 1985-86 and the Indian Air Force employed this multi-role advanced technology fighter to good effect in a number of actions within the next few years.

Not too long afterwards, the Indian Air Force was, to be pleasantly surprised when its test pilots were invited to evaluate the Soviet Union's latest, still-under-wraps, air superiority fighter, vaguely known to the public as the *Fulcrum.* Officially designated the MiG-29, the IAF team was obviously delighted by the new generation fighter's performance and handling qualities, described as "truly outstanding". Two years were to pass, however, before the Governments of India and the Soviet Union formalised an agreement for supply of the MiG-29, integrated with contemporary pulse doppler radar and new weapon systems.

8

Strategic Role of Air Power

There is a need to understand the meaning of the oft used word "strategic". But we must keep in mind the context in which it is used. Initially, during the 1920s-1940s, "strategic" in air doctrine meant the pure offensive of the bomber against the enemy's heartland to achieve quick, swift victory which avoided the carnage of defensive trench warfare. Post-World War II, as the world got divided in the two blocs led by two superpowers, "strategic" mostly meant bombers with intercontinental range, carrying nuclear weapons. Ballistic missiles with nuclear warheads also came in this category from the 1950s onwards.

So "strategic" referred to ranges of 5,000 km plus and nuclear weapons in large kilo ton (KT) or mega ton (MT) capacities. The Vietnam War saw B-52 strategic bombers unleashing up to 30 ton bombs in each sortie for supporting troops in close air support, that is, in a tactical role. In 1982, eight Israeli F-16 aircraft attacked the Osirak nuclear reactor near Baghdad with 1,000 kg bombs each and totally destroyed the facility. It set back Iraq's quest for nuclear weapons at least by a decade. So while Cold War bombers were being used for tactical air support, the tactical aircraft, using tactical weapons, achieved results that were totally strategic in nature.

During World War II, it took 1,000 bombers, with 9,000 aircrew, dropping nearly 2,000 ton of bombs to destroy a target. During the Gulf War of 1991, one F-117 carrying 2 ton bombs could destroy a target with greater assurance in one sortie. Thus, a tactical aircraft with tactical weapons was achieving a far greater effect than the 1,000 bomber raid of World War II.

This has blurred the earlier distinction between "strategic" and "tactical". What is the future like? Today, one B-2 bomber of the US Air Force (USAF) carries 80 bombs of 500 lb each. It can attack 80 separate targets, each with extreme precision, achieving the desired effect. In a few years, its capacity will be 200 small diameter bombs (SDB) able to attack 200 targets in one sortie. This 135 kg SDB, filled with much better explosives, will give the same effect as an earlier 500 kg bomb. An SU-30 aircraft could easily carry 32 precision bombs in each sortie and attack 32 separate targets with great precision. So, in today's warfare, the strategic connotation is no longer related either to the very long range of bombers or nukes as weapons, but to the effects that are produced at the target end. The aircraft type and the size of bomb are no longer primary considerations.

EVOLUTION OF STRATEGIC AIR POWER

The use of the expression "air power" was first recorded in H.G. Wells' novel *The War in the Air,* in 1908. However, according to Professor Tony Mason, the official birthday of air power has arbitrarily been selected as 1893, when a Major Fullerton of the British Army had presented a paper to a meeting of army engineers in Chicago in which he prophesised that the impact of aeronautics foreshadowed "as great a revolution in the art of war as the discovery of gun power," that "future wars may well start with a great air battle," that "the arrival over the enemy capital will probably conclude the campaign" and that, "command of the air would be an essential prerequisite for all land and air warfare." This date has been selected in preference to 1803 when the first airship company was formed in France; or 1883, when Albert Robida envisaged a sudden crushing air strike in his *War of the Twentieth Century*; or 1903, that marked the first heavier than air machine flight by the Wright Brothers. While the 19th century may well be credited with the conceptual visualisation of air power, it was the epic heavier than air machine flight by the Wright Brothers in 1903, which was the first concrete step in the fulfilment of the vision. By 1909, aircraft had been inducted into military service. The first official record of the use of aircraft in actual combat was made in 1911 by the Italians in the Libyan campaign when Captain Moizo and De Rada, flying in a military biplane Forman, spotted an Arab encampment and proceeded to drop hand carried bombs on them.

Britain was amongst the pioneers in developing its air power. The Royal Flying Corps (RFC) with its military and naval wings was established in 1912. Inter-Service rivalry soon surfaced, and by 1914, despite opposition by Churchill, the Royal Navy unilaterally broke away from RFC and established its own Royal Naval Air Service (RNAS), under the direct control of the British Admiralty. At the outbreak of World War I, RFC and RNAS, thus, formed two separate bodies under the aegis of the British Army and Navy respectively. In the meanwhile, Germany, France and the USA had also developed their air corps as a part of their land forces. At the outbreak of World War I in 1914, military aviation consisted of light wooden bi/tri planes with maximum speeds of under 100 mph and very limited load carrying capacity. Their roles were initially restricted to reconnaissance and artillery observations.

July 1917 marked a watershed in air power's history when German Gotha bombers raided London. The damage again was more psychological than real as the images of H.G. Wells' destruction from the skies appeared to become a reality. As a direct result of these attacks, Britain established what amounted to a strategic bombing unit in France, known as the Independent Force, to conduct reprisal raids against the German homeland. The concept of strategic bombing, whose mission was made independent of support to surface forces, was born. This action sowed the seeds of a new Service. The Royal Air Force (RAF), independent of the Royal Army and Royal Navy, was established in 1918.

World War I ended in 1918. During the war, all subsequent roles of air power had either been established or attempted, and the doctrines of command of air and support to surface forces had been firmly established. For the surface forces, roles such as close air support, transport support, reconnaissance, interdiction, artillery spotting, anti-submarine warfare, convoy escort, search and rescue and maritime strikes become vital contributors to the existing land and maritime strategies. Historian Lee Kennett aptly summed the progress made by air power during World War I when he wrote, "While the role of air weapon in the Great War was a modest one, the role of the Great War in the rise of air power was anything but modest."

Giulio Douhet, an Italian military officer was one of the earliest advocates of air power. He had taken part in the air action in the Libyan campaign in Tripoli in 1911-12. An ardent supporter of the strategic bombing concept and the military superiority of air power over other forms of warfare, he served in World War I, organising Italy's bombing campaign. For publicly criticising the Italian high command as being responsible for Italy's aerial weaknesses, he was courtmartialled and jailed. He was released when his theories were proven correct by the defeat of the Italians by the Austrian Air Force at Caporetto. He was later recalled and promoted to brigadier general's rank in 1921. In 1922, he was appointed head of Italy's aviation programme by Benito Mussolini. His book, *Command of the Air* was first published in 1921 and a revised version came out in 1927. It was regarded as a classic by early air power theorists and had a major impact on the shaping and development of air power, especially in the USA and Britain. He argued that command of the air should be the first objective during war, and having achieved it, subsequent bombing of industrialised and population centres would be so disruptive and destructive that the enemy would be forced to sue for peace. He maintained that control of the air, followed by strategic bombing, could win a war independent of land and sea power. Douhet is regarded as the father of air power.

The next air power advocate to emerge during and after World War I was Gen Trenchard, the first commander of the RAF. Trenchard believed in the offensive role of air power and was convinced that the primary mission of air power was to decimate the enemy through aerial bombardment. He strongly advocated the need to devote maximum resources to air power development, for the main danger in future would come from the air. He argued that by denying the enemy the capability to conduct a strategic bombing campaign against oneself and by conducting one against him, air power would lead to the enemy's capitulation. He was convinced that unless control of the air was established, armies and navies would become powerless, and that the days of big ships were past—they could no longer operate in the face of air power. As the chief of staff of the world's first independent air force, Gen Trenchard's thinking was to have a major impact on the RAF's force composition and performance during World War II.

The third key air power advocate to emerge during the post-World War I era was an American, Billy Mitchell. He is the most famous and controversial figure in American air power history. The son of a wealthy Wisconsin senator, he enlisted as a private during the Spanish American War and quickly gained a commission due to the intervention of his father. He had an outstanding war record and after challenging tours of Philippines and Alaska, Mitchell was assigned to the Army General Staff, at the time its youngest member. He became interested in aviation and its possibilities. In 1916, at the age of 38, he took private flying lessons. Arriving at France in 1917 as part of the American contingent, he quickly took charge and began preparations for the American air units that were to follow. By the end of World War I, Billy Mitchell was the top US airman. He returned to the USA in 1919 and immediately became a very strong advocate of air power. Mitchell was greatly influenced by Douhet's theories. He was appointed the deputy chief of the Air Service.

In this capacity, his relations with his superiors continued to sour as he began to attack both the War and Navy Departments for being insufficiently far-sighted regarding air power. When Mitchell suggested that US air power could better defend the nation's coasts from attacks by warships than US sea power, a controversy developed as to whether an airplane could sink a battleship. Live tests were conducted in June/July 1921 and September 1921. Mitchell's bombers sank three captured German vessels and an obsolete USS *Alabama* in the first trial and sent two more obsolete US vessels to the bottom of the sea in the next one.

The success of the bombing trials encouraged the advocates of air power to press for a separate air arm but the Army

General Staff remained convinced that air power on its own could not win a war and, at best, it had an important but supporting role. Mitchell became increasingly critical of his superiors and began to go public in his criticism of the high command. His actions could no longer be tolerated and in December 1925, he was found guilty before a court martial of violating the 96th Articles of War and was suspended from duty for five years. Mitchell resigned in 1926.

In conformity with Douhet's and Trenchard's theories, Mitchell postulated the potency of air power in any future conflict and that air power would be the most decisive element in any future conflict. He also advocated that strategic bombing could on its own defeat the enemy.

Douhet, Trenchard and Mitchell were passionate advocates of air power, perhaps too passionate, and all three seem to have overstated their case. While a majority of their theories and prophecies have come true, their claim that air power alone could win a war has yet to be proved. They seriously failed to visualise the defensive warfare against air threat in the form of fighter aircraft and ground defences, which could and did reduce the impact of air power, especially in the strategic bombing role. They also grossly underestimated the continued requirement of naval and land forces and the people's will to resist aerial bombardment.

The role of air power during World War II can be summed up in two quotes, one by Winston Churchill and the other by Professor Tony Mason. While speaking at the Massachusetts Institute of Technology in 1949, Churchill had commented: "For good or ill, air mastery is today the supreme expression of military power. And fleets and armies, however necessary and important, must accept subordinate rank. This is a memorable milestone in the march of man." Professor Tony Mason in his book *Air Power-A Centennial Appraisal*, states: "Air power had been peripheral between 1914 and 1918. In the Second World War it dominated most theatres, and in at least two, was decisive." If the Korean and Vietnam Wars had brought out the inadequacies of air power, the Arab/Israeli Wars of 1967 and 1973 again demonstrated its dominance in a conventional war. In both these conflicts, air power played a major role. In 1967, having won the command of the air on the very first day through preemptive offensive counter-air operations, the Israeli Air Force (IsAF) brought to bear such effective bombardment on the Arab land forces that it became relatively simple for the Israeli Army to defeat them. Even in 1973, air power was dominant. The IsAF's inability to win the command of the air initially cost them dearly but in the later stages, through the substantial technical and logistical support of the USA, the IsAF succeeded in neutralising the Arab air defence network. From then onward, support to their land forces helped turn a likely defeat into victory. By the time a ceasefire was declared, Israel had gained the upper hand in the conflict.

Essentially, a one-day campaign, the Bekaa Valley operation was planned by Israel to take out all the air defence units in the valley in a single coordinated air assault. The presence of Syrian SA-6 units in the east of Bekaa Valley was constraining the IsAF's contribution when the Israeli Defence Forces (IDF) had launched Operation Peace in Galilee in 1982. These units had to be taken out. The IsAF painstakingly plotted the position of every SA-6 unit in the valley. On October 9, 1982, Israeli long-range artillery and surface-to-surface missiles engaged the Syrian missile batteries. The IsAF aircraft followed up with aerial attacks, using free fall bombs and anti-radiation missiles. When the Syrian Air Force rose to defend the air defence complex, the IsAF's F-15 and F16 fighters, equipped with the most modern air-to-air missiles, airborne radars and electronic warfare package, massacred them. This was the most onesided air victory in the history of air power. In terms of the evolution of air power, the Bekaa Valley campaign was a generation ahead. This campaign is relevant because it was a harbinger of how the next air battle would be fought. The Gulf War of 1990-91 was to demonstrate the same philosophy on a much larger scale. Dr James A. Mowbray has correctly concluded, "Technology helped to win the fastest, lowest casualty, almost devastatingly destructive one-sided war in recorded history. Air Force capabilities had come of age." Col Warden, the architect of the Desert Storm air campaign, has elaborated the technological advancement made by air power further by saying,

"To have a 90 percent probability of putting one bomb on a target of the size of a normal room, in World War II, it needed 9,000 bombs or over 1,000 B-17 sorties—which meant putting 10,000 men at risk over the target. An F-117 class aircraft will achieve the same probability in a single sortie." Between World War II and the Gulf War, bombing accuracy had registered a 1,000 per cent increase.

In the Gulf War, air power demonstrated its ability to strike at the strategic heart of a country with maximum precision and minimum collateral damage and casualties. It proved beyond any shadow of doubt that air power has become an integral component of modern warfare. Professor R.A. Mason has very rightly observed, "The Gulf War marked the apotheosis of twentieth century air power."

STRATEGIC DEVELOPMENT OF IAF

The Indian Air Force (IAF) came formally into existence on October 8, 1932, the day the Air Force Act became operative. In the last three quarters of the century, the IAF has grown from the "army cooperation" role into a strategic force. The British never envisaged a strategic role for the IAF. However, the IAF was instrumental in creating a strategic effect by blocking the advance of the Japanese Army in Burma. In recognition of the crucial role played by the IAF, King George VI conferred it the prefix "Royal" in 1945. This prefix was dropped in 1950 after India became a republic.

During the Indo-Pak War of 1947, the IAF conducted airlift operations from Safdarjang, then known as Willingdon airfield, to Srinagar airfield starting at 09:30 hours IST on October 27. This was the most instrumental action of the war as it provided crucial support to the Indian Army in pushing the invaders out. In 1962, during the Indo-China conflict, the IAF provided the much needed logistics support to the Indian Army fighting in some of the most trying environment. Without essential air support, the Indian Army faced overwhelming odds in their fight against well trained Chinese troops. The Indian leadership grounded the IAF for the majority of the war, fearing that if the IAF attacked the Chinese forces, the PLA Air Force (PLAAF) would retaliate on Indian cities (a feeling based on utter lack of information). This was the only time post-independence when the full potential of the IAF was not utilised, resulting in national humiliation in a conflict. Soon after, the Indian government, learning from its mistakes, began a vigorous campaign to expand the IAF. An emergency flying scheme was started in Delhi, Madras, Kanpur, Nagpur, Patiala and Adampur and more than 1,000 cadets received primary flying training by 1964. The IAF's strength was increased from 28,000 officers and men in 1961 to 100,000 officers and men by 1964. By 1965, the IAF had also added newly bought An-12B and C-119G transport aircraft to its fleet. In 1965, India and Pakistan went to war over Kashmir for the second time. The Indo-Pakistan War of 1965 tested the strength of the Indian Air Force to its full limit. The Indian Air Force was successful in bombarding several Pakistani airfields, military installations and ammunition depots deep inside Pakistani territory and provided crucial air cover to the Indian Army. During the war, the IAF carried out more than 4,073 combat sorties, compared to the Pakistan Air Force's (PAF's) total of 2,279 sorties. The IAF helicopters proved to be highly useful in logistics and rescue efforts (Med Evac).

During the Indo-Pak War of 1971, Pakistani armour, accompanied by infantry, moved towards Longewala, the Indian border outpost. The post was defended by only one company of infantry soldiers. Commencing at daybreak, the IAF provided critical close air support from AF Station, Jaisalmer, and knocked out 37 out of the 45 tanks. This prevented loss of significant territory in the desert, a significant strategic effect. In East Pakistan too, the IAF flew more than 4,000 sorties, causing extensive damage to airfields, infrastructure, aircraft and the war waging potential. The vital air cover provided to the Indian Army assisted in rapid advances. Entire brigade strengths were heli-lifted over the river Meghna, allowing the Indian Army to continue their advance in spite of stiff resistance at Ashuganj, where the retreating Pakistan Army blew up the bridge (also known as the heli-bridge over the Meghna). The IAF airdropped Para Bn Gp 130 in the now famous Tangail airdrop. The operation involved An-12, C-119s, 2 Caribous and Dakotas from 11 and 48 Sqns. In total, about 1,000 troops were airdropped. On the morning of December 14, a message was intercepted by Indian intelligence about a high-level meeting of the civilian administration in East Pakistan, and a decision was made to mount an attack. Within 15 minutes of interception of the message, a strike was launched against Dhaka. Armed with tourist guide maps of the city, four MiG 21s of No. 28 Sqn hit the Governor's House with 57mm rockets, ripping the massive roof of the main hall and turning the building into a smouldering wreck. The Governor of East Pakistan, Mr. A.H. Malik, resigned then and there, renouncing all ties with the West Pakistani administration, to take refuge at the Red Cross Centre in Dhaka. The entire Cabinet resigned even though more than 90,000 Pakistani troops were available to defend Dhaka. This was a clear indication that tactical actions by air power have significant strategic influence.

During the Kargil War with Pakistan, the Indian Air Force is said to have proved the decisive force in accelerating the end of the conflict. It successfully provided considerable air cover for Indian troops fighting against Pakistani soldiers. In spite of losing two fighter aircraft and one helicopter, the IAF, by using innovative tactics and precision weapons, was instrumental in evicting the invaders.

STRATEGIC ROLE OF AIR POWER

The ability of air power to reach, disrupt or possibly destroy an opponent's strategic or operational centre of gravity suggests that air power is inherently capable of military action with strategic effect. That effect may be created through independent distinct action or through joint or multinational activity operating in conjunction with other forces. Throughout the history of air power, air platforms and their associated weapon systems have been able to carry the fight to the enemy.

Two air power theorists from the USAF, Cols Warden and Boyd have propounded path breaking theories of paralysing the enemy by strategic application of air power. While Boyd talks of paralysing the enemy psychologically and weakening his will to fight, Warden emphasises the need to physically paralyse the adversary by attacking leadership, infrastructure, communication links and fielded forces as part of his now famous "Five Ring Theory" based on Clausewitz's centres of gravity, which formed the heart of the air campaign in Operation Desert Storm.

While the strategic air campaign that aims at paralysis is based on the overwhelming asymmetry the US forces are likely to enjoy in any conflict scenario, it is important for policy and strategy planners in India too to understand the tremendous advantages of creating asymmetry vis-à-vis potential adversaries by building up a potent strategic air capability that is built around technology, force multipliers and multi-theatre capability. The strategic roles in which air power could possibly be employed are discussed hereafter.

Political Signalling

Air power has the ability to consistently provide the dominance of the battlespace with the utilisation of manned as well as unmanned airborne platforms that can stay on station for long durations of time. This ability can transmit clear signals to any enemy, thereby dissuading him from any misadventure. These signals may be transmitted in terms of raised alert status, extensive surveillance activities and deployment of combat forces at critical operational locations.

Strategic Coercion

Coercion is the ability to deter another party from performing a hostile action or compelling an enemy performing such an action to cease doing so. Three examples are the rice bombing of Jaffna in 1987 which demonstrated India's ability to intervene in a crisis situation in its neighbourhood and forced Sri Lanka to sign the Indo-Sri Lankan agreement; Operation Deliberate Force in 1995 by the North

Atlantic Treaty Organisation (NATO) air power to force Bosnian Serbs to remove heavy weapons from designated exclusion zones; and Operation Allied Force, to change the thinking of President Milosovic of Yugoslavia. At display in these cases were air power's inherent characteristics of reach, speed, responsiveness and lethality (in the Yugoslavian example), to achieve strategic objectives of a nation/group of nations, when employed in a coercive role. Without doubt, air power is the premier instrument of strategic coercion today.

Conflict Prevention

The existence of credible deterrence can truly prevent war or any conflict. In case deterrence fails, there should be sufficient offensive capability to thwart any misadventure. Conflict prevention is the critical strategic role of an air force, essentially by possessing strategic deterrence capability. The existence of threat available in deterrence must be obvious to the enemy. Deterrence has a psychological element and in addition to the availability of credible forces, can be strengthened by resolute policy, demonstrated military capability, the will to use force and a readiness to escalate, should deterrence fail.

Strategic Bombing

The notion that the strategic employment of air power is inextricably linked to bombing and bombardment is derived from historical experience. The purpose of the strategic employment of air power is to create strategic effect on the identified target set. This effect will be in support of the defined strategic aim but may not be part of a theatre campaign. In April 1986, exasperated by terrorist actions supposedly backed by the Libyan President, Col Qaddafi, the Reagan Administration authorised a retaliatory night air attack. For Operation El Dorado Canyon, a joint US Navy (USN) and US Air Force (USAF) force was mounted against terrorist and airfield targets in Libya. The Libyans boasted of an air force of 500 aircraft and a formidable ground environment bristling with integrated surface-to-air missile (SAM) sites, armed mainly with Soviet missiles and radar guided anti-aircraft guns. The system was operated under the direction of 3,000 Soviet technicians. At 2.00 am local time on April 15, the coordinated raids of the USN and USAF swept into Libya to hit their targets The attack lasted for thirteen minutes, and cost the Americans the loss of one F-111 crew, but caused considerable damage to the Libyans.

Battlespace Domination

The primary task of the air force is to gain and maintain "command of the air". If this is achieved, the resultant air supremacy will allow the land, sea and air operations to continue without enemy air interference. This was amply demonstrated in 1971, when the IAF gained command of the air over East Pakistan within the first 48 hours. Thereafter, the ground forces were able to move at a faster pace towards Dhaka. It was also possible to mount heliborne operations and launch airborne operations of a brigade group by using transport aircraft. All this would not have been possible without first achieving air supremacy. "Command of the air" has to be gained by fighting for it. With an opponent who has the state-of-the-art aircraft and weapons, combined with quality training and high morale, it would be a struggle for survival by each side. Therefore, in peace-time, it is imperative that the nation provides the best possible weapon systems, training and high class leadership which is truly professional, motivated and dedicated.

Psychological Operations (PSYOPS)

PSY OPS played a significant role in operations such as Operation Enduring Freedom, in which air-mobility missions delivered humanitarian rations while, at the same time, air-combat sorties struck militarily significant targets in other parts of Afghanistan. Furthermore, during Operation Iraqi Freedom, Coalition forces dropped both leaflets and ordnance to prompt enemy soldiers to surrender. They also broadcast messages to them over their own radio systems. These transmissions had the complementary effect of denying the Iraqis use of their own radios. Air, space, and information power are all psychological instruments that can influence an adversary's perception, behaviour, and morale.

For this reason, USAF PSY OP activities serve as an integral part of air operations planning and targeting processes, rather than as mere adjuncts. US aircraft, by their dynamic presence and actions, transmit an unmistakable psychological message to most adversaries.

The mere threat or presence of superior aircraft can ground an enemy's air force, demoralise his army and civilian population, or promote stability. In the Kosovo operations, Lt Gen Short intended to generate functional and psychological effects targeted directly at Slobodan Milosevic. The IAF certainly needs to formulate appropriate doctrines and procure suitable equipment to conduct PSY OPS at all levels of any conflict.

Strategic Airlift

The strategic airlift capability of a nation will govern to a large extent its armed forces' ability to respond. The airlift of troops by the IAF from Delhi to Srinagar to combat the Pakistani intruders was instrumental in saving two-third of Kashmir, including Srinagar. The airlift operations conducted by the IAF during Oeration Meghdoot resulted in the initiative being with Indian troops. This manifested in the Indian Army taking control of two-third of the highest battlefield in the world while the Pakistan Army was still preparing to launch operations. The IAF employed transport aircraft and helicopters to transport troops and stores, as well as airdrop supplies to the high altitude locations. On the night of November 3, 1988, the Indian Air Force airlifted a parachute battalion group from Agra and flew them non-stop over 2,000 km (1,240 miles) to Maldives. The Indian paratroopers landed at Hulule and secured the airfield and restored the government rule at Male within hours. The performance of the IAF in numerous humanitarian missions at home and abroad is worth a special mention. This includes providing relief to Indonesia and Sri Lanka during the tsunami and to the US in the aftermath of Hurricane Katrina. Evacuating the Indian civilians from the Gulf countries during 1990-91 is another example. The need of the hour for the IAF today is to procure transport aircraft and helicopters to build and enhance its medium lift capability.

Out of Area Contingencies

The ability of air power to engage strategic targets with minimum collateral damage, maximum effect and "shape the battlefield" for swift operation by airborne assault or amphibious attack, has made it a preferred option in swift out of country conflict resolution, the likes of which was achieved in Kosovo. Even when it comes to humanitarian intervention, it is the strategic mobility assets of air power that can make a substantial difference, whether it is during natural calamity or evacuation of population from conflict torn areas. India's increasing "footprint" in the area means that it is only a matter of time before its influence spreads into Africa, the Central Asian Republics and Southeast Asia where it will continue to compete with China for resources and markets.

Credible Deterrence

Modern air power has become an instant instrument of projecting power in the great depth with surprise and concentration of firepower which is highly discriminating and precise and, therefore, avoids collateral damage. It can target the nerve centre of the enemy very effectively and thereby paralyse his command, control and communication system, bringing enemy military operations to a halt. The credibility of deterrence provided by modern air power, supported by high technology systems like airborne warning and control system (AWACS), joint surveillance target attack radar system (J-STARS), electronic warfare (EW) systems and precision guided weapons is extremely high. A modern air power in being could provide a credible deterrence without resorting to the weapons of mass destruction.

Low Intensity Conflict

We need to develop strategies to exploit the inherent capabilities of air power— speed and reach—in low intensity conflicts, by swift induction of troops in the affected areas by air, and air surveillance of large tracts of land in mountainous regions.

TRAINING REQUIREMENTS

The IAF today is a strategic force with reach, precision, capability for air dominance and is transforming itself into a networked aerospace force. There is an urgent need for us to start thinking strategic and thereafter to train for the same. Perhaps the weakest area that afflicts the IAF today is the inadequacy of training infrastructure, specially for the non-officer cadres. A fighting force equipped with the most sophisticated aircraft, smart weapon systems, complex sensors, space-based surveillance and reconnaissance systems, and a networkcentric environment needs to be supported by an equally advanced and sophisticated training environment with computer-based training systems, elaborate simulation devices for all disciplines, automated distance learning and evaluation systems, all designed to train for the next war and not the last one. The future leadership would need to develop a strategic outlook that develops unconventional responses to various threats across the spectrum ranging from terror strikes to conflicts under the nuclear threshold. The present training pattern in the IAF for various branches is heavily tilted towards tactical orientation, and is defensive in nature owing to our reactive doctrines. The path ahead is not to drastically change our training methodology but to train continuously in strategic roles.

We need to continue training with a few foreign air forces with simulation of contingencies, be it bilateral or multilateral. Simulated target systems need to be realistic in nature rather than "pin and circles," as existent today. We need to create strategic task forces which are kept current and have centralised decision-making, independent component commanders and decentralised execution. The leaders need to be visionaries, analysts, theorists and strategic practitioners. Hence, there is a need to shift the focus during the growth of the officer in service. The levels of intellectual capability and education need to be enhanced rather than remaining busy with fire-fighting and crisis management most of the time. The need to posess better awareness of the global situation in general and of South Asia in particular cannot be overemphasised.

Air power is inherently strategic in nature but for the optimum exploitation of its attributes, the practitioners need to be absolutely clear as to what effect the application of air power will have in different scenarios. Air power needs to be dovetailed into a nation's international policy-making process as an effective instrument of diplomacy.

For this, national leaders and civil servants in the decision-making chain need to be educated by air power exponents about the potential that it possesses as a national instrument of peace and power.

The short period of history since the advent of air power provides us with enough examples as proof of this. While looking into acquiring the capabilities that would maximise the true potential of air power, we should not lose sight of the vital aspects of support systems and human resources, without which air power only becomes mere hardware and not an effective national instrument of power. Col John Warden of the USAF, who was instrumental in designing the fourphase campaign of the Allied forces in the 1991 Gulf War says *"Real exploitation of air power's potential can only come through making assumptions that it can do something we thought it couldn't do...We must start our thinking by assuming we can do everything with air power, not by assuming that it can only do what it did in the past."* Therefore, planners and executioners of air power need to think and look ahead and plan for the changing nature of warfare. They need to continuously think about what role air power will play in any future conflict, and plan and train for the optimum exploitation of this vital instrument of war.

INTRODUCTION-THE IAF IN ITS PRELIMINARY YEARS

The Indian Air Force (IAF) was officially born on 08 October 1932, when the Indian Air Force (IAF) act became effective. On that day six Indians were granted the King's commission on passing out as pilots and ground duty officers from RAF Cranwell. They had been sent earlier in 1930 and five of them became pilots while the sixth became a Ground Duty Officer. Among the five pilots were such well known names like Subroto Mukherjee, who became the first Indian Chief of Air Staff and Awan who had later opted for the Pakistan Air Force.

No.1 Squadron IAF, came into being on 1 April 1933 at Drigh Road, Karachi. There were five pilots commanded by an RAF officer and the first batch of Hawai Sepoys. The complement of the squadron consisted of four Westland Wapiti biplanes comprising 'A' Flight of the squadron. After 3 years of training, in which time more pilots joined the squadron. It was inducted into the North West Frontier Province (NWFP), which is now in Pakistan. The primary aim was to support the RAF and the Army in its operations against the frontier tribesmen.

Stationed at Miranshah, the pilots flew many sorties in their rickety aircraft, often suffering casualties in the form of forced landings or stopped engines due to the tribesmen firing. Throughout this period, with more pilots being trained at a rate of 5 to 6 per year, two more flights were raised and at the outbreak of the second world war, No.1 Squadron IAF was well experienced in its role of army cooperation, having received its baptism of fire at the frontier.

At the outbreak of the war, the IAF put into effect various expansion plans to raise more new squadrons. An RAF squadron at Risalpur was made responsible for training of aircrew and invitations were sent to commercial pilot license holders to join the newly created Indian Air Force Volunteer Reserve (IAFVR).

About a 100 such pilots joined the IAFVR and among them were men like P.C. Lal, Rajaram, etc. who rose to high posts after the war. All these pilots after a short conversion course were posted to newly raised coastal defence flights. They flew aircraft like the Wapiti, the Hart, Audax and some other types which have been requisitioned from civil owners. They flew long surveillance missions over the coastal waters and some times escorted ship convoys over sea lanes. With the entry of Japan into the War, the expansion of the Indian Air Force was rapid. Flying schools were set up at Walton near Lahore and at Ambala. Two operational training units came up at Risalpur (for fighters) and Peshawar (for ground attack). The squadrons grew from one to ten.

A total of 3000 officers and 25,000 men were trained in the period 1942-45. Some 600 pilots flew with the ten squadrons, all of them seeing action against the Japanese in Burma. Some pilots attached to the RAF were sent to North Africa and England and saw action against the Germans and the Italians. On the Burma front, the Indian AF flew in aircraft inferior to the Japanese. These aircraft, Hurricanes and Vengeances were those discarded by the RAF. Throughout the war, the IAF had to make do with aircraft discarded by the RAF as inferior and it was only at the end of the war did the IAF acquire the latest Marks Spitfires. In spite of this handicap it faired well in the war.

Field Marshal Slim in praising No.6 *Dragons* Squadron wrote, "I was impressed with the conduct of a reconnaissance squadron of the Indian Air Force. Flying in pairs the Indian pilots in their outmoded Hurricanes went out, time and again, in the face of overwhelming enemy fighter superiority...They were a happy, efficient, and a very gallant squadron." Coming from one of the greatest Generals of World War II it was proof indeed of the bravery of the pilots. When the war ended Indian pilots had earned 1 DSO, 23 DFCs (including 1 bar) and a host of numerous other awards. In doing so it lost some 60 pilots killed in action. These figures would seem small compared to the RAF or the land armies but it should be remembered that the number that constituted the IAF was also small. The Indian Air Force's contribution to the victory of the commonwealth was recognised by King George VI who conferred the prefix "Royal" to the title making it the Royal Indian Air Force.

After the war ended, the IAF had ten fighter squadrons flying Hurricanes and Spitfire XIV's. It had sent one squadron (No.4) with the British Commonwealth Occupation Force in Japan. Some were at the frontier undergoing training and keeping guard. About the time it was thought necessary to raise a transport squadron. Some individual pilots have had some experience on transport aircraft during the war but no special transport unit existed. So accordingly No.12 Squadron was raised with ten Dakotas in 1946. Even before training could commence a tropical storm came and wrote off all the aircraft. Despite this inauspicious start, No.12 began training on Oxfords, till replacement Dakotas began arriving.

More Spitfires and new Tempest II fighter bombers became available and the squadrons re-equipped with them, phasing out the Hurricanes. In the training role Harvards and Tigermoths were the mainstay for years to come. These were supplemented by the Percival Prentice and the Cornell trainers. As partition became inevitable, so was the division of the Armed Forces. New India's share of the Air Force amounted to seven fighter and one transport squadrons. Pakistan received two fighter and one newly raised transport squadron. The RIAF lost all of its permanent training establishments and major bases as they were all located in Pakistani territory. So all establishments had to be rebuilt from scratch.

The first Chief of Air Staff was Air Marshal Sir Thomas Elmhirst of the RAF. He was later succeeded by Air Marshal Sir Ivelew Chapman and later by Air Marshal Sir Eric Gibbs. All the three British service Officers served the Air Force well during their tenures as Air Chiefs. It was under their tenure that the expansion plan of the Air Force was drawn up and that the IAF fought in its first war. Free India's Air Force had its first taste of action during the invasion of the Kashmir valley by the frontier tribesmen. These tribesmen, financially aided & armed by Pakistan and led by Army deserters, poured into Kashmir on 20 October 1947, and went into a frenzy killing, ransacking and pillaging through the Kashmiri villages. In reply to the Maharajah's plea for help and after his signing of the accession, India decided to send troops to Srinagar by air.

No.12 Squadron with its DC-3 Dakotas along with those of private airlines helped in the airlift. It was a remarkable achievement at such a short notice. Taking off from Palam the first Indian troops were landed at Srinagar airfield at 0930hrs on October 27th. At that time it wasn't even known whether the airfield has fallen to the tribesmen or not, but the risk was taken. On the first day the IAF and civilian Dakotas had airlifted the 1st battalion, The Sikh regiment and thus secured the safety of the airfield.

On October 28th, Tempests from Ambala attacked Enemy positions at Patan. Two days later the first Spitfires were flown to Srinagar, joining the Harvards which were already flown there. Fuel to keep these aircraft was hard to come by, but the Army developed ingenious methods to provide the necessary fuel. As soon as any Dakota landed, a jeep with a drum in its back would approach the aircraft, and with the pilots consent, the men would siphon off any extra amount of fuel that the captain of the aircraft would spare. The fuel thus collected kept the Spitfires flying later for the crucial battles of Badgam and Shalateng. On November 3rd, the decisive battle of Badgam was fought in the vicinity of Srinagar airfield where the enemy launched a surprise attack. It was in this battle that Major Somnath Sharma was awarded the Param Vir Chakra (PVC) posthumously.

Two RIAF Spitfires came to the aid of the Indian Army by strafing the enemy attackers. The combined Army-Air Force onslaught beat back the attack. Four days later on November 7th, the battle of Shalateng took place which routed the enemy. The tribesmen kept retreating till Uri. Tempests of No.7 Sqn played an important part. according to Brigadier L.P. Sen, 400+ bodies were counted between Srinagar and Baramula, almost all due to air action. Later on, Tempests provided much needed air support to the Army in the area of the Uri bowl where the fighting had stabilized. RIAF Tempests strafed and rocketed enemy concentrations at Kot, helped in the advance to Tithwal, dropped vital ammunition and food supplies to the beleaguered Skardu garrison. They destroyed enemy field guns at Poonch, and in a daring and spectacular low level air raid, destroyed the bridges over the Domel and Kishenganga rivers in the face of heavy ack-ack fire.

The lone transport Squadron was not left behind. No.12, in the course of its regular casualty evacuation and transport duties, airlifted 25 Pounder field guns to Poonch, flew the first troops to Leh, which was the first aircraft to land at Leh, and even bombing sorties in support of the army with the bombs being rolled out of the cargo bay by the aircrew. The main driving force behind the squadron was Air Commodore Meher Singh, the head of the operational group in J&K. Meher Singh himself led many of the pioneering flights including the ones to Leh and Poonch. For leading and guiding the air operations in Jammu & Kashmir, he received the Maha Vir Chakra. Wing Commander K.L. Bhatia, CO No.12 Squadron, got the Vir Chakra as did many pilots of the squadron.

The fighting ended on 31 December 1948, the cease-fire bought about by UN Mediation. The IAF acquitted itself well earning four MVCs and 23 VrCs. Not much is known about its losses but at least one fighter, a Tempest was lost in the Tithwal area due to ack-ack fire. The pilot, Flying Officer U.G. Wright, baled out and had a harrowing experience during his parachute descent. He was fired at by rifles, LMG's and even 3" mortars! But he made it back to our lines.

One RIAF DC-3 went missing on the second day of the conflict, during the airlift and nothing was heard about the pilot, Ft. Lt. C.J. Mendoza and the 20 passengers till almost 40 years later, when the wreckage was stumbled upon and the remains of the crew members were laid to rest. No air-to-air encounters took place between the RPAF and the RIAF but on one occasion a lone RPAF Dakota was intercepted by two Tempests over Chilas. Squadron Leader Masamalani and Flight Lieutenant Dogra were rocketing Chilas and stumbled onto the RPAF Dakota. However, inspite of radio warnings and firing across the path of the Dakota, the RPAF pilot slipped across the border. Later getting a "Sitara-E-Juraat" award for the escape.

Meanwhile down south, the Hyderabad police action was in progress. Here too the RIAF lent a hand to the Army. Tempests and Dakotas saw much action, strafing, bombing and dropping leaflets against the Nizam's forces. However the scale of operations is minuscule compared to the Kashmir operations. The end of the hostilities gave the RIAF some breathing space. It went ahead with its re-equipment plans and to build up as a 20 squadron force. About a 100 Spitfires and Tempests were acquired from Britain. To build up a bomber complement, the RIAF salvaged about 40 odd B-24 Liberator bombers from the ex-USAAF scrapyard at Kanpur and put these relics into the air. Initially, Lancaster bombers were offered by Britain, but it was decided to acquire more fighters with the same money and build up the required bomber force with the salvaged aircraft.

In November 1948, the RIAF became the first air arm in Asia to equip with Jet fighters. No.7 Sqn started inducting De Havilland Vampires bought from Britain and eventually some 400 were acquired. These vampires saw action even after 23 years in the 1971 war. 1950 saw India becoming a Republic. This led to all Royal titles being dropped and the RIAF was no exception. On 26 January 1950, she was just know as the Indian Air Force (IAF). Also, in order not to become dependent on only Great Britain for its arms purchases, the IAF started purchasing aircraft from other sources. In 1953 the Dassault Ouragan re-christened *Toofani* by the IAF was inducted. Belonging to the same generation as the Vampire, 104 of these straight winged fighters were received by the IAF.

On 1st April 1954, Air Marshal Subroto Mukherjee took over as the first Indian Chief of Air Staff. Mukherjee was the first Indian to command a squadron in the IAF and now he was the first Indian Air Chief. He had a good relationship with Nehru and this helped him to get the required allocation of finances for the air forces expansion plans. During this period it can be certainly be said that the Air Force received privileged treatment more than the Army. When its Pakistani counterpart started inducting F-86 Sabres, efforts were made to acquire

Hunter Mk.6 from the British. But the British did not release the Mk.6 for export and they offered only the Mk.4. So Mystere IV-A fighter-bombers were acquired from France. It was with the Mysteres that IAF pilots could break the sound barrier for the first time and later when the Hunter Mk.6 was cleared for export, the IAF acquired them too.

The offensive capability received a boost with Canberra bombers being purchased and Gnat fighters supplemented the interceptor force. Besides India, Finland was the only country to operate this diminutive fighter, while Britain operated Trainer versions.

The transport fleet was also increased to meet with the demands of India's great geographical size. Besides inducting more trustworthy Dakotas, Devons and Viscounts were bought in. One squadron of Ilyushin-14's were purchased. American Fairchild C-119 flying Packets joined the transport fleet. This aircraft could carry twice the cargo load that a Dakota could manage and thus were a welcome addition to the force.

The decision to manufacture the new Avro Hs.748 was taken and the agreement with Britain was signed in 1958. In 1960, No.44 Squadron was raised on Antonov-12s, which were the Russian equivalent of the American C-130 Hercules, which Pakistan had already got. In spite of all these additions, India's transport force was stretched to its limits by the increasing geographical and strategic demands.

The helicopter wing of the air force was born with some Bell 47 two seaters forming the initial equipment and soon some S-55 Whirlwinds joined the force. To cope with the High altitude operations the Russian Mi-4 was tested and found suitable and large numbers were inducted.

One thing is certain, the IAF was never starved out of money. Its expansion plans proceeded at an uninterrupted pace, without much canvassing on its part. What made the government favour the IAF over the Army? One theory is that the government was more keen on developing a "visible military force" as part of its political diplomacy, and the IAF fitted the part. It was a lopsided policy, we had the best transport aircraft that money can buy but had no adequate parachutes to drop supplies at forward posts. The government would be most eager to buy shiny new fighters but be most miserly in purchasing spares for them.

Aircraft like the Spitfire and Tempest continued in service till 1956, the Dakota was in service till the 80s and the Liberator till 1967. It became difficult for the IAF to manage an effective air arm but it managed nevertheless, thanks to the men who led it. Air Marshal Mukherjee died an untimely and tragic death in Japan while still in service and was succeeded by Air Marshal Aspy Merwan Engineer. Air Marshal Engineer, a DFC from Burma, was one of the famous Engineer brothers. It was in his tenure that the Indo-China conflict flared up. But before we go into this conflict, let us see how the IAF did in other short but limited encounters.

After more than twelve years, the Indian Air Force saw combat in a foreign land, fighting for a world cause. Six Canberras from No.5 Squadron were attached to the United Nations force in Congo. India also sent a brigade of troops there, and the Canberras were to support the operations of the UN there. The Canberras were under the command of Wg. Cdr. AIK Suares.

On 6 December 1961, after clashes broke out between UN forces and the Katangan rebels, The Canberras, operating from Leopoldville, attacked the Katangan airbase at Kolwazi. In the raid, they destroyed four Fouga Magister jets, the fuel dump and a bridge at Lufira. Besides they flew close support sorties for UN troops fighting on the ground, as well as escort missions for the USAF transport aircraft bringing in supplies. This was the first time that jet aircraft of the IAF went into action. The IAF acquitted itself well in this operation.

In the same month back in India, *Operation Vijay*, the plan to liberate Goa took place. There was no Portuguese air opposition and Canberras, Hunters, Ouragans and Vampires operated with impunity. Dabolim airport and the airstrip in Diu were put out of commission. Portuguese strong holds were attacked to smoothen up the Army's advance. However, on one occasion, Vampires of No.45 Squadron operating from Belgaum were called up by the 2 Sikh LI to soften up Portuguese positions at Mapusa, and they ended up bombing positions of our own, 17th Para Fd Regt, injuring two. Throughout the action no

Portuguese anti-aircraft fire was encountered and the whole operation can be termed as an exercise for the Indian Air Force to test itself.

The dawn of the new year bōught forth new threats to the borders. A confrontation with China happened in October 1962. The Army had established posts in remote corners of Ladakh and NEFA. It became the IAF's responsibility to supply these posts from the air. The IAF had for some years did supply dropping in the jungles of Assam, and it continued doing so in Ladakh and NEFA. Most of the time during the supply drops, the parachutes carrying the supplies would drift away into inaccessible valleys and gorges. A policy of reusing used parachutes recovered from these places saw supplies falling to the ground with unopened parachutes. In all the Army estimated that it recovered only 40% of the supplies airdropped by the Air Force, and it was barely sufficient to maintain its posts.

The Indo-China war started on 20th October 1962, with Chinese troops launching a heavy attack on Indian positions at the Tsangdhar area, in NEFA. On that day the IAF lost two Bell helicopters in quick succession to Chinese ground fire. Before that, while the Indian troops were fighting for the posts, a lone Dakota came over lazily on its usual supply dropping run and the crew were shocked at being fired upon by the Chinese. This was the first indication that the IAF had of the war. No one had informed the Air Force authorities of the battle that had started three hours before.

Throughout the hostilities, IAF helicopters were primarily engaged in evacuating casualties. And after the Chinese ceasefire, in picking up numerous stragglers of the broken up 4th Infantry Division making there way back to the plains, most of these stragglers were forced to trek back across the country and suffered severe mental and physical strain on the way.

Scores of them were picked up by the helicopters including a Divisional commander himself. One Mi-4 helicopter was lost to ground fire in November 1962, another was abandoned at Zimithaung and it fell into Chinese hands intact. They later returned it after the ceasefire as a "gesture of goodwill." On the Walong front, the IAF was the only means of supply and reinforcement to the Indian troops there. The only aircraft capable of operating from that airstrip was the Otter. These flew in supply and CASEVAC (Casualty Evacuation) missions till Walong fell.

One Otter which was made unserviceable by the Chinese shelling was abandoned. This was also later returned by the Chinese as a goodwill gesture. In most other wars, aircraft are deliberately destroyed to prevent their capture in the enemy hands. Sadly, no one found time to undertake such measures in the race to retreat. While the situation in NEFA was bad, the IAF's performance in Aksai Chin in Ladakh was nothing short of excellent. The IAF's only AN-12 Squadron operated in this sector. They flew in reinforcements in the form of additional troops and AMX-13 tanks to everywhere, from Daulet Beg Oldi to Chushul. The PSP runway at Chushul almost disintegrated under the daily landings of these aircraft. At Leh, when after the cease-fire, a detachment of American C-130's landed there and the pilots were amazed at the tough and backward infrastructure facilities existing there. And with which the IAF was operating regularly.

Two questions remain in the readers minds about the 1962 conflict. Why was the Indian Air Force not used in an offensive role? And would it have made any difference if it had been used? It was thought at that time that the Chinese Air Force would retaliate if our air force was bought in. The decision not to use the IAF was purely a political one, which unfairly displays a lack of trust in the ability of our own Air Force to defend our side. It was not known at that time that the Chinese Air Force was grounded due to shortage of fuel and if it had tried to bomb Indian cities, the IAF would certainly had the upper hand, as both our pilots and aircraft were much better than those of the Chinese.

The answer to the second question depends on a lot of factors. In Ladakh the Chinese attacked in masse, and in open areas and in broad daylight, employing field and rocket artillery. In the terrain, in which there was no vegetation, the IAF would have had a field day in attacking the ground targets. The Battles of Rezang La, Gurung Hill and Chushul would definitely have had different outcomes.

But we suffered our main reverses in NEFA where the Chinese employed no artillery, no road transport, where they had lots of forest cover to use for hiding, and most important of all, the Chinese there fought by outflanking moves, never using the road, but the numerous tracks in the jungles. Air power can only be used during the day, and the Chinese mounted night attacks at most of the places.

They could afford to lie low during the day and move only in the nights. Thus nullifying most of the airpower advantage we had.

The IAF might have won a victory in the air but it would not have altered the situation in NEFA. Achieving air superiority would be meaningless if it was not exploited to wreck the enemies ground forces and more so if our own ground forces lack the ability to defend itself, which was what actually happened. Having the air situation in your favour does not alter the fact that your Generals are not up to the mark.

If it wasn't for the Chinese war we would have been caught off balance in 1965. And the consequences would have been more than the loss of barren uninhabited territory, and the 6000 men killed, missing or POW as in the Chinese invasion. The IAF came through the war with a bitter sense of disappointment. It was not allowed to have a crack at the enemy, and its pride wasn't better from the fact that the Prime Minister Nehru had asked for protection for Indian cities from American planes while it was there to do the job. It would have been fair to say that it was not the defeat of the Armed Forces but the defeat of our politicians pet dreams.

After the war aid came from all over, Canada supplied Caribou STOL transports, France speeded up the supplies of Alloutte III helicopters, while the Americans loaned us the services of a C-130 Squadron and also supplied some old used Packets. A squadron of Otters was also procured from the Canadians. The government entered into an agreement for the supply of MiG-21 fighters from the Soviet Union. Preparations were made to undertake production of the fighter. Old disused airfields in the North-East were reactivated, the result of which in the war nine years later, the IAF had no shortage of airfields to operate from.

To beef up the radar and communications network we got some old radar units from the United States, called the Air Defence Ground Environment System or ADGES. A plan was mutually agreed to set up a troop-scatter communication system. And one unit was being set up when the 1965 war started and further work was stopped.

To help the IAF assess its weaknesses and rectify them, an exercise was conducted jointly with the USAF and the RAF in 1963. For the first time, IAF Hunters operated alongside the Javelins of the RAF and the F-100 Super Sabres of the USAF. The Exercise aptly named *Siksha* was helpful for the IAF in gaining invaluable experience.

Though the object was to learn to meet the Chinese threat, it helped in assessing the Pakistani threat too. Perhaps the most important development was the approval of the government for the Indian Air Force to expand to a 45 Squadron force. The implementation of this plan would demand a tremendous effort from all those in the service.

On 1 August 1964, Air Marshal Arjan Singh D.F.C. took over as the Chief of Air Staff from Air Marshal Aspy Engineer. A tall and well built Sikh, he was a man of courage, no flamboyance, a rare combination of dignity, modesty, firmness and decision.

He saw action in Burma, and was a distinguished pilot, and was the first Air Chief to be medically and operationally fit to fly all types of aircraft, including the latest type of jet fighters. He had kept himself in flying trim by going to the squadrons and flying with them during their training. And as a flier to the end of his term he could have led a squadron into battle if the need ever rose. On Arjan Singh fell the responsibility to supervise the increase in the size of the Indian Air Force and train it in the shortest possible time.

Air Marshal Aspy Engineer was doing just that for an year and seven months and it was now Arjan Singh's job to complete what his predecessor had started, to forge the Indian Air Force into a formidable fighting machine. But he would never know that, because both he and his command would be put to test in less than an year.

FLIGHT SAFETY STRATEGY

A Flight Safety organisation has been functioning in the IAF since 1960. Procedures of flight safety management at various levels have been outlined in the Manual of Flight Safety Management (IAP 3030). The mission of the Flight Safety organisation of the IAF is to ensure operational capability by conserving human and material resources through prevention of aircraft accidents.

As risk is inherent in military aviation, it has to be assessed and managed effectively. In order to accomplish the mission safely, a well-defined strategy is given in the subsequent paragraphs.

Mission Statement

"The mission of the Flight Safety organisation of the IAF is to ensure operational capability by conserving human and material resources through prevention of aircraft accidents."

Pillars of Flight Safety

Under the provisions of the concepts of Flight Safety, a set of "recommended Pillars" to enhance safety has been identified. These recommended pillars serve as the criteria for qualification of safety status of the operational IAF units. The criteria that serve as the cornerstones of the Flight Safety Concept are outlined below:-

(a) Technology. It implies the optimal utilisation of available technology that affects flight operations. This would include identification of vulnerable technologies, their management, identification of design deficiencies and difficult maintenance practices.

(b) Capability. It involves the building up of capacity in the Air Force of man and machine for safe and successful mission accomplishment. This would encompass drawing on the ability and competence of all personnel involved in aviation.

(c) Training. Effective training is necessary to impart and progressively build required skills, knowledge and professional competence, which match the requirements of the first two pillars given above. With such training in place, there would be better 'risk management' leading to an improved fight safety.

(d) Environment. A safe environment would optimally utilise all elements of a program that not only supports flight operations but also human resource and build the morale of the personnel. This covers a whole range of infrastructure, which must mandatorily be in place and effective. This is important, since deficiencies in infrastructure would nullify the positive aspects of the first three pillars.

Safety Culture

Every organisation holds common beliefs, values and ethos that constitute its "culture". These characteristics have often become invisible to those inside, but may be startling to outsiders coming from a different culture. The notion of an organisational culture is difficult to define. It simply is 'Who and what we are, what we find important, and how we go about doing things'.

Though Flight Safety has always been a concern in the IAF, we need to assess the extent to which our safety culture has evolved. Safety cultures may fall under one of the following categories:-

(a) Pathological. Where we care less about safety than about not being caught.

(b) Reactive. Reactive is when we look for fixes to accidents and incidents after they happen.

(c) Calculative. We do have systems in place to manage hazards, however the system is applied mechanically. Field units and HQs follow the procedures but do not necessarily believe those procedures are critically important to their jobs or operations.

(d) Proactive. Proactive is when there are systems in place to manage potential hazards and rectify these before an accident. Units and higher formations have begun to acquire beliefs that Flight Safety is genuinely worthwhile and look ahead in a proactive manner.

(e) Generative. What we really require to strive for is to inculcate Safety behaviour fully and integrate it into everything we do. The value system associated with safety and safe working is fully internalised as beliefs, almost to the point of invisibility.

To reach the apex of performance pyramid, the IAF would have to be Generative in nature. To achieve this on a sustainable basis we have to clearly define and delineate various facets of the organisational work and define our tasks and endeavours in these areas. Hence it is necessary to lay down our concepts and the method of achieving this clearly.

Technology

Aviation in general and military aviation in particular is driven by technology. Technologies are getting outdated faster than the full utilisation of aircraft. Therefore, we are saddled with ac and technology that is more than four decades old. In the past two decades, technology has leaped from single engine transonic jets with minimal instrumentation to supersonic ac with an array of avionics.

Technological Asymmetry. The challenge with the IAF today is that it needs to keep pace with the proliferation of new glass cockpits, and yet be able to manage and maintain the vintage technologies. We operate a large variety of aircraft comprising both Russian and Western fleet with varied technology vintages ranging from low-tech to the modern. While modern state-of-the-art technology aircraft contribute towards safer and efficient operations, it is the older technology that needs our best effort to improve its reliability.

Identification of Deficiencies in Design/Equipment. It would be prudent to clearly identify deficiencies in design or equipment, which are not conducive to safe operations. This would involve examination of obsolete equipment, difficult maintenance practices and equipment prone to frequent failures. Thereafter, either we shelve such equipment no matter what the cost, or, train and improve capability of the human element to anticipate and act effectively in a crisis. Decision in this regard needs careful consideration of not only the financial implication but also of op degradation aspects. Hence, the following strategies need to be adopted to ensure safe operations:-

(a) Identifying the vulnerable technology and replacing old technology ac with new in a phased manner.

(b) Retaining the best personnel in the older technologies.

Diversified Inventory. The next concern is the disadvantage of a wide spectrum of ac on our inventory. The problem areas in this regard are maintenance, training, inter-operability and interchangeability. Further, spares management is difficult and expensive as it is not financially prudent to hold large inventories of spares and consumables. Limited availability of spares especially from the erstwhile Soviet state, compounded by long gestation period has adversely affected maintenance at the field. In order to meet the training and operational requirements, field units resort to cannibalisation, leading further to unserviceabilities, thus ensnaring the organisation into a vicious circle. These ultimately result in a large number of concessions given to ac, excessive downtime, non-availability of redundancy and therefore work pressure. Therefore, the following need to be adopted:-

(a) Future acquisition plans need to be based on symmetry of technology in our training and operational aircraft without unwarranted diversification.

(b) The acquisition of capital equipment should factor in past performance and adequate contractual obligation on the vendors to ensure reliability and maintainability of the equipment.

Maintenance of Older Technologies. The useful life of an aircraft is said to be over when the economics of maintenance exceed the value of the aeroplane. Nevertheless, we do not fly based on economics alone and continue to maintain an aircraft well beyond fiscal feasibility. With aircraft ageing, general wear and tear sets in, stress cracks develop, seals fail and corrosion begins. The list is endless and frequently is as much a symptom of old age and possibly inadequate maintenance, as of poor design. Older the equipment more is the maintenance required, necessitating increased man-hours and experienced crew. Occasionally, we attempt to take more out of a machine than is safe without the requisite maintenance investment in terms of manpower and spares. Experienced and the motivated personnel are generally posted to the units with new induction and the older equipment then takes a back seat. This is a sure recipe for accidents and needs to be corrected.

The approach that is required is as follows:-

(a) Early identification of ageing symptoms.

(b) Initiation of timely preventive/corrective maintenance.

(c) Every snag/defect needs to be given due importance and followed-up as it is a potential source of latent error. Snag reporting must be encouraged without fear of adverse career impact.

(d) Placement of experienced and motivated personnel with the vulnerable equipment.

Challenges of Life Extension. Mechanical devices can and do fail. Some are predictable and preventable to a degree of assurance depending on the preventive measures taken. With ageing of an aircraft or equipment, the probability of failure increases. This failure probability in our ageing fleet stems from limitations of design, degree of manufacturing precision and preventive maintenance initiated especially in respect of aeroengines and critical accessories. Though aeroengines have a defined life, several variables can affect their longevity. Aeroengines are also most prone to failure because of inherent complexity and stresses. In every safety review, the aeroengine is at least twice as likely to be the cause factor in an accident than other aircraft-related causes. Therefore, life extensions need to be undertaken judiciously and backed with extensive study in consultation with the manufacturers.

The most significant requirement however is to identify the critical weaknesses in technology, which have a direct bearing on Flight Safety. Having identified these, we then need to manage them by enhanced maintenance, modifications, replacements or even shelving them.

Capability

Capability refers to the capacity built up into the organisation to facilitate performance of the task safely and to anticipate and act in face of unforeseen contingencies. It is required to ensure that man machine combination is capable of mission accomplishment with efficiency.

Capability vs Task. The organisation should aim to build on its inherent capability to place the right person for the right job. This would need the following:-

(a) Development of job-oriented selection process and training.

(b) Rationalised training for concerned personnel to ensure right training at right stage.

(c) Judicious placement and posting of trained personnel.

Professional Competence of Technicians. There is a need to instill a proactive approach and generate dynamic involvement of technicians in matters of aviation safety. The following actions are required to generate a flight safety consciousness right down to the grassroots level:-

(a) Capacity amongst technicians to analyse a snag and take corrective action needs to be nurtured and developed right from the ab-initio stage. Knowledge of the concept behind repair scheme or system maintenance will enable quicker diagnosis of the cause of the problem rather than reacting to the symptoms.

(b) The technicians at the field level should get extensive interaction with the OEMs/major repair units. This will increase their understanding of the systems besides developing a friendly and informal link between the manufacturers/repair agency and the operators.

(c) The personnel at the field units need an exposure to investigation into incidents/accidents. This would widen the knowledge base and provide first hand account of the factors that led to the incident/accident.

Comprehension of Orders and Instructions. During the last decade, human error alone accounted for 45% of the total accidents of the IAF. It is therefore imperative that the person on the ground or in air is competent, qualified and suitable to accomplish the mission safely. Thorough understanding of the SOPs relating to the aircraft, technical practices and the operational environment is a prerequisite. Orders, instructions and policies etc are at best only guidelines for safe operations. Understanding of the rationale behind such SOPs and instructions would facilitate correct judgement/decision-making in complex situations.

Trend Analysis. Accident/incident trends require study both at the field units and at HQ. Patterns need to be comprehended to react proactively. The following actions are warranted to derive the maximum benefit from statistics and trends:

(a) History of component-wise/system-wise snags and rectification should be organised and meaningful analysis is to be disseminated to the lowest level.

(b) Periodic feedback and compendiums of accident/incident trends need to be compiled at Command and Air HQ levels to identify critical areas affecting safe operations.

Specialist Flight Safety Organisation. The Command structure should reflect the priority of flight safety in the organisation. As far as possible the flight safety set-up should be independent of the executive function to impart objectivity to the assessment of flight safety activities. The concept of a separate flight safety organisation as a career option for volunteers needs to be explored. This is already in vogue in some advanced nations. The actions required in this regard are as follows:-

(a) Personnel who have undergone Flt Sfty courses abroad need to be posted to the Flt Sfty organisation to form its core group.

(b) Training of additional personnel on specialised spheres of accident prevention and investigation is required. Training could be arranged on forensic aspects at DMRL, NAL, NFL, OEM and other organisations to enable in-house expertise in area of accident investigation and attendant area of accident prevention and safety.

(c) Interaction of this organisation with other aviation related organisations like DGCA, AAI etc. on a regular basis is required to be enhanced.

Training

New designs aim to reduce workload and simplify systems. But accidents involving basic handling skills and judgement-related mishaps have affected the new models just as they have always plagued the older aircraft. Traditional aviation risk management identifies three sources of risk: the man, the aircraft and the environment. Over the years, most of the flight safety problems related to aircraft and environment have been tackled satisfactorily. Today, a significant amount of the trouble stems from humans. Towards reducing or controlling 'human error', training would make a huge difference.

Equipment vs Personal Capability. The operational environment is the same for all aircraft, but some ac are better equipped than others. Auto-pilot, on-board radar, and data link multifunction displays do change the environment and do provide the trained pilot with more tools upon which to base good decisions. This decision-making should be the target of our training pattern. Some aspects that require consideration are:-

(a) Better safety because of redundancies lead to increased comfort levels and at times to over-confidence.

(b) These ac are likely to be tasked for tougher/riskier missions and in marginal weather conditions.

(c) The basic aerodynamics of low-speed handling has not been altered appreciably — stalls, directional control, crosswinds and landing flares.

Effective training is therefore the foundation of a professional. If any deficiency in the equipment or personal capability exists, it must be improved by appropriate training. Needless to mention, training must be focused and appropriate for ensuring safety.

Discipline and Just Culture. Discipline on ground generally translates to flying discipline also. Therefore, there is a need to inculcate discipline as a way of life. Strict action needs to be initiated for any disciplinary lapses in the air.

However, the disciplinary action taken must be 'event-oriented' and not 'result-oriented'. Based on intent, knowledge and recklessness, there is a need to distinguish between inadvertent errors, unintentional risk taking and deliberate violations.

Only deliberate violations warrant a disciplinary action. Inadvertent errors and unintentional risk taking provide opportunities for system correction and increasing situational awareness. Experience gained out of these 'learning outcomes' need to be shared during continuity training for the benefit of the organisation. This would in turn lead to removal of error provoking conditions and creation of error tolerant systems.

Maturity and Professionalism. The training establishments have little trouble teaching the aircraft, but developing requisite maturity and professionalism poses some difficulty. A study of HE (A) accidents reveals that this aspect needs greater attention. Following measures are called for:-

(a) The maturity level of officers should be a prime consideration for selection to instructional courses. Most pupil officers try to emulate their instructors and any bravado/false ego inculcated during training manifest later as part of flying discipline.

(b) The maturity level of all supervisors, instructors and trainees in training establishments needs to be monitored on a regular basis.

Simulators. The infrastructure available for training has a bearing on the quality of training and the competence of the end product i.e. the trainee. Formal training in the IAF has prepared aircrew dictated by mission requirements. Simulators were not used extensively since they were prohibitively expensive and availability of reliable simulators in the Russian fleet was limited. The first generation simulators had basic flight and instrument skills wired. Pilots were taught aircraft systems but did little else. This induced most to doubt the utility of simulators. The advent of the modern simulators viz. mission simulators, maintenance simulators has changed this mindset. Extensive use of simulators for training of aircrew and technical personnel is prudent and needs to be encouraged.

Challenge of Technology Evolution. Difficulty in decision-making arises from the hesitance/confusion caused by complexity of avionics packages that are integral to the control and navigation of the aircraft. Since avionics mutate much faster, the avionics that was top of the line five years ago is now obsolete, and this creates legacy and primacy of training issues (what is learned first is learned best). The best example is the auto pilot system for the Jaguar ac. Most senior pilots at that time felt it would affect pilot trg and build complacency in the pilots. Therefore, training pattern needs to keep pace with the rate of obsolescence.

Rationalisation of Syllabi. This brings us to the adequacy of training pattern, syllabus and SOPs available. Varieties of syllabi have been tried out on an equally large variety of ac. In spite of all safe guards apparently introduced in devising these training syllabi, accidents continue to occur. IAF therefore needs to address some of these issues by ensuring that pilots stepping into modern jets have the benefit of a defined syllabus and best practices.

This is a challenge where syllabus needs continuous revision while maintaining adequate time for assimilation and study. Following actions are warranted:-

(a) Changes of minor nature need to be incorporated annually within the training command.

(b) Major changes in syllabi need deliberate study and require to be done on a three/five-yearly basis at the Air HQ level, utilising the best from field and HQ staff.

Transition Training. In the ideal situation, pilots would get all the training they needed to prepare for stepping up to their next aircraft. Safely putting low-time pilots into high-performance aircraft has always been a challenge. There is presently no quick, inexpensive fix to building maturity and the yearning for professionalism. It takes time and more than a quick formal checkout, particularly if the pilot is relatively young and inexperienced. The following points need attention in this regard:-

(a) Realistic training is essential to prepare for a real emergency. Military trainers operate under the motto: "Train like you fight; fight like you train." Surprise in combat or in flight is a bad thing. Training needs to be made as realistic as possible without infringing on flight safety.

(b) Training at units must also emphasise on learning from others' mistakes. It is less expensive and far less embarrassing to learn from ones own mistake. Studying accident reports is a sobering way to learn about flight Safety. The articles in Flight Safety Magazine and reports issued by the DFS from time to time is one such way. It allows us a look into problem areas, before an accident occurs and correct things either systemically or individually.

Environment

Environment constitutes all elements, which have a bearing on flying operations. By virtue of this fact, they are likely to be taken lightly in normal scheme of things. However many of the accidents have their genesis in the environment and thus the environment should be made conducive to safe operations. A safe environment needs the professionalism of every single individual. No task, however small, can be missed in the chain. The ground, technical and administrative support must synergies towards creating such an environment. The overall environment can broadly be divided into organisational environment & operating environment.

Organisational Environment. This refers to the set of values and work ethos prevailing in the organisation. To foster environment conducive to safety, an appropriate culture needs to be developed and nurtured. This refers to a culture where error reporting is encouraged and there is an acceptance that human error is inevitable.

Mechanisms such as non-punitive reporting, recurrent training, periodic evaluation of safety management programmes and easy access to flight safety data need to be in place and actively functioning.

The aspects pertinent in the area of organisational environment are as follows:-

(a) Inspection & Assessment. Inspections carried out by the organisation should not only measure compliance to prescribed standards but also identify potential hazards and make constructive suggestions for improving the safety environment. Only when all the presonnel are encouraged to continuously assess their environment and share relevant information, a 'learning organisational climate' can be created based on shared understanding. This would then enable development of a compatible organisational environment encompassing the equipment, mission procedures and personnel such that they are able to identify errors/hazards early and facilitate safe operations. Following measures need to be implemented in the right spirit:-

(i) Flight safety audits need to be formalised and carried out and form a part of performance appraisal system of all key personnel in the field.

(ii) Inspections/audits need to be carried out by SFS&IO regularly and reported to the respective Command.

(iii) Inspections by Commands may then be scheduled with a report being rendered to Air HQ for suitable monitoring & follow-up.

(b) Sensitivity to Operations. An organisation should have an ongoing concern with the unexpected, attentiveness to these and acknowledgement that the cause of an accident is often not the result of a single, active error. Rather, many latent errors get embedded in the operational system until a combination of adverse events occurs leading to a catastrophic accident. Hence, the organisation needs to focus on everyone knowing the 'big picture'. This calls for a willingness to do true introspection and change in the ethos and pattern for aircraft accident investigation. The following merit consideration:-

(i) Investigations need to be conducted by a professional team of members who are formally trained in this specialised field.

(ii) One or more members from an independent aviation organisation/agency may be co-opted into Courts of Inquiry to assure a degree of independence.

Operating Environment. This involves the following:-

(a) Ground Infrastructure & Support Services. The recent analysis of accidents reveal that the ground infrastructure in terms of surveillance and precision radars, Nav aids, Communications and other supporting systems need to be revamped. Launch and recovery of ac vis-à-vis prevailing and forecasted weather need deliberate assessment. The ground support services would need to gear up within the existing limitations and function with greater involvement. The elements of air traffic services should be well trained, adequate motivated staff, clean, hygienic and ergonomically designed control towers, proactive met services, well-maintained safety services and continuity training in various exigencies.

(b) Navigational and Recovery Aids. The navigational and recovery aids should have high reliability of desirable performance, low downtimes, planned effective maintenance and well-trained ground controllers. The controllers should interact with the aircrew on a daily basis to enhance their perspective and better understand the capability of each aircrew. There should be optimal utilisation of all air defence radars and aids in effective monitoring of flights and their recovery.

(c) Runways and Operating Surfaces. Runway and operating surfaces remains a perennial source of FOD that affect a large number of flights. Besides, the runway conditions affect the wear and tear of tyres and have a bearing on aircraft operations due to undesirable water logging. A well-maintained runway along with night lighting system will go a long way in contributing to flight safety. Future plans must cater for making the AF flight safety zones and ac manoeuvring areas, vehicle-free. Runway crossings must be banned. All antennae, lighting etc have to be frangible, to collapse on impact. Hangars and maintenance areas need to be spotless wherein indoctrination and active support of all personnel are required.

(d) Wild Life and Bird Control Measures. Wild life menace and bird activity poses a great hazard to flight operations. Wild life and environment organisations need to be co-opted at all levels. Bird hazard combat measures need to be well integrated with the flying operations and suitably monitored. This is an ongoing activity and requires collation and study to be instituted at the station level for suitable proactive measures to be implemented for combating the bird hazard.

(e) Command and Control. Effective operational control system is essential for flow of relevant information and its understanding by the operators. The system should be free of delays, red tape and responsive to the need of the field units. The chain of command should be clear with well-demarcated responsibilities.

(f) Information Dissemination. An online information dissemination infrastructure requires making available all the relevant information to the user in the field, in a usable and friendly manner. An open forum must be provided to facilitate feedback and constructive suggestions from the field units/personnel.

9

IAF Medical Services and its Support to the Air Power of India

In the context of warfare today, the Air Power of a nation, has been used and will continue to be used, as the primary means of striking the enemy. Even though there has been a progressive improvement in the class of aircraft and ancillary equipment on the inventory of the Armed Forces, man still remains the supreme weapon and his morale, the battle winning factor. It was due to the foresight of the pioneers of Dte Gen Armed Forces Medical Services 50 years back and the sustained subsequent support that, from a Humble beginning of three Medical Officers, a large pool of specialised manpower and infrastructure has been created today, to support the air operations of the Armed Forces, both in war and peace.

IAF's Medical Branch has grown along with the Air Force and has integrated exceptionally well, with both offensive and defensive role of the Indian Air Force, and has been providing the aeromedical support to Army, Navy and Civil Aviation. Today through the Institute of Aerospace Medicine, it is also playing its international role in training and research. This article is an attempt to recollect the glorious past and place in perspective the contribution of the Air Force Medical Services in support of the Air Power over the past 50 years. The Indian Society of Aerospace Medicine, beyond doubt plays a pivotal role in this support.

THE HUMBLE BEGINNINGS

With the introduction of the Indian Air Force bill in the legislative assembly by the Government of India in 1931, the Indian Air Force Act came into force on 08 Oct 1932, laying down the foundations for the Royal Indian Air Force (IAF). In the initial years, from 1933 to 1941, the medical facilities for the IAF personnel were not instituted since their numbers were very small and they worked with the Royal Air Force (RAF) at the same airfield. The Station Medical Officer of the RAF provided medical cover to the IAF personnel also. Whenever the IAF flight operated out of an airfield without RAF medical staff, the nearest army medical unit provided the requisite medical cover. The hospital facility for the IAF and RAF personnel was either at the British Military Hospitals (BMH) or Combine Indian Military Hospitals (CIMH).

This was as per a contract between the Air Ministry, London and the Government of India War Department before World War II. This situation changed completely with the outbreak of World War II. Expansion of the IAF commenced in earnest since 1939. At the same time many RAF and Allied operational units moved into India. The Air Ministry, London was finding it difficult to meet the medical manning requirements of the RAF and IAF units in India. There was also an acute shortage of RAF medical personnel in Britain. Thus a major policy decision by the Principal Medical Officer (PMO) RAF in India, with the concurrence of the Air Ministry, London, was taken to start the IAF Medical Service in 1940. The Government of India issued an order, in the middle of 1940, which stated that "medical requirements of the Indian Air Force will be met by grant of temporary commissions in the IAF medical branch to Indian commissioned officers of the Indian Medical Service (IMA)". Medical officers who volunteered to serve in the IAF medical branch were given an allowance of Rs. 50/-per month and had to fly in service aircraft in war and peace. In the summary of reasons for the formation of Indian Air Force medical branch, it was stated that "Aviation presents new physiological and pathological problems which require specialized study and which can only be dealt with satisfactorily by a specially trained body of men".

ADMINISTRATION OF AIR FORCE MEDICAL SERVICE

Medical services of the Air Force in India were administered by the PMO, RAF, Air HQ (India). Till 1940, the office of the PMO was located at Lahore, nearly 400 miles from Air HQ, Delhi. Hence there was ignorance amongst the executives at Delhi about the medical problems of aviation. Thus the interest taken by them, particularly in preventive medicine, was also minimal. There was little cooperation between the PMO at Lahore and other senior staff officers of the RAF at Air HQ, Delhi. The RAF medical branch was, if at all, rarely consulted in planning and preparations for the war. For smoother administration, the office of the PMO was moved to Delhi in 1940.

The Pioneers

Group Captain Brisco, the RAF PMO in 1940, was instrumental in starting the IAF medical service by selecting the three volunteers from the IMS. This included Lt MM Shrinagesh, Lt Ajit Nath and Lt PL Khurana. They were selected amongst the volunteers to serve in the IAF medical service. These three medical officers formed the nucleus from which the Air Force medical service has grown over the years.

A beginning was also made in 1941 for training of Indian Air Force nursing orderlies, later known as medical assistants. In the 1st batch, seven airmen were recruited in Group 'M'. This group was created specially for the recruitment of nursing orderlies for the IAF. The number of IAF medical officers and medical assistants increased during the war years with the expansion of the IAF to the strength of ten squadrons. Several Air Force training units were established all over the country. This also helped partly to meet the medical manning requirements of the RAF in India. From a nucleus of 3 medical officers and 7 medical assistants in 1941, the strength increased to 51 medical officers and over 200 medical assistants by the end of the war in 1945.

The posts of Senior Medical Officer (SMO) were established in 1943. Another major development was creation of the post of Deputy Principal Medical Officer (DPMO) (IAF) on the RAF

PMO's staff at Air HQ. The first IAF medical officer to be posted as DPMO (IAF) was Flt Lt MM Shrinagesh. He was promoted to the rank of Squadron Leader to fill this appointment in 1943. Subsequently, in 1945, the post of DPMO (IAF) was upgraded to the rank of Wing Commander and then Sqn Ldr MM Shrinagesh was promoted to fill this appointment. This was the nucleus from which the IAF Medical Directorate grew up in 1947. Another interesting development in July 1944 was the decision by the Government of India that IAF Medical Officers will be eligible, if found fit, to undergo flying training and become pilots. It was decided that the number of such medical officers should not exceed 30% of their total strength. Under this scheme, two IAF medical officers earned their flying badge after successful completion of General Duty (Pilots) training.

The Consolidation

The IAF consisted of 10 squadrons before the independence. After partition of the Indian nation in 1947, six and a half squadrons remained in India and the remaining three and a half were transferred to the newly carved Pakistan. As on 15 August 1947, the IAF had 56 medical officers. This does not include the six Muslim officers of the Air Force who migrated to Pakistan. At this time, the Royal Indian Air Force was rechristened as Indian Air Force, with India becoming a sovereign republic. On 15 August 1947, Wg Cdr MM Shrinagesh was appointed PMO, Air HQ in the rank of Group Captain. In 1950, the designation of PMO was changed to Director Medical Services (DMS (Air), but the rank remained the same. The first Director General Armed Forces Medical Services (DGAFMS), Lt Gen KS Master, soon after assuming his appointment in 1949, took up the issue of supercession of acting Gp Capt MM Shrinagesh, DMS (Air) IAF with the Ministry of Defence on the basis of seniority. However, Col DN Chakraborty was appointed DMS (Air) in the rank of Gp Capt. For the next 19 years, six senior Army medical officers were seconded to the air force to fill the appointment of DMS (Air) as the Air Force medical officers were relatively junior. In 1969, the second Air Force medical officer Air Marshal Ajit Nath became DMS (Air) and later retired as the first Air Force DGAFMS.

FOUNDATIONS OF AVIATION MEDICINE IN INDIA

The trio of pioneers of IAF medical service were pioneers in the field of aviation medicine in India as well. All three, Lt MM Shrinagesh, Lt Ajit Nath and Lt PL Khurana, were mostly self taught and learnt the meaning of the new specialty-Aviation Medicine, and its professional applications from RAF Air Ministry Medical Publications. With the induction of RAF and other Allied aircrafts into the Indian skies in 1942, the IAF medical officers got opportunities to gain first hand practical knowledge in aviation medicine by working with the RAF medical officers. By 1944, a comprehensive training programme in Aviation Medicine was being implemented for medical officers and medical assistants.

Courses in Aviation Medicine were offered for IAF medical officers in 1944 at No.1 and 2 RAF Decompression Chamber Units at Calcutta and Poona, respectively. Among the early medical officers of IAF only 17 could receive this training because the RAF Decompression Chamber Units were busy with the training of pilots and navigators engaged in the war. In 1947, the RAF left behind the RAF Mobile Decompression Chambers for use by the IAF. Thus the IAF medical service was trained and equipped in the field of Aviation Medicine.

The two mobile decompression chambers left behind by the RAF at the end of World War II were relocated at Bangalore and Palam. Two Aeromedical Units (AMU) were formed for the purpose of training in August 1948 after the approval of the Government of India. The medical staff authorised to man these two special units was one Squadron Leader, one Sergeant and two Corporals. No.1 AMU was formed at Palam, New Delhi on 02 August 1948 and No.2 AMU at Ambala on 06 Dec 1949. Later another, No.3 AMU was established at Jodhpur on 15 Aug 1956. Another significant milestone in the history of aviation medicine in India was the formation of Aeromedical Society. This happened towards the end of 1952 when Air Force medical officers of the Delhi area decided to form the Aeromedical Society. The guiding light and architect of the Aeromedical Society was Wg Cdr Ajit Nath, DDMS Air Headquarters. He was also the founder editor of the Journal of the Aeromedical Society of India. The first volume of the journal was published in 1954. In 1960, the Aeromedical Society was registered under the Societies of Registration Act.

DELIVERING HEALTHCARE

Concept of Squadron MO, Station Medicare Centres & Peripheral Hospitals

Comprehensive medical care is now being provided in the IAF to the groups of personnel and their families in isolated and airfields remote from the cities through its unique organizational structure of Squadron Medical Officer, Station Medicare Centers, peripheral hospitals and bigger referral hospitals. Special aircrew requirements are met through the Institute of Aerospace Medicine and the two Aeromedical Training Centers at Hindon and Dundigal. The aim is to support the aircrew from cockpit to his home.

Squadron Medical Officer has always been the pivot of the medical care in the IAF. His role is to make flying safe, by maintaining and fortifying the human elements of the aircrew in the squadron. The trained medical officer of IAF establishes a rapport with his aircrew through sound professional knowledge and by involving in the flying activity of the squadron, thus gaining insight to the needs of aircrew and his family. Station Medicare Centre is a Medical Unit designed and perfected by the IAF, which was introduced in India for the first time during World War I. Its utility was to provide some medical care to the Air Force, which always has to operate from airfields located miles away from towns and cities. These units have constantly been upgraded and today provide modern Out Patient as well as In patient care, emergency medical care, basic lab facility, Maternity and Child Welfare and minor surgical procedures. Station Health Organisation, aircraft emergency setup and Passive Air Defence have now become an integral part of this medical unit at an Air Base.

Modern Hospital Chain of IAF

Excellent peripheral hospitals have been developed at Gorakhpur, Halwara, Hindon, Hashimara, Hyderabad, Coimbatore and Amla, providing all the specialist care in their zones. These are backed up by Command Hospital Air Force,

Bangalore and AF Hospitals at Jorhat and Kanpur which are providing modern specialised investigative and therapeutic care, at par with the best in the country. New specialised centers are being added to the bigger hospitals, like renal transplant facility, reconstructive surgery and Ophthalmic Laser surgery.

Aviation Medicine & Aeromedical Support: Institutions Par Excellence Institute of Aerospace Medicine

The Institute of Aerospace Medicine (IAM) started as the School of Aviation Medicine (SAM) on 29 May 1957. The Aeromedical Unit (AMU) and the Aeromedical Research Centre were amalgamated with the newly established SAM. HAL provided one building, which till date continues to be the administration block at IAM. The SAM initially started with a staff of three officers, four airmen, two civilian typists and two class IV employees. The three officers at the SAM during 1957 were Wg Cdr Arunachalam, Officer Commanding (OC), Sqn Ldr JHF Manekshaw and Flt Lt KK Majumdar.

In 1963, a Decompression Chamber with altitudes simulation capability of 1,00,000 feet and deep cooling upto-70°C was acquired for studies in high altitude physiology. In 1966 the first and only human centrifuge in the country was commissioned, the same was procured from erstwhile West Germany, and the Department of Acceleration Physiology was established. In 1967 a five-man Hyperbaric Chamber was setup and was the first Hyperbaric Oxygen Therapy facility in the IAF. The period from early to late sixties also saw most of the other major simulators and facilities being acquired or indigenously designed and developed. These included the Hot Cockpit, an anechoic chamber for noise studies, Anthropometric Platform, Spatial Disorientation devices etc. During this period the Department of Aviation Accident Pathology and Toxicology was shifted to the School from Armed Forces Medical College, Pune. Through the pioneering efforts of dedicated aeromedical experts, the activities of the School increased which was redesignated as the Institute of Aviation Medicine (IAM) in 1968. The Institute provided medical support to the Indo-Soviet Manned Space Programme form 1982. With its increased involvement in Space Medicine, the present Institute of Aerospace Medicine came into existence, in 1989.

The Institute of Aerospace Medicine has established itself as one of the well-recognized training and research establishment in the world. The Institute has not only trained a large number of Indian military and civil aircrew and medical officers but has also trained several military and civil medical officers from foreign countries. Today, the Institute is the nodal agency in India providing the best solutions in the field of Aerospace Medicine. It is an affiliated Post Graduate College of the Rajiv Gandhi University of Medical Sciences, Bangalore, for conduct of MD in Aerospace Medicine. The Institute also conducts aircrew medical evaluation and runs various training courses in Aerospace Medicine for IAF, Army, Navy and Civil Aviation.

AIR FORCE CENTRAL MEDICAL ESTABLISHMENT (AFCME)

On 15 August 1947, the RAF Central Medical Board, New Delhi was taken over by the IAF. This board was subsequently named the Royal Indian Air Force (RIAF) Central Medical Board w.e.f. 01 April 1948; and later became the IAF Central Medical Board in 1949. This unit was re-designated as AF Central Medical Establishment (AFCME) on 01 April 1958. Major changes in its role and establishment lead to the formation of AFCME on 21 Oct 1967. It conducts medical evaluation of both military and civil aircrew apart from medical examinations of candidates for grants of various commissions, special medical boards and critical analysis of clinical and other data collected over the years. The establishment has kept pace with the changing technology in evaluation techniques and has positioned itself at par with similar establishments of the world.

Aeromedical Training Centres

The first Aeromedical Training Center (AMTC) was established at Air Force Station, Hindan in June 1968. The unit was established with one Wing Commander (Med), two Sqn Ldrs (Med), one Aeronautical Engineer, 23 non medical airmen and 4 medical assistants. Wg Cdr RC Bhargava was the first commanding officer of No. I AMTC. No. 2 AMTC was sanctioned at Air Force Academy, Hyderabad in the year 1979 and came into existence in June 1981, with an explosive decompression chamber (EDC). Its establishment, task, training and manpower were the same as No. 1 AMTC. Subsequently, recompression chambers were installed at both AMTCs.

Air Evacuation & Disaster Management in War & Peace

As a result of the experiences during the Jammu & Kashmir operations in 1947, the need for dedicated medical units for air evacuation of casualties was felt. Thus Casualty Air Evacuation Units (CAEUs) were formed in 1957. The air evacuation of casualties from the battle fronts was carried out mainly by helicopters. In the Indo-Pak conflict of 1971, these units carried out yeoman service in the evacuation of the wounded and the injured from the active theatres of war to hospitals at the rear. Air evacuation of sick and injured service civilian personnel has become a routine responsibility of the IAF today. For this reason special training and plans have been integrated for aircraft accidents and disaster management at all airfields.

Para Medical Teams

The first paratrooper medical team was formed in 1951. Its primary role was to render medical aid to victims of air crashes in inaccessible areas. Its secondary role was to assist civil authorities during natural calamities. The first operational drop by the parachute team was at Segallie in Assam to render medical aid to the victims of a crashed Dakota. Flt Lt KK Majumdar and his team had the distinction of this first drop near the site of the crash. The need for paratrooper medical teams to rescue victims of air crashes became less and less with the introduction of helicopters in the IAF in the late sixties. Air Force paratrooper medical teams have since been deployed to work with helicopter squadrons.

Rapid Action Medical Teams (RAMT)

The two Rapid Action Medical Teams of the Indian Air Force, No.1 and No.2 RAMT were raised as lodger units of Command Hospital Air Force and No.5 AFH, respectively. These units were established with the aim of providing immediate medical and surgical aid, and establishing a chain of casualty evacuation in the event of any disaster within their zones of responsibility. These units are capable of rendering the emergency and trauma care for a duration of three to four days at a stretch. No.1 RAMT was one of the first medical teams to reach after the Bhuj earthquake on 26 January 2001.

CONTRIBUTION TO CIVIL AVIATION

DGCA and AAA have designated medical services of the IAF for medical evaluation of all types of licensed categories of personnel in civil aviation activities. This role is being performed since independence through IAM, AFCME and a number of designated peripheral station Medicare centers.

Aeromedical research and role in national projects and space medicine

IAM and other air force medical units have been actively engaged in various research activities in the field of aerospace medicine. Most of the research is of applied nature, oriented towards operational efficiency and flight safety. It is supported by Armed Forces Medical Research Committee and the Human Engineering panel of Aeronautical Research and Development Board. Aeromedical consultancy in aircraft design and in promotion of flight safety in the areas of thermal stress, physiological tolerance limits of aircrew, mental workload and clinical aerospace medicine is also being provided. IAM has been nominated as the prime agency for all human engineering aspects in the design and development of Light Combat Aircraft (LCA) and the Advanced Light Helicopter (ALH), which are to be the mainstay of our forces in the future. It is also providing aero medical support to national projects in the field of space sciences. It has already been recognized by both the Russian and the US space agencies for astronaut and cosmonaut evaluation, besides conducting life science experiments in space.

The Saga Continues

The IAF, over the years, has become a force to reckon with. The Air Force medical services have also come of age, and its performance during operations has been outstanding. Medical planning, execution and administration are of a very high order and comparable with any military in the developed world. The credit for this goes to the pioneers of the armed forces medical services who in the past had the vision, courage and conviction to lay very strong foundations for what the medical service is today. It also goes to the devoted and dedicated service rendered by all the medical, dental, nursing and civilian personnel of the Indian Air Force. The medical services of Air Force now looks forward to meet the challenges of the next century by keeping pace with new technologies that are likely to be introduced in military and civil aviation.

Bibliography

Air Marshal V K Bhatia: *The Shorkot Raid,* IAF Journal 1997.

Air Vice Marshal C V Parker: *Laal Salaam.* Air Force Academy Journal.

Bharat Kumar: *An Incredible War: Indian Air Force in Kashmir War 1947-48*, Knowledge World, Delhi, 2007.

Bonarjee, V.S.C.: *My days in the Indian Air Force 1940-1948.* Privately Published, Delhi, 1998.

Chakko, Gp Capt Jacob: *Memoirs.* National Printing Press, Delhi, 1999.

Chakravarty, B C Dr.: *Indian Armed Forces - Official History of the 1965 Indo-Pak War.* Ministry of Defence.

Chaturvedi, Air Marshal M. S.: *History of the Indian Air Force.* Vikas, Delhi, 1978.

Chaturvedi, M S Air Marshal: *History of the Indian Air Force.* Vikas, Delhi, 2003.

Fricker, John: *Battle for Pakistan.* Ian Allan, London 1978.

Gibbs, Air Marshal G.E.: *Survivors Story,* Hutchinson, Delhi, 1961

Gupta, SC: *History of the Indian Air Force 1933-45*, Pubications Division, Ministry of Defence, Delhi, 1961.

Hussain, Syed S. and Squadron Leader M. Tariq Quershi: *History of the PAF 1947-1982.* PAF Press, Masroor, Karachi 1982.

Jagan Mohan, PVS and Samir Chopra: *The India-Pakistan Air War of 1965*, Manohar, New Delhi, 2005.

Kapila, AVM Viney: *The Indian Air Force : a balanced strategic and tactical application,* Ocean Books, Delhi, 2002.

Karim Afsir, Major General: *The Story of India's Airborne Troops*. Lancer, Delhi, 1992.

Khan, Air Marshal M. Asgar: *The First Round (The Indo-Pakistan War 1965)*. Vikas, Delhi, 1969.

Lal, Air Chief Marshal Pratap Chandra: *My years with the IAF*, Lancer International, Delhi, 1986.

Pushpindar Singh: *Aircraft of the Indian Air Force, 1933-73*, English Book Store, Delhi, 1974.

Ranbir Singh, Gp Capt: *Indian Air Force - In the footsteps of our Legends*, Book Mates Publishers, New Delhi 1998.

Roopinder Singh: *Marshal of the Air Force Arjan Singh - Rupa Charitravalli series* , Rupa Publications, Delhi, 2002.

Saigal, Air Cmde A L: *Birth of an Air Force: the memoirs of Air Vice Marshal Harjinder Singh*. Palit & Palit, Delhi, 1977.

Seth, Vijay: *The Flying Machines - Indian Air Force 1933-99*. Seth Communications, Delhi, 2000.

Tanham, George K.: *The Indian Air Force: Trends & prospects*. Rand, Santa Monica, Delhi, 1995.

Tufail, Kaiser: *Great Air Battles of the PAF*. Ferozesons, Karachi 2004.

Index

I

J

M

N

O

P

R

S

T

W

□□□